TO THE MOVEMENT

A Return To The Past, a Vision
For The Future

By Seamus A. Connolly

CONTENTS

Title Page
Introduction:
Populism: 1
Land Reform: 11
Socialist Patriotism: 15
Quotes On Patriotism: 23
Globalism: 85
Russia: 101
Definition of Socialism: 108
Bourgeois Socialism: 114
Nazbol: 133
Socialist Billionaires: 144
SwAC: 147
Revolution: 151
Quotes On Revolution: 158
Morality: 184
The Lumpen: 190
Womens Issues: 195
Sex: 207
Religion: 212
Asiatic Mode of Production: 219

Terminology:	226
Dogmatism:	228
Bourgeois Ideology:	233
History/Education:	236
The Masses:	239
Class:	244
Peasants:	251
Transitional Nature of Communism:	257

INTRODUCTION:

I an Irish Communist am writing to you, the American Left, specifically the Communist movement, because I am an internationalist and I want to tell you of the importance of your struggle. You American Communists. Firstly let me just say that I love the American people, I see you as a great, proud people who value your family and community.

You have a great revolutionary tradition from the War of Independence which inspired countless revolutionary movements afterwards and the Civil War which ended the scourge of slavery in your country. Revolutionary movements here in Ireland have always received support from America, in our time of famine we had America to thank as refuge for our people, our revolutionaries a safehaven from the British. There is of course a bad side to this history, for example the Cherokee who were sent on their trail of tears due to the actions of your government. Despite the conditions they endured, they still were able to send aid to us Irish in our time of great need as we endured severe famine. Us Irish people will never forget this act of great solidarity.

However today you need to liberate yourselves from your own monopoly capitalists, it is up to you Communists, as the best representatives of the proletariat to take this into your hands and win over the masses. I stand with those who have fought for a better America. I believe America has a destiny in this world to move on from its stained past and live up to its full potential. A socialist America would be a great liberationary force.

The question of where the movement is today has to be

raised. The problem is not that the Americaan masses are too 'stupid' as media likes to portray, no it is that the masses have been misled by the media. The deeper fundamental problem for you though is that there is a disconnect between the masses and you. You deserve complete blame for the failure of the last decades which has seen Communism almost collapse completely in support. To see a Communist movement which rejects populism, rejects the very existence of it's own country, burns it's own flag, this is the height of infantileness. National nihilism will achieve nothing. This is not a tea party, this is serious. The boot of American imperialism is on the neck of the world. The struggle you fight is a world historical struggle, if the American imperialists were to fall it would lead to a domino effect, the entire Western Left follows the example of America (to our detriment). The armies that oppress the people of the world would return home, the biggest obstacle to Communist revolutionaries in upholding comprador regimes would be no more. An America on the side of the people over the few parasites would be a country that could truly inspire the world and put America once more as the beacon of freedom and democracy the world over. An America that could actually make the American dream a reality for millions of people as China does today. An America that would actually join China in the Belt and Road initiative and create mutual win-win development and uplift the people of the world.

"I envy you. You North Americans are very lucky. You are fighting the most important fight of all - you live in the heart of the beast" - Ernesto 'Che' Guevara

This is the future you American Communists have ahead of you. It will be a tough road but I am sure that in the coming years and decades you will be successful in your struggle. To be frank I am sick of hearing about American politics. It is time to end the infantileness and actually build a mass movement. The truth is that the answer has been in front of you the whole time, it comes from the legacy of all Marxist-Leninists to have come before us, it comes from your own Party the CPUSA, the great stalwarts of the international Communist movement who led and organised millions in the past. It is their legacy that you must strive to return to and to finish what they dedicated their lives to. Communism is not an imported ideology to America, it is embedded in the very fabric of your history, it is about time that you reclaim this legacy and carry it forward to victory! There has never been a better time for revolutionaries in America than today.

In the first half of this book I will discuss a series of things that mainstream Communists in America get completely wrong, from an outside perspective. I will discuss this in multiple chapters with a key topic in each. The later half of this book is a similar to Mao's Red Book and features quotations on a wide range of topics None of this is meant to replace the classics, make sure the classics. I want to inspire a Marxist-Leninist culture of reading and learning.

You can find me at my website: http://liberation.us.to/

You can also find my writings here for free: https://lemmygrad.ml/post/38693

Please note that on the paper version the links do not work, if you are reading on the paper version and doubt a provided claim, fact or source, it will be provided here on the free version where you can view it, all references are here: https://lemmygrad.ml/post/38693/comment/214068

This book is dedicated to all those who have fought for a better world.

POPULISM:

The class struggle is something fundamental.

The class struggle comes from the contradiction between differing class interests that are at odds with each other, not some moral good vs bad scenario.

In the case of our society today, the primary class struggle is between the bourgeoisie and the proletariat.

Western Marxists tend to come into Communism with a moralistic depraved worldview where they want to destroy everything. They at heart are anarchistic. When they analyse history they think that everything 'bourgeois' is bad, even though from a materialist perspective in the past, the bourgeoisie were at one point a progressive force in history.

They think that the class struggle comes from the bourgeoisie being bad, but this is wrong because this notion leads to reformism as it implies that if the bourgeoisie would just be 'nice' that things would be fine and nothing would be wrong. This is why that notion must be fought against and why real class analysis is necessary.

Of course the relation the bourgeoisie has to the worker is bad (and it is necessary that us workers must organise collectively to get gains for our class from the bosses, as that is the only way for us to get to the negotiation table) but the point here is that it comes from something fundamental, as in the differing class interests which are completely at odds, akin to Hegel's master-slave dialectic. It does not come down from the sky or from binary good or bad.

The class struggle is at it's root populist. Communism

is true populism, and real populism is Communism, ask any random Chinese person who was, is, and will be the Communist party fighting for and they will answer the people. For example populism is redundant in China because it is a given that all politics must be 'populist'.

Real socialism is populist because populism is supposed to mean serving the masses but every 'populist' in power who is not a socialist (today not historically) is just a fake populist (demagogue) who is only in power to prevent the rise of class consciousness among the masses.

There is definitely an anti-establishment current emerging in the United States, but it is up to the Communist party to emerge as leader over it as opposed to other (fake) populist forces that form and show how Communism is true populism and win over the minds of the people. Due to the dwindling, downward labour aristocracy, an increasing amount of people have been looking for alternatives, albeit most have developed false consciousness. However the fact that people have developed false consciousness shows that if they were guided correctly they would become socialists. Anti-establishment movements such as those of (that stem from) Bernie Sanders and Donald Trump (MAGA) are prime examples of movements we should be reaching out to so that we can guide them on the right path. It is from these mostly blue-collar and rural people that we should be reaching out to as opposed to liberal, metropolitan (or suburban), university graduates, AKA the Professional Managerial Class (PMC).

Recently we saw American self-proclaimed 'Communists' oppose the trucker protests despite the vast majority of truckers being either working class or one truck operators (likely indebted to banks). This is all despite Engels stating that Communists must always bring the property question to the forefront of every protest. It does not matter what spurred on the protests to being with, what matters is the protests are anti-establishment. It is up to us Communists to be at the forefront of any movement against the current order and to always bring up the property question and guide it towards a revolutionary proletarian direction. Complete denounciation did not help the movement in anyway and is an indictment of just how low the Communist parties of North America (CPUSA and CPC) have fallen.

Communists want a socialist United States but there are people calling themselves socialist who want it to be called 'Turtle Island' because they think America is fundamentally stained and Americans are all settlers benefitting from imperialism (when this could not be further from the truth as only the imperialist bourgeoisie benefit from imperialism). Despite this being so divorced from the masses as all they know is the U.S. and the vast majority identity with the United States. Socialism is not just about having 'correct beliefs'. If your position does not allow you to build a mass, POPULAR movement of your countrys MAJORITY, then you are not a socialist. It is socialism that delivers true patriotism and socialism that delivers true populism and only socialism which can as it is the scientific vehicle moving society forward.

Revolutionary defeatism is the stance American Communists need to take internationally and when it comes to the oppression of oppressed peoples inside the U.S., but that needs to be backed up by real patriotism not the phony patriotism of the ruling class. We are patriotic to the people themselves, not the current state. We want to win over the masses and establish a socialist state to serve the masses because only with Communism can the mythos of the American dream be made reality for the masses.

When it comes to American leftists, they sure love to focus on issues which do not have anything to do with the majority of people. For example Chris Smalls' Amazon Labour Union (ALU) organised workers regardless of where they were ideologically (including anti-vaxxers) focusing solely on class, and was able to defeat the bosses of Amazon who employed every technique in the book and spent untold amounts just to stop the union, including attempting to divide around racial and other differences, yet they still succeeded because of the class focus. It is also notable that the union organisers took great inspiration from William Z. Foster's 'Organising Methods in the steel industry' showing that Communists are once again taking up their important position in American society and the legacy of the past lives on and is burning bright.

The economic and political are by far the most important issues while the social irrelevant in comparison but Americans seem to hyperfocus on divisive identity culture wars which plays into the bosses hands because Americans are highly polarised within a narrow overton window giving the illusion of difference leading to team sport mentality. Even before the neoliberal era, 'social issues' used to refer to matters of housing and health and occasionally societal issues such as abortion and gay rights, but since then, it has only ever referred to identity politics of the individual.

Leftists become associated with this identity confrontation due to the liberals, while right liberals (conservatives) are the reaction to this, often even American 'Marxists' themselves will make out the social issues to be the most important focus and completely ignore the economic issues. Ironically since Occupy Wall Street, leftists have become more and more pro-establishment, pro-NATO, pro-intervention and it is the Trump faction of the Republican party which is dominant over the party which has taken on the anti-establishment aesthetic (of course Trump is a phony). While so called 'ACAB' supporters praise the police crackdown on rightwingers, and today seeing anyone who identifies as a 'leftist' oppose NATO is seen as a good start when before that was a given

It is because of this that us Marxists and us

revolutionaries must break from the left-right wing paradigm if we want to win because Marxism-Leninism transcends the linear and binary political compass and it is up to us to ensure that we tread the golden centre of Stalin and not tread past the tightrope to revisionism on the right or ultra-leftism on the left.

Even when it comes to Communists in the West, there are a lot of people with this label who are really liberals with a red mask on and hold a typical liberal, Kantian (liberal universalism which stems from modernity) worldview where everything fits into their (postmodern) idealistic, metaphysical paradigm. Often these so called 'Communists' muddy the waters and take a line against religion or even a pro-prostitution and anti-family line. This shows just how depraved their worldview is as they do not care what the masses think. The vast majority of people in the world are religious, the vast majority oppose prostitution and have a loving family who they care for. However these people do not care about that and want to push their satanic depraved worldview on the masses. The masses have never and will never fall for them. This synthethic left must be pushed against hard as they will try to bring us and other genuine revolutionary movements down with them into the abyss. These people simply care about their own individual self and do not love the masses as we do. We must expose them for what they are and ensure that we do not get associated with them.

Empty sloganeering is very common in the Western Left, it causes nothing but confusion and does nothing but hold us back. For example, ACAB is a slogan which in general just puts us backwards. Most people know individual cops but of course we know that the true nature of the police force is to serve capital. (When it comes to the police I completely agree with this Parenti piece). Those who are already Communists know that ACAB refers to the police as an institution, but average people when they hear that the term think it means we are calling all individual officers bad people. This definitely does alienate a large percentage of people from our cause and plays into the hands of the bourgeoisie keeping us divided. ACAB is an anarchist/radlib slogan not one Communists should be using because it can be exploited against socialist states, which as we know still retain police forces and have to maintain law and order. When that order breaks down, all states, including socialist ones are susceptible to regime change, which gets exploited by the imperialists themselves. We must be careful as to our wording. I do however have no problem when it comes to people in the ghetto being against cops and pigs in phrasing because it is these (poor and minority) communities which suffer the most at the hands of the police and it is through rap and other artistic form that anti-establishment sentiment can be sown.

'Eat the rich' is almost as cringe as 'ACAB' because rich is subjective and even the slightly well off man down the road thinks that he is 'rich'. We must ensure that our actions and phrasing is directly against the true enemy of the working class, the capitalist elite themselves, and that it is not against (or seen to be against) the worker who is slightly better off. One good thing that came out of OWS (Occupy Wall Street) was the slogan '99% vs the 1%' because in comparison to 'Eat the rich', this slogan explicitely is raising the issue of class itself and while class relations are far more complex than this, it was a far better starting point to build a mass movement from and far less easy to exploit by the capitalist media. I think it is because of this (as well as the anti-establishment rap songs which were everywhere) and the rise of the internet which led to widespread anti-establishment sentiment. From this we saw such a reversal of this trend from the late 00s, as censorship became widespread, the internet became monopolised, as well as manipulation of algorithms to prevent the masses waking up.

When it comes to our sloganeering, phrases such as ACAB which require context to understand can come back to bite us because if you have to keep explaining a slogan then that slogan becomes useless. It is far too easy for our enemies to play up a strawman of our views and use that to keep us from winning the masses. 'Eat the rich' can also similarly be exploited.

There are also terms that come from liberal metropolitan university ivory towers pushed by academics on the masses to refer to groups of people. These terms are academic jargon terms and more often than not these terms are hated by the people they are actually supposed to describe. For example 'POC/BIPOC' and 'Queer'. 'POC' is hated by a **majority of people it describes** and has evolved from a **gesture of solidarity** to one of skirting around racial issues. 'Queer' is hated by a **vast majority of LGBT people**. The same also applies to 'latinx'. Of course it is obvious with these terms that they have their uses, it is clear that when the vast majority of people they are describing dislike or even hate the term, that they should be avoided when referring to those groups of people if at all possible. This is what I mean when I talk of academic jargon terms being pushed on people. We should avoid the jargon and get down to real issues and talk to the masses with normal terms they are familiar with not academic jargon they do not identify with.

Race is a social construct dependent on where you are, who is defining it and how it is defined. Race science originates from Anglo-Colonial pseudo-science to justify slavery and colonialism for the bosses and to divide the exploited classes on the basis of skin tone/pigment/melanin/haplogroup and ethnicity.

However while it is a social construct, it does have real meaning in simple terms since the colonial era. For example, to an African man living in Johannesburg, it is obvious that the fair skinned man (white) who came to enforce apartheid was serving the whites in trying to keep the majority who are darked skinned (black) people down. Whereas in the past before this dialectic came up through the onset of colonialism, different African groups fought each other, had vastly different cultures, languages and looked different, whereas against the white man, they were all black and in the struggle for African liberation after the colonisers left they were also black. The same holds true today globally as we live in a globalised society and one in which the vast majority of people outside of the imperial core (which is overwhelmingly white) are not white and are under the lock of imperialism.

While we must oppose race essentialism, it is undeniably that different racial groups will have different interests. For example, the promise of 40 acres and a mule to the black people of America which was promised to them after freedom from slavery was never fulfilled, instead they were ignored, segregated and later Jim Crow laws made them poor. All of this has a real impact still to this day and even today they suffer in much higher rates from police violence. From this there is the potential to build a mass movement of black people which will deliver 40 acres and a mule (tractor) to every black family and which will uplift the community. The affirmative action programs of today, which are based on race and not class are clearly made to divide as poor whites get left out while even rich blacks benefit, this should in the future be based on wealth. Giving land to black families would greatly uplift the community and would be an impetus for a cultural and social revolution as a rejuvenation is brought to the rural areas and black culture would thrive.

Similarly in America, when it comes to the native people, they are of course after a revolution going to have the right to self determination on a tribe by tribe basis and this will also serve as part of a massive land reform program which will see the poverty of reservations be no more and will uplift them and allow them to thrive and be respected and contribute to their communities in ways which were impossible through the reservation system which oppresses them. Both of these are massive impetuses for popular support in these communities which are both significant minorities. There is so much land owned by corporations and capitalists that other groups would of course also be included in an extensive land reform program.

Also to address those who hold some dogmatic idea that 'populism' means 'mob rule' whatever that is supposed to mean to entail as if it is a buzzword. 'Mob rule' is a slanderous term invented by the bourgeois historians to slander populist leaders and movements throughout history. However what is wrong with it? Real socialism is populist because populism is supposed to mean serving the masses and under a socialist system they themselves are in power. Only socialism has historically, and only socialism can provide this future to the working masses.

What if I was to tell you that I was working class:

– I was Anti-government - Pro-strong state to serve the people, for and by the people

– Anti-deep-state, anti-DoTB - Pro-government of action for working families, pro-DoTP

– Anti-elite/ultra-rich/bourgeoisie - Pro-worker/small business/farmers, pro-nationalist/patriot

– Anti-establishment, anti-censorship, anti-MSM - Pro-populism, pro-free speech

– Anti-malthusian, anti-degrowth - Pro-wealth, pro-material abundance, not anti-billionaire

– Anti-corporation/oligopolies/monopolies - Pro-conservative, centrally planned economy

– Anti-war, anti-imperialism, anti-colonialism, anti-racist - Pro-self-determination

– Anti-immigration, seeing immigration for what it is, braindrain - Pro-immigrant, internationalist

– Anti-idpol - Pro-equal rights, live and let live, what happens in the bedroom stays there

– Anti-moralism, anti-vegan - Pro-facts and logic, pro-environmental and animal conservation

– Anti-reform, anti-taxation, taxation is theft - Pro-gun ownership, pro-revolution, expropriation

– Pragmatic, thinking of how things can be directly applied to my community and state

You would probably think that I was conservative, but no I am a Communist.

Liberals would be calling for my arrest.

LAND REFORM:

Land reform is the solution not 'Land back' to the American issue of land. Complete nationalisation is also not the answer in the short term. The native people should be included in an extensive land reform program as well as given self-determination. Black people should also finally be given 40 acres and a mule (tractor).

Socialists states have always implemented land reform. 'Land back' has never been implemented, America is no exception if it were to ever become socialist. The problem with 'Land back' is that it is a baseless slogan which has a different meaning depending on who uses it. It also has some dodgy backers such as Jeff Bezos who funds the official organisation. The same people who espouse this view also view the native peoples as 'noble savages', and have race essentialist views that they think they must think the way they want or else 'they are not real natives'. No, it is up to the native people themselves to decide what they want to do, virtue signalling does nothing for oppressed peoples. It is not up to you who likely is a white man, suffering from white guilt to decide for them. That is the national question and it is theirs, each, to decide on a tribe by tribe basis.

I also think that complete state ownership of land straight away is not the answer. If we look at the Soviet Union, the Bolsheviks came to power on a program of 'Peace, land and bread', which was simple and was the simple needs of the people that they were actually existing with at the time. They did not say they were going to nationalise everything today and create a socialist utopia tommorrow, no they were pragmatic and realistic, meeting the direct demands of the people in front of them. There is so much land in America owned by massive corporate entities, this could all be broken up easily and redistributed after the revolution in a broad program of land reform. The vast majority of people have become disillusioned with the corporate work place and as a result the socialisation of such means immedietely would not necessarily be favourable to people. We saw a similar process in the Soviet Union where land was reformed first and only nationalised on a large scale over a decade later. Under socialism, whereby the corporate workplace is collectivised, it has to be given new meaning and have some level of democracy among it's workers going forward in America.

Also, monopolisation necessitates collectivisation (due to class contradictions) but you cannot apply that where monopolisation has not happened yet as people are going to associate the collective with their fears of the corporate so you cannot just expect them to want to join something larger initially which is why in the Russian revolution the peasants were given land redistributed from the landlords. Different places have different material conditions when it comes to the application of land reform and thus it all depends on the conditions whether land is reformed and given out to the masses on a large scale or whether it be nationalised straight away which would be the case if the socialisation of agricultural production has already happened. It is likely that large corporate farms would be broken up, while farmers who work their own land would be given more land while new families would be given land to work. Socialism has to mean something directly to the people and historically this has often been land reform as land is space in its most direct sense, what it means directly depends on the material conditions.

When it comes to the capitalist system, of course the monopolisation of capital is inevitable but that does not mean you should be celebrating the closure of small businesses and celebrating that monopolisation. We as Marxists know that it is an inevitability and that the petty-bourgeoisie are a class doomed to proletarianisation (to put it in their own words) whether they like it or not eventually. It is merely a process of the system that is just the way it is. It also does not mean that we should be sad either on the other hand, but of course when you know a local mom and pop shop is closing and is being taken over by some corporate entity, that leaves a big loss on the community.

There is a tendency within Marxists (Western in particular) where they hate the petty-bourgeoisie, they see it as a 'bad class', despite the vast majority of petty-bourgeois people not being exploiters of labour at all. Of course they are a reactionary class but as they are a class on a downward spiral, they are definitely a section of the people we can reach out to and win over to the cause. Historically this has been especially true with the toiling masses of peasantry who in rural areas are a key group to win over as they are the rural masses. The Chinese revolution for example came primarily from the peasantry who had some stake in the system to some extent however small. There is also another problem with Western Marxists in particular where they look for a pure kind of proletariat but with looking at class through such a lens the irony is that there is no such thing as a pure anything and by that logic the vast majority of people are petty-bourgeoisie because they have some stake in the system. As in simple terms the petty-bourgeoisie is anything in between proletariat and bourgeoisie and thus far more people are petty-bourgeois than they realise.

However if we look at the corporate structure that proceeds after monopolisation has occured, we see that there is created an abstraction of the class struggle. Due to monopolisation there are more layers between you and the boss, the boss hires security to keep the workers in line and prevent theft, the bosses hires one-quarter of the workers to manage the other three-quarters and has HR to keep things in line and ensure the bosses interest is met over everyone elses. The bosses likely has no direct interaction with the workplace at all. This gives rise to labour unions but for the last few decades since the fall of the socialist bloc and collapse of militant unions, along with whitewashing of capitalists and reforms, has led to their complete decimation at the hands of union busters and the capitalists cronies. This has yet to be solved in the west for the most part as recently we saw the Amazon workers attempt at a union fail.

It is the monopolisation of capital inherent of the capitalist system (capital accumulation) as well as the conditions that arise from that monopolisation which make inevitable the development of socialism, this is how us Marxists know that socialism is inevitable, and in just the same way it is the contradictions that arise in socialism which make Communism inevitable. It is up to the Communist party to seize power and scientifically guide this process as either way we are heading into some kind of bourgeois socialism.

SOCIALIST PATRIOTISM:

Recently we have seen anti-patriotic 'socialists' refer to 'patriotic socialism' as if it is a separate distinct ideology. However this is a farce, the truth is that there is no socialism that is not patriotic. Just as in the same way we see people identify as 'democratic socialists' despite there being no socialism that is anti-democratic. What is real is socialist patriotism, which is a core socialist value.

It is obvious to Communists all over the world throughout history and to this day that to be a Communist is inextricably linked with Patriotism for one's people, one's country, one's culture and the progressive history of those who have come before them and struggled for a better world.

With this compilation of quotes I have very decisively shown this.

Here is a general outline of other resources on this topic.

To any self-declared 'Communist' who sees this and still holds an anti-patriotic line you either are oblivious to reality and our history or else you are a federal agent. Either way you should be treated as a subverter who does not want us to win. The feds spent almost the entire 20th Century trying to smear us Communists as Un-American with McCarthyism and now you want to fall in line with and pigeon-hole yourself into their caricature of us? Taking a national nihilist stance would effectively snooker us from having any chance at reaching the masses.

It is clear that the pro-patriotism side of the argument are right to any Communist outside of America and the anti-patriots have no ground to stand on except with strawmen such as patriots supporting imperialism despite Communists being the most anti-imperialist or it not being compatible with the national question when Communists have always advocated for the self-determination of native peoples.

From an outside perspective it reflects very badly on American Communists that this was even a debate. It shows the infantile nature and petty bourgeois radicalism present within Communist circles in the United States and shows that a lot of work has to be done towards building a mass party which can win over the working masses and take power. The rest of the world needs American Communists to take power, the boot of American imperialism can only be freed from the neck of the world when the Communist party wins the hearts and minds of the masses and from there victory can only be assured. However this can never happen while you dismiss the masses as 'reactionary' and 'settlers' or refer to the landmass that is materially known to millions of people as America, as 'Turtle Island'.

If you are not patriotic for something you are not a Communist. You are liberal with a red mask who has a calvinistic depraved moralistic worldview. Now it is understandable if Native American or Black people don't support the American flag, but the vast vast majority of Americans identify strongly with the American flag and Communists support the self determination of Native American tribes as per the National Question as well as for the Black Belt if they so please.

There is no contradiction between patriotism and support of the national question and the nationalism of the oppressed. There is no contradiction between patriotism and internationalism. There is no contradiction between patriotism and anti-imperialism in fact anti-imperialists are the only real patriots. Revolutionary defeatism is the manifestation of patriotism Communists must take in America as the wars of aggression are hurting the people of the world and neither are they helping the American people, they are enriching a few parasites at the expense of the rest of the world. Us Marxist-Leninists want our paper tiger, reactionary, imperialist government to lose and we want its enemies to win, we also do anti-war action (and expose the truth) in the imperial core better than the so called Third-Worldists (who out of infantilism reject American workers). We do this while building up a revolutionary movement as we are actually genuine. Finally to state the obvious there is no contradiction between Communists and patriotism, in fact Communism is the most true expression of Patriotism and love for one's own people.

The reason the patriotism debate is so important is because we defend China and other anti-imperialist states.

The U.S. is doing everything it can to demonise these states to the public because they know they are losing, it is because of this that in the coming years as we get out to the masses more and more that they will call Communists 'Un-American' for supporting anti-imperialist states. This is the reason that the feds are working overtime to make sure that the anti-patriotism side of the debate gets pushed as much as possible and it is because of this that we must distinguish ourselves from the slime and show how we are patriotic for the people and want to improve things and show how this is in no way contradictory to supporting anti-imperialist states. We cannot let the ruling class own the flag and let super-patriotism (jingoism and chauvinism, as opposed to proletarian patriotism), as Michael Parenti called it, dominate. We must desire to improve the conditions of the working masses and we must not let the ruling class control the narratives whether it be on what patriotism is or whether it is lies about anti-imperialist states.

"The government of the United States represents, as its army also does, the finances of the United States. But these finances do not represent the North American people; they represent a small group of financiers, the owners of all the big enterprises... who also exploit the North American people. Clearly they do not exploit them in the same manner that they exploit us, the human beings of inferior races... for we have not had the good fortune of being born from blood, Anglo-Saxon parents. But they do exploit and divide them, they too are divided into black and whites, and they too are divided into men and women, union and non-union, employed and unemployed" - Ernesto 'Che' Guevara

Why do online left people think that patriotism for one's PEOPLE, means we agree with what our government does/has done? I love my PEOPLE, my COMRADES, and that's why I want to change my country. This quote demonstrates that it is no different for the United States, just as it wasn't for Latin America even though it was made up of settler states, nor was it different for the GDR even though they had just suffered under the Nazis before it's establishment yet they were still patriotic for the people and the progressive elements of the past and built their own socialist states that they were patriotic towards and defended against from the agression of the imperialists.

"The U.S. flag is your flag, you cannot allow the U.S. ruling class to own the flag. The working class of the U.S. must fight for the flag and once socialism is established it is up to the workers to decide what they want to do with flag and the U.S. as it exists - (Fidel Castro, Addressing a group of students who did not want to associate with their flag while people from other countries sat next to theirs)

It is clear here what I said in another comment here, that

American 'Communists' never learn because no matter what other Communists tell them they must do to suceed and win, they still do the opposite and alienate the masses and without the masses you cannot win because only the masses can make a revolution but if you look down on the masses like Trotsky looked down upon the peasants as inherently reactionary then you will never win them over and your movement will stay irrelevant. Anarchistic actions such as flag burning (Which is understandable for nations oppressed under the boot of imperialism but I am talking about Americans, particularly white Americans in denial) have never brought one ounce of sucess to the American Communist movement in the last 50 years. Socialism isn't just about having 'correct beliefs.' If your position does not allow you to build a mass, POPULAR movement of your countrys MAJORITY, then you are not a socialist.

"Can a Communist, who is an internationalist, at the same time be a patriot? We hold that he not only can be but also must be. The specific content of patriotism is determined by historical conditions. There is the 'patriotism' of the Japanese aggressors and of Hitler, and there is our patriotism. Communists must resolutely oppose the 'patriotism' of the Japanese aggressors and of Hitler. The Communists of Japan and Germany are defeatists with regard to the wars being waged by their countries. To bring about the defeat of the Japanese aggressors and of Hitler by every possible means is in the interests of the Japanese and the German people, and the more complete the defeat the better. This is what the Japanese and German Communists should be doing and what they are doing. For the wars launched by the Japanese aggressors and Hitler are harming the people at home as well as the people of the world. China's case, however, is different, because she is the victim of aggression. Chinese Communists must therefore combine patriotism with internationalism. We are at once internationalists and patriots, and our slogan is,

'Fight to defend the motherland against the aggressors.' For us defeatism is a crime and to strive for victory in the War of Resistance is an inescapable duty. For only by fighting in defense of the motherland can we defeat the aggressors and achieve national liberation. And only by achieving national liberation will it be possible for the proletariat and other working people to achieve their own emancipation. The victory of China and the defeat of the invading imperialists will help the people of other countries. Thus in wars of national liberation patriotism is applied internationalism" - Mao Zedong

This quote demonstrates that socialist patriotism is patriotism for the people themselves, not for the genocidal imperialist state and its actions internally or externally against oppressed peoples. It is in the interest of the vast majority of the American people regardless of race to overthrow the American bourgeoisie and free themselves from their chains.

Here are some links on the book settlers because Americans seem to somehow think that it is compatible with Marxism when it is fundamentally at odds and alien to it.

– Settlers Debunked -1 -2 -3 -4 -5 -6 -7 -8

Also when it comes to decolonisation, this article explains in detail actual real examples of it in action in the world past and present, that are not just empty sloganeering and false virtue signalling.

Firstly patriotism is not nationalism. However there are many different types of patriotism such as Jingoism (which is uncritically supporting everything your country does) or Chauvinism (which is the oppression of oppressed peoples and seeing your country as superior as well as pushing your values on people), these are extreme forms of patriotism. They are also the most common expressions of patriotism in the United States for obvious reasons. Socialist patriotism (or just patriotism) on the other hand is a love for your people, it does not mean you support your country when it oppresses oppressed groups or that you love the system that oppresses workers and oppressed peoples, it means that you love the people and want to liberate them from the oppressors and the system those oppressors uphold.

Destroying the U.S. empire is just as much in the interests of the American working class as it is in the interests of the Cuban or Afghani people.

I am not American, in fact America has had a negative effect on my country with it's military occupation and corporations but the fact of the matter is that American socialists have to be patriots if they want to win, because only socialism can actually serve the masses, the only groups who benefit form Imperialism are the ruling classes, it is in the interests of the American working class to overthrow their oppressors just as much as it in is in my interest and the interests of the whole world.

Every major Communist party across the world (including in the U.S.) opposes flag burning of the American flag by Americans because it is anarchistic and divorces them from the responsibility of themselves having to end imperialism and Americanism. Of course it is understandable if black or native people oppose the United States project but any Communist recognises that they are entitled to self-determination and they are still patriotic for America as in the people and if they are not they are patriotic for something (their own nation).

It is only ever whites who have no patriotism for anything and you can not call yourself a Communist if you are not a patriot because being a Communist means that you have a deep love for your people and want to see things get better for them. Socialist patriotism does not mean you defend everything the state does, no in fact it means that you oppose it because you have a deep love for the people and want to see them do better and free themselves from the shackles of oppression and in the case of the United States them doing so means that the boot of imperialism gets off the neck of the third world. Only then can the world prosper and peace be enjoyed.

The quotes linked above together demonstrate this perfectly, the Fidel quote is particularly striking because it just goes to show how American self proclaimed Communists have been doing the same shit of flag burning for 50 years with no success to speak of whatsoever... and it is no wonder when every international Communist keeps telling them the same things over and over again.

To conclude, it is clear this should never have been a debate in the first place and now that this line has convincely won out it is clear that Americans must join the CPUSA and work towards improving it and building it into a mass party which can win over the masses. This is what the world needs the most!

QUOTES ON PATRIOTISM:

"I, John Brown, am now quite certain that the crimes of this guilty land can never be purged away but with blood. I had, as I now think, vainly flattered myself that without very much bloodshed, it might be done. This is a beautiful country" - John Brown

"We congratulate the American people upon your re-election by a large majority. If resistance to the Slave Power was the reserved watchword of your first election, the triumphant war cry of your re-election is Death to Slavery. From the commencement of the titanic American strife the workingmen of Europe felt instinctively that the star-spangled banner carried the destiny of their class. The contest for the territories which opened the dire epopee, was it not to decide whether the virgin soil of immense tracts should be wedded to the labour of the emigrant or prostituted by the tramp of the slave driver?" - Karl Marx

"The unity of the nation was not to be broken; but, on the contrary, to be organised by the Communal Constitution, and to become a reality by the destruction of the State power which claimed to be the embodiment of that unity independent of, and superior to, the nation itself, from which it was but a parasitic excrescence; that unity of great nations which, if originally brought about by political force, has now become a powerful coefficient of social production; if the Commune was thus the true representative of all the healthy elements of French society, and therefore the truly national government, it was, at the same time, as a working men's government, as the bold champion of the emancipation of labour, emphatically international. Within sight of that Prussian army, that had annexed to Germany two French provinces, the Commune annexed to France the working people all over the world" - Karl Marx

"It is a truth which at the very least teaches us to see the hollowness of our patriotism, the perverted nature of our state and to hide our faces in shame. I can see you smile and say: what good will that do? Revolutions are not made by shame. And my answer is that shame is a revolution in itself; it really is the victory of the French Revolution over that German patriotism which defeated it in 1813. Shame is a kind of anger turned in on itself. And if a whole nation were to feel ashamed it would be like a lion recoiling in order to spring" - Karl Marx

"Unity of great nations which, if originally brought about by political force, has now become a powerful coefficient of social production" - Karl Marx

"Though not in substance, yet in form, the struggle of the proletariat with the bourgeoisie is at first a national struggle" - Karl Marx

"It is altogether self evident that; the working class must organise itself at home as a class and that its own country is the immediate arena of its struggle" - Karl Marx

"The workingmen have no country. We cannot take from them what they have not got. Since the proletariat must first of all acquire political supremacy, must rise to be the leading class of the nation, must constitute itself the nation, it is so far, itself national, though not in the bourgeois sense of the word" - Karl Marx

"'For Mussulmans, there is no such thing as subordination', Inequality is an abomination to 'a true Mussulman' (a Muslim), but these sentiments, (…) 'will go to rack and ruin without a revolutionary movement" - Karl Marx

"'No socialist,' remarked the Doctor, smiling, 'need predict that there will be a bloody revolution in Russia, Germany, Austria, and possibly Italy if the Italians keep on in the policy they are now pursuing. The deeds of the French Revolution may be enacted again in those countries. That is apparent to any political student. But those revolutions will be made by the majority. No revolution can be made by a party, but by a nation'" - Karl Marx

"The English laughed heartily when I began my speech with the observation that our friend Lafargue, and others, who had abolished nationalities, had addressed us in 'French', i.e., in a language which nine-tenths of the audience did not understand. I went on to suggest that by his denial of nationalities he seemed quite unconsciously to imply their absorption by the model French nation" - Karl Marx

"'The barbarities and desperate outrages of the so-called Christian race, throughout every region of the world, and upon every people they have been able to subdue, are not to be paralleled by those of any other race, however fierce, however untaught, and however reckless of mercy and of shame, in any age of the earth. This does not mean that the American people have an original sin that they must be cleansed of by fire and destruction. The illegitimate state shall be destroyed, not the people'" - Karl Marx

"The workingmen of Europe feel sure that, as the American War of Independence initiated a new era of ascendancy for the middle class, so the American Antislavery War will do for the working classes. They consider it an earnest of the epoch to come that it fell to the lot of Abraham Lincoln, the single-minded son of the working class, to lead his country through the matchless struggle for the rescue of an enchained race and the reconstruction of a social world" - Karl Marx

"The biggest things that are happening in the world

today are on the one hand the movement of the slaves in America started by the death of John Brown and, on the other, the movement of the serfs in Russia" - Karl Marx

"No, I make no pretension to patriotism. So long as my voice can be heard on this or the other side of the Atlantic, I will hold up America to the lightning scorn of moral indignation. In doing this, I shall feel myself discharging the duty of a true patriot; for he is a lover of his country who rebukes and does not excuse its sins" - Frederick Douglass

"It is a strange transition from the states to Canada. First one imagines that one is in Europe again, and then one thinks one is in a positively retrogressing and decaying country. Here one sees how necessary the feverish speculative spirit of the Americans is for a rapid development of a new country (if capitalist production is taken as a basis); and in ten years this sleepy Canada will be ripe for annexation - the farmers in Manitoba, etc., will demand it themselves. Besides the country is half-annexed already socially - hotels, newspapers, advertising, etc., all of the American pattern. And they may tug and resist as much as they like; the economic necessity of an infusion of Yankee blood will have its way and abolish this ridiculous boundary line - and when the time comes, John Bull will say 'Amen' to the matter" - Friedrich Engels

"The tendency of the Capitalist system towards the ultimate splitting-up of society into two classes, a few millionaires on the one hand, and a great mass of mere wage-workers on the other, this tendency, though constantly crossed and counteracted by other social agencies, works nowhere with greater force than in America; and the result has been the production of a class of native American wage-workers, who form, indeed, the aristocracy of the wage-working class as compared with the immigrants, but who become conscious more and more every day of their solidarity with the latter and who feel all the more acutely their present condemnation of life-long wage-toil, because they still remember the bygone days, when it was comparatively easy to rise to a higher social level. Accordingly the working class movement, in America, has started with truly American vigor, and as on that side of the Atlantic thigns march with at least double the European speed, we may yet live to see America take the lead in this respect too" - Friedrich Engels

"At first the contest is carried on by individual labourers, then by the work-people of a factory, then by the operatives of one trade, in one locality, against the individual bourgeois who directly exploits them... It was just this contact that was needed to centralise the numerous local struggles, all of the same character, into one national struggle between classes" - Friedrich Engels

"A country like America, when it is really ripe for a socialist workers' party, certainly cannot be hindered from having one by the couple of German socialist doctrinaires" - Friedrich Engels

"In America, where a democratic constitution has already been established, the Communists must make the common cause with the party which will turn this constitution against the bourgeoisie and use it in the interests of the proletariat - that is, with the agrarian National Reformers" - Friedrich Engels

"This party is called upon to play a very important part in the movement. But in order to do so they will have to doff every remnant of their foreign garb. They will have to become out and out American. They cannot expect the Americans to come to the them; they, the minority and the immigrants, must go to the Americans" - Friedrich Engels

"To love your country, and be willing to sacrifice and battle for it, that is patriotism. To have no home, to be unable to provide self and loved ones with food, clothing and shelter, that is poverty. At first sight it would appear that a man afflicted with poverty could not possibly be a patriot. He owns no part of any country, and patriotism means love of one's own country, not love of a country owned by others. What matters it to the poor devil who is starving whether the country in which he is hungry is owned by this ruler or that ruler, if his miserable status changes not? But we see that poverty, instead of crushing patriotism. actually appears to produce it. The troops who left New York yesterday to fight the Chinese were mostly men who own nothing in the way of property in this country. They are not going to fight for love of their country. That have none. Their very poverty gave birth to the bastard patriotism of the Hessian. Here is a sample of the leave-takings between the soldiers and their wives: 'Oh, why did you go and enlist, Charlie? And now you have to go and leave me and the child all alone," said a weeping young wife, as she held her strapping soldier husband about the neck. 'It had to be done, Lizzie.' he replied. 'You know I could not find any work.' The capitalist papers which contain the above item also contain the usual silly talk about the 'patriotism of our volunteers,' and thus furnish proof for the socialist contention that the capitalist class is at once ignorant and corrupt. Ignorant in not knowing that this paid-for bastard patriotism portends the doom of their class, and corrupt in attempting to pass this counterfeit for the genuine article. Capitalism attacks and destroys all the finer sentiments of the human heart; it ruthlessly sweeps away old traditions and ideas opposed to its progress, and it exploits and corrupts those things once held sacred. Instead of the American freeman bidding his wife be of good cheer that he was going to fight for his country, we have the wage-slave driven by hunger to fight for a hireling's pittance. Instead of repelling a foreign foe, he goes to loot and ravage a peaceful race, so as to swell the coffers of his own capitalist masters. The patriotism which poverty produces is as yellow as the gold which buys it" - Daniel De Leon

"No honest man will consider anything he gives to the socialist movement a sacrifice. It is no sacrifice at all to invest all our time, wealth, knowledge, and all else, so as to leave our children the estate of the socialist or cooperative Commonwealth" - Daniel De Leon

"What is Patriotism? Love of country, someone answers. But what is meant by 'love of country'? 'The rich man,' says a French writer, 'loves his country because he conceives it owes him a duty, whereas the poor man loves his country as he believes he owes it a duty.' The recognition of the duty we owe our country is, I take it, the real mainspring of patriotic action; and our 'country', properly understood, means not merely the particular spot on the earth's surface from which we derive our parentage, but also comprises all the men, women and children of our race whose collective life constitutes our country's political existence. True patriotism seeks the welfare of each in the happiness of all, and is inconsistent with the selfish desire for worldly wealth which can only be gained by the spoliation of less favoured fellow-mortals. It is the mission of the working class to give to patriotism this higher, nobler, significance. This can only be done by our working class, as the only universal, all-embracing class, organising as a distinct political party, recognising in Labour the cornerstone of our economic edifice and the animating principle of our political action" - James Connolly

"The Socialist does not cease to love his country when he tries to make that country the common property of its people; he rather shows a greater love of country than is shown by those who wish to perpetuate a system which makes the great majority of the people of a country exiles and outcasts, living by sufferance of capitalists and landlords in their native land. Under Socialism we can all voice the saying of the poet; at present 'our' native land is in pawn to landlords and capitalists" - James Connolly

"...Not the rack-renting, slum-owning landlord; not the sweating, profit-grinding capitalist; not the sleek and oily lawyer; not the prostitute pressman - the hired liars of the enemy. Not these are the Irish upon whom the future depends. Not these, but the Irish working class, the only secure foundation upon which a free nation can be reared. The cause of labour is the cause of Ireland, the cause of Ireland is the cause of labour. They cannot be dissevered" - James Connolly

"After studying the Irish question for many years I have come to the conclusion that the decisive blow against the English ruling classes (and it will be decisive for the workers' movement all over the world) cannot be delivered in England but only in Ireland (- Karl Marx); We are told that the English people contributed to help our enslavement. It is true. It is also true that the Irish people have contributed soldiers to duly crush every democratic movement of the English people from the deportation of Irish soldiers to serve the cause of political despotism under Charles to the days of Featherstone under Asquith. Slaves themselves the English people helped to enslave others; slaves themselves the Irish people helped to enslave others. There is no room for recrimination. We are only concerned now with the fact - daily, becoming more obvious - that the English workers who have reached the moral stature of rebels are now willing to assist the working class rebels of Ireland, and that those Irish rebels will in their turn help the rebels of Ireland, and that those Irish rebels will in their turn help the rebels of England to break their chains and attain the dignity of freedom. There are still a majority of slaves in England - there are still a majority of slaves in Ireland. We are under no illusions as to either country. But we do not intend to confound the geographical spot on which the rebels lie with the political government upheld by the slave. For us and ours the path is clear. The first duty of the working class of the word is to settle accounts with the master class of the world - that of their own country at the head of the list. To that point this struggle, as all such struggles, is converging" - James Connolly

"The socialist of another country is a fellow patriot; the

capitalist of my own country is a natural enemy" - James Connolly

"We are full of a sense of national pride, and for that very reason we particularly hate our slavish past (when the landed nobility led the peasants into war to stifle the freedom of Hungary, Poland, Persia and China), and our slavish present, when these selfsame landed proprietors, aided by the capitalists, are loading us into a war in order to throttle Poland and the Ukraine, crush the democratic movement in Persia and China, and strengthen the gang of Romanovs, Bobrinskys and Purishkeviches, who are a disgrace to our Great-Russian national dignity. Nobody is to be blamed for being born a slave; but a slave who not only eschews a striving for freedom but justifies and eulogises his slavery (eg. calls the throttling of Poland and the Ukraine, etc. a 'defence of the fatherland' of the Great Russians) - such a slave is a lickspittle and a boor, who arouses a legitimate feeling of indignation, contempt, and loathing" - V.I. Lenin

"We know that the especially favourable conditions for the development of capitalism and the rapidity of this development have produced a situation in which vast national differences are speedily and fundamentally, as nowhere else in the world, smoothed out to form a single 'American' nation" - V.I. Lenin

"American Revolutionary workers have to play an exceptionally important role as uncompromising enemies of American imperialism" - V.I. Lenin

"Bolshevism, our reading of Marxism, actually originated in America. Daniel De Leon left the Socialist Party, he resigned, he founded a more radical party, a more truly Marxist party, which he called the Socialist Workers Party of America" - V.I. Lenin

"We are ruining the Russian language. We use foreign words with no need to use them. We use them incorrectly. So why say 'defects' when we can say flaws, or deficiencies, or lacunae?.. Isn't it time to declare a war on the unnecessary use of foreign words?" - V.I. Lenin

"The American people have a revolutionary tradition which has been adopted by the best representatives of the American proletariat, who have repeatedly expressed their complete solidarity with us Bolsheviks. That tradition [which] is the war of liberation against the British in the eighteenth century and the civil war in the nineteenth century. In some respects, if we only take into consideration the 'destruction' of some branches of industry and of the national economy, America in 1870 was behind 1860. But what a pedant, what an idiot would anyone be to deny on these grounds the immense, world-historic, progressive and revolutionary significance of the American Civil War of 1863-65!" - V.I. Lenin

"The history of modern, civilised America opened with one of those great, really liberating, really revolutionary wars of which there have been so few compared to the vast number of wars of conquest which, like the present imperialist war, were caused by squabbles among kings, landowners or capitalists over the division of usurped lands or ill-gotten gains. That was the war the American people waged against the British robbers who oppressed America and held her in colonial slavery, in the same way as these 'civilised' bloodsuckers are still oppressing and holding in colonial slavery hundreds of millions of people in; all parts of the world" - V.I. Lenin

"The American people, who set the world an example in waging a revolutionary war against feudal slavery, now find themselves in the latest, capitalist stage of wage-slavery to a handful of multimillionaires..." - V.I. Lenin

"The proletariat... evaluates every national demand, every national separation from the angle of the class struggle of the workers" - V.I. Lenin

"Is a sense of national pride alien to us, Great-Russian class-conscious proletarians? Certainly not! We love our language and our country, and we are doing our very utmost to raise her toiling masses (i.e., nine-tenths of her population) to the level of a democratic and socialist consciousness. To us it is most painful to see and feel the outrages, the oppression and the humiliation our fair country suffers at the hands of the tsar's butchers, the nobles and the capitalists. We take pride in the resistance to these outrages put up from our midst, from the Great Russians; in that midst having produced Radishchev, the Decembrists and the revolutionary commoners of the seventies; in the Great-Russian working class having created, in 1905, a mighty revolutionary party of the masses; and in the Great-Russian peasantry having begun to turn towards democracy and set about overthrowing the clergy and the landed proprietors" - V.I. Lenin

"We remember that Chernyshevsky, the Great-Russian democrat, who dedicated his life to the cause of revolution, said half a century ago: 'A wretched nation, a nation of slaves, from top to bottom - all slaves.' The overt and covert Great-Russian slaves (slaves with regard to the tsarist monarchy) do not like to recall these words. Yet, in our opinion, these were words of genuine love for our country, a love distressed by the absence of a revolutionary spirit in the masses of the Great-Russian people. There was none of that spirit at the time. There is little of it now, but it already exists. We are full of national pride because the Great-Russian nation, too, has created a revolutionary class, because it, too, has proved capable of providing mankind with great models of the struggle for freedom and socialism, and not only with great pogroms, rows of gallows, dungeons, great famines and great servility to priests, tsars, landowners and capitalists" - V.I. Lenin

"During a reactionary war a revolutionary class cannot but desire the defeat of its government" - V.I. Lenin

"'No nation can be free if it oppresses other nations,' said

Marx and Engels, the greatest representatives of the consistent nineteenth century democracy, who became the teachers of the revolutionary proletariat. And, full of a sense of national pride, we Great-Russians want, come what may, a free and independent, a democratic, republican and proud Great Russia, one that will base its relations with its neighbours on the human principle of equality, and not on the feudalist principle of privelage, which is so degrading to a great nation. Just because we want that, we say: it is impossible, in the twentieth century and in Europe (even in the far east of Europe), to 'defend the fatherland' otherwise than by using every revolutionary means to combat the monarchy, the landowners and the capitalists of one's own fatherland, i.e., the worst enemies of our country. We say that the Great Russians cannot 'defend the fatherland' otherwise than by desiring the defeat of tsarism in any war, this as the lesser evil to nine-tenths of the inhabitants of Great Russia. For tsarism not only oppresses those nine-tenths economically and politically, but also demoralises, degrades, dishonours and prostitutes them by teaching them to oppress other nations and cover up this shame with hypocritical and quasi-patriotic phrases" - V.I. Lenin

"This is a lie; it is disgusting, intolerable hypocrisy. Everyone knows - and the Grütlianer openly publishes this bitter truth - that the congress is being postponed because these social-patriots are afraid of the workers, afraid that the workers will decide against defence of the fatherland; that they threaten to resign their seats in the Nationalrat, if a decision against defence of the fatherland is carried. The social-patriot (referring to 'socialists' who supported their own imperialists war of aggression, this caused the SPD/KPD split and was the main dividing line between the Mensheviks and Bolsheviks) 'leaders' of the Socialist Party of Switzerland, who even now, two and a half years after the beginning of the war, favour 'defence of the fatherland', i.e., defence of the imperialist bourgeoisie of one or the other coalition, have decided to disrupt the congress, to sabotage the will of the Swiss socialist workers, to prevent them from discussing and determining, during the war, their attitude towards the war, towards the 'defenders of the fatherland', i.e., towards the lackeys of the imperialist bourgeoisie" - V.I. Lenin

"All Communist parties should render direct aid to the revolutionary movements among the dependent and underprivelaged nations (for example Ireland, the American Negroes, etc.) and in the colonies" - V.I. Lenin

"The proletariat of the oppressing nations cannot confine itself to the general hackneyed phrases against annexations and for the equal rights of nations in general, that may be repeated by any pacifist bourgeois. The proletariat cannot evade the question that is particularly 'unpleasant' for the imperialist bourgeoisie, namely, the question of the frontiers of a state that is based on national oppression. The proletariat cannot but fight against the forcible retention of the oppressed nations within the boundaries of a given state, and this is exactly what the struggle for the right of self-determination means. The proletariat must demand the right of political secession for the colonies and for the nations that 'its own' nation oppresses. Unless it does this, proletarian internationalism will remain a meaningless phrase; mutual confidence and class solidarity between the workers of the oppressing and oppressed nations will be impossible; the hypocrisy of the reformists and Kautskyan advocates of self-determination who maintain silence about the nations which are oppressed by 'their' nation and forcibly retained within 'their' state will remain unexposed" - V.I. Lenin

"We live in the capitalist system, so called because it is dominated by the capitalist class. In this system the capitalists are the rulers and the workers are the subjects. The capitalists are in a decided minority and yet they rule because of the ignorance of the working class" - Eugene V. Debs

"On this May Day let us stand upright and be counted. We need to be united. We need to get together. We need to feel the common touch. The world will always be against us if we are not for ourselves. You who produce everything, you who really create, you who are conserving civilisation - how can you endure to think that you are the bottom class, the lower order? When you go for a job to the master class you work upon conditions which they prescribe. You depend upon them for tools, you work for their benefits" - Eugene V. Debs

"They have always taught and trained you to believe it to be your patriotic duty to go to war and to have yourselves slaughtered at their command. But in all the history of the world you, the people, have never had a voice in declaring war, and strange as it certainly appears, no war by any nation in any age has ever been declared by the people. And here let me emphasise the fact - and it cannot be repeated too often - that the working class who fight all the battles, the working class who make the supreme sacrifices, the working class who freely shed their blood and furnish the corpses, have never yet had a voice in either declaring war or making peace. It is the ruling class that invariably does both. They alone declare war and they alone make peace" - Eugene V. Debs

"It is 'patriotism' of the workers of one nation to fall upon and foully murder the workers of another nation to enlarge the possessions of their masters and increase the piles of their bloodstained riches, and as long as the poor, deluded toiling masses are fired by this brand of 'patriotism,' they will serve as cannon fodder and no power on earth can save them from their sodden fate. We socialists are not wanting in genuine patriotism, but we are deadly hostile to the fraudulent species which is 'the last refuge of the scoundrel' and which prompts every crook and grafter and every blood -sucking vampire to wrap his reeking carcass in the folds of the national flag that he may carry on his piracy and plunder in the name of 'patriotism.' Ours is a wider patriotism - as wide as humanity. We abhor murder in uniform even more than we do in midnight assassination. We stand with Garrison upon the proposition that the world is our country and that all mankind are our countrymen. We stand for peace and for the only system that makes peace possible. They, who support a system that breeds war cannot consistently say they are for peace, and they who prate so much about their 'patriotism' have, as a rule, the hearts of poltroons and the souls of cowards. Patriotism, like brotherhood, must be international and all embracing to be at all. Socialism rightly understood is the most profound patriotic movement on the planet" - Eugene V. Debs

"We have to give life to Indo-American socialism with our own reality, in our own language. Here is a mission worthy of a new generation" - José Carlos Mariátegui

"In the lead-up to Nazi aggression, we have seen Stalin stress the need [to] link 'national sentiment' and the idea of the nation [to] a healthy nationalism, correctly understood with proletarian internationalism; [He similarly distinguishes between] cosmopolitanism [and an] internationalism [which knows - and in fact must know - how to be] profoundly national [as well]" - Antonio Gramsci

"Who is the real patriot, or rather what is the kind of patriotism that we represent? The kind of patriotism we represent is the kind of patriotism which loves America with open eyes. Our relation towards America is the same as the relation of a man who loves a woman, who is enchanted by her beauty and yet who cannot be blind to her defects. And so I wish to state here, in my own behalf and in behalf of hundreds of thousands whom you decry and state to be antipatriotic, that we love America, we love her beauty, we love her riches, we love her mountains and her forests, and above all we love the people who have produced her wealth and riches, who have created all her beauty, we love the dreamers and the philosophers and the thinkers who are giving America liberty. But that must not make us blind to the social faults of

America. That cannot make us deaf to the discords of America. That cannot compel us to be inarticulate to the terrible wrongs committed in the name of patriotism and in the name of the country. We simply insist, regardless of all protests to the contrary, that this war is not a war for democracy. If it were a war for the purpose of making democracy safe for the world, we would say that democracy must first be safe for America before it can be safe for the world" - Emma Goldman

"I am not a world refugee, I am a German with great national, but also international experiences. My nation, to which I belong and which I love, is the German people, and my nation, which I honour with great pride, is the German nation, a chivalrous, proud and hard nation. I am blood of the blood and flesh of the flesh of the German workers and therefore, as their revolutionary child, I later became their revolutionary leader. My life and work knew and knows only one thing: to use my spirit and my knowledge, my experience and my energy, indeed my whole personality, for the victorious socialist struggle for freedom in the new springtime of the German nation!" - Ernst Thälmann

"…Who therefore is a patriot? They or us? Capital doesn't have a country and seeks profit in whatever country it is able to. That is why it isn't concerned for the existence of borders and the state. But all we own are our hats and the small kerb in front of us… So, who can be interested more in their country? They, who remove the capital from the country, or us who are stuck on our doorsteps here?.." - Aris Velouchiotis

"The proletarian state will gradually turn, as socialist construction succeeds, capitalist relations are eradicated and the capitalists disappear, into a state of the whole people" - (Mikhail Kalinin, What the Soviet government is doing to achieve democracy, 1926)

"Mussolini does his utmost to make capital for himself out of the heroic figure of Garibaldi. The French fascists bring to the fore as their heroine Joan of Arc. The American fascists appeal to the traditions of the American War of Independence, the traditions of Washington and Lincoln. The Bulgarian fascists make use of the national-liberation movement of the seventies and its heroes beloved by the people, Vassil Levsky, Stephan Karaj and others. Communists who suppose that all this has nothing to do with the cause of the working class, who do nothing to enlighten the masses on the past of their people in a historically correct fashion, in a genuinely Marxist-Leninist spirit, who do nothing to link up the present struggle with the people's revolutionary traditions and past - voluntarily hand over to the fascist falsifiers all that is valuable in the historical past of the nation, so that the fascists may fool the masses" - Georgi M. Dimitrov

"We Communists are the irreconcilable opponents, in principle, of bourgeois nationalism in all its forms. But we are not supporters of national nihilism, and should never act as such. The task of educating the workers and all working people in the spirit of proletarian internationalism is one of the fundamental tasks of every Communist Party. But anyone who thinks that this permits him, or even compels him, to sneer at all the national sentiments of the broad massses of working people is far from being a genuine Bolshevik, and has understood nothing of the teaching of Lenin on the national question" - Georgi M. Dimitrov

"It is necessary to develop a line of thought that combines wise nationalism, properly understood, with proletarian internationalism. Proletarian internationalism should be based on the nationalism of individual countries [...], between that properly understood nationalism and proletarian internationalism there can be no contradiction. Nationless cosmopolitanism, which denies national sentiment and the idea of the nation, doesn't have anything in common with proletarian internationalism" - Georgi M. Dimitrov

"Soviet patriotism, expressing the devotion of the Soviet people to their socialist Fatherland, is cementing the foundations of the Soviet multinational State, rallying all peoples and nationalities of our country into a united, fraternal family. Soviet patriotism serves for the people of our country as a powerful ideological booster for unselfish work and heroic acts for the fame of the socialist Fatherland, for the sake of the victory of Communism. With the blazing expression of Soviet patriotism is the lofty feeling of Soviet national pride, the awareness of the immeasurable superiority of Soviet society and socialist culture over bourgeois society and its culture" - F. Chernov

"In the era of imperialism the ideology of cosmopolitanism is a weapon in the struggle of imperialist plunderers seeking world domination. Cosmopolitanism is the negation of patriotism, its opposite. It advocates absolute apathy towards the fate of the Motherland. Cosmopolitanism denies the existence of any moral or civil obligations of people to their nation and Motherland. The bourgeoisie preaches the principle that money does not have a homeland, and that, wherever one can 'make money,' wherever one may 'have a profitable business', there is his homeland. Here is the villainy that bourgeois cosmopolitanism is called on to conceal, to disguise, 'to ennoble' the antipatriotic ideology of the rootless bourgeois-businessman, the huckster and the traveling salesman. Lenin proved here that the bourgeoisie places the protection of its self-serving class interests 'higher than the interests of the fatherland, the people, or anything else,' that in the name of protecting its class interests the bourgeoisie creates a 'union of imperialists of all countries' against the workers" - F. Chernov

"Cosmopolitanism and nationalism are not opposites, but are merely two sides of bourgeois-imperialist ideology. Cosmopolitanism always was and is merely a screen, a disguise for nationalism. In due course, unmasking the German bourgeois 'true socialists,' Marx and Engels indignantly wrote: '...such a narrow nationalist world-view lies at the foundation of supposed universalism and German cosmopolitanism'" - F. Chernov

"The period of the dictatorship of the proletariat and of the building of socialism in the U.S.S.R. is a period of the flowering of national cultures that are socialist in content and national in form" - J.V. Stalin

"The strength of Soviet patriotism lies in the fact that it is based not on racial or nationalistic prejudices, but upon the profound devotion and loyalty of the people to their Soviet Motherland, on the fraternal cooperation of the working people of all the Nations inhabiting our country. Soviet patriotism is a harmonious blend of national traditions of the peoples and the common vital interests of all working people of the Soviet Union" - J.V. Stalin

"A Leninist cannot be just a specialist in his favorite science [like mathematics, botany or chemistry]; he must also be a political and social worker, keenly interested in the fate of his country, acquainted with the laws of social development..." - J.V. Stalin

"Proletarian culture does not abolish national culture, it gives it content. On the other hand, national culture does not abolish proletarian culture, it gives it form" - J.V. Stalin

"Under capitalism the exploited masses do not, nor can they ever, participate in governing the country, if for no other reason than that, even under the most democratic regime, under conditions of capitalism, governments are not set up by the people but by the Rothschilds and Stinneses, the Rockefellers and Morgans" - J.V. Stalin

"Earlier, the bourgeoisie presented themselves as liberal, they were for bourgeois democratic freedom and in that way gained popularity with the people. Now there is not one remaining trace of liberalism. There is no such thing as 'freedom of personality' any more, - personal rights are now only acknowledged by them, the owners of capital, - all the other citizens are regarded as raw materials, that are only for exploitation. The principle of equal rights for people and nations is trodden in the dust and it is replaced by the principle of Full rights for the exploiting minority and the lack of rights of the exploited majority of the citizens. The banner of bourgeois democratic freedom has been flung overboard. I think that you, the representatives of Communist and democratic parties must pick up this banner and carry it forward if you want to gain the majority of the people. There is nobody else to raise it. (Stormy applause)" - J.V. Stalin

"Earlier, the bourgeoisie, as the heads of nations, were for the rights and independence of nations and put that 'above all.' Now there is no trace left of this 'national principle.' Now the bourgeoisie sell the rights and independence of their nations for dollars. The banner of national independence and national sovereignty has been thrown overboard. Without doubt, you, the representatives of the Communist and democratic parties must raise this banner and carry it forward if you want to be patriots of your countries, if you want to be the leading powers of the nations. There is nobody else to raise it. (Stormy applause)" - J.V. Stalin

"What is a nation? A nation is primarily a community, a definite community of people. This community is not racial, nor is it tribal. The modern Italian nation was formed from Romans, Teutons, Etruscans, Greeks, Arabs, and so forth. The French nation was formed from Gauls, Romans, Britons, Teutons, and so on. The same must be said of the British, the Germans and others, who were formed into nations from people of diverse races and tribes. Thus, a nation is not a racial or tribal, but a historically constituted community of people" - J.V. Stalin

"American exceptionalism is posturing that America is exempt from the general laws of historical development" - J.V.

Stalin

"Hitlerites are not patriots since they invade other countries and destroy other cultures; It would be ludicrous to identify Hitler's clique with the German people, with the German state. The experience of history indicates that Hitlers come and go, but the German people and the German state remain" - J.V. Stalin

"But people cannot live together, for lengthy periods unless they have a common territory. Englishmen and Americans originally inhabited the same territory, England, and constituted one nation. Later, one section of the English emigrated from England to a new territory, America, and there, in the new territory, in the course of time, came to form the new American nation. Difference of territory led to the formation of different nations" - (J.V. Stalin, Marxism and The National Question)

"In fighting for the right of nations to self-determination, the aim of Social-Democracy is to put an end to the policy of national oppression, to render it impossible, and thereby to remove the grounds of strife between nations, to take the edge off that strife and reduce it to a minimum. This is what essentially distinguishes the policy of the class-conscious proletariat from the policy of the bourgeoisie, which attempts to aggravate and fan the national struggle and to prolong and sharpen the national movement. And that is why the class-conscious proletariat cannot rally under the 'national' flag of the bourgeoisie. That is why the so-called 'evolutionary national' policy advocated by Bauer cannot become the policy of the proletariat. Bauer's attempt to identify his 'evolutionary national' policy with the policy of the 'modern working class' is an attempt to adapt the class struggle of the workers to the struggle of the nations. The fate of a national movement, which is essentially a bourgeois movement, is naturally bound up with the fate of the bourgeoisie. The final disappearance of a national movement is possible only with the downfall of the bourgeoisie. Only under the reign of socialism can peace be fully established. But even within the framework of capitalism it is possible to reduce the national struggle to a minimum, to undermine it at the root, to render it as harmless as possible to the proletariat. This is borne out, for example, by Switzerland and America. It requires that the country should be democratised and the nations be given the opportunity of free development" - J.V. Stalin

"I daresay you yourself do not know quite clearly why you have lost these illusions You are a patriot, - as good a one as any among these super-patriots. You are very sincere in your patriotism, but so too are they. So there must be something wrong in the very conception of patriotism, which can lead men to pursue such contrary and often contradictory goals. Actuated by the same spirit of patriotism, one man reads the Gita, one sends missionaries to America to preach the gospel of Sri Ramkrishna, one orders the whole nation to spin, one cooperates in the working of the Montagu Reforms, another throws bombs, and there are even some who drink three bottles of whiskey a day. There is absolutely no reason to doubt that all of them are equally patriotic. Every one of them loves the Motherland, serves her, worships her, glorifies her, idealises her, - almost every one of these Indians believes implicitly in the providential mission of India to spiritualise the world. Yet in spite of all this, these patriots and the philosophy they preach do not satisfy you any longer, although there was a time when you accepted their teachings as infallible. This shows that there is some fundamental difference between your patriotism and that of the leaders in whom you have lost faith" - M.N. Roy

"Among the elementary measures the American Soviet government will adopt to further the cultural revolution are the following; the schools, colleges and universities will be coordinated and grouped under the National Department of Education and its state and local branches. The studies will be revolutionised, being cleansed of religious, patriotic (bourgeois patriotism) and other features of the bourgeois ideology. The students will be taught on the basis of Marxian dialectical materialism, internationalism and the general ethics of the new socialist society. Present obsolete methods of teaching will be superseded by a scientific pedagogy" - William Z. Foster

"A truly democratic government, unless it were to fail and be crushed under the violent attacks of big business, would have no alternative but to develop into the general type of government now existing in a number of countries of Eastern and Central Europe and known as People's Democracy. This new kind of government, in which the basic economic system is controlled by the people, the power of monopoly capital is shattered, and the working class is the leading class, is one which definitely tends to orientate toward building socialism, and not toward patching up obsolete capitalism. Socialism in the United States naturally would have some specific American characteristics. However it would embody the socialisation of all the social means of production and distribution, the carrying on a planned production for use instead of for profit, with the Government under the acknowledged leadership of the working class. Only with such a system, with the exploitation of man by man completely abolished, will American society finally be freed of the fascism, poverty, economic chaos, and warmongering that are increasingly menacing our country as well as other lands. All these socialist measures would, naturally, be legally adopted by the people's democratically elected government, by the People's Democracy, despite employer resistance, whatever its form and violence" - William Z. Foster

"Throughout the ages the central principle of all great systems of morals has been 'Do unto others as you would have them do unto you.' Under slavery, feudalism, and capitalism, although the ruling classes have constantly preached this maxim to their slaves as a way by which to regulate their lives, they themselves have cynically ignored it in practice. Their systems of exploitation, including present-day capitalism, have always been based upon a ruthless class ethics, condoning the most brutal violation of every principle of human solidarity. That is why Christianity has never 'worked.' As has been truly said, 'It has never been tried.' It is only with the introduction of socialism, and later of Communism, that the Golden Rule, without benefit of religion, becomes a matter of practical politics and of general acceptance by society as a whole" - William Z. Foster

"Dearborn, Kentucky, England (Ark.), Lawrence, Pittsburgh coal strike, etc., reflect the new spirit of the American class struggle. The capitalists, in the midst of the sharpening general crisis of capitalism, are determined to force the living standards of American toilers down to European levels, or lower. The workers will respond to this offensive by increasing class consciousness and mass struggle. More and more they will turn to the Communist party for leadership, and eventually they will be joined by decisive masses of the ever-more ruthlessly exploited poor farmers. The toiling masses of the United States will not submit to the capitalist way out of the crisis, which means still deeper poverty and misery, but will take the revolutionary way out to socialism. The working class of this country will tread the path of the workers of the world, to the overthrow of capitalism and the establishment of a Soviet government. Lenin was profoundly correct when he said in his Letter to American Workingmen, of Aug. 20, 1918: 'The American working class will not follow the lead of its bourgeoisie. It will go with us against its bourgeoisie. The whole history of the American people gives me this confidence, this conviction'" - William Z. Foster

"There is no other group as loyal to the interests of the

workers and the people as the Communists. As I have pointed out earlier, the whole life of our party has been a ceaseless fight for the interests of the workers, the Negro people, the nation. In our demand for socialism for the United States, we are giving expression to the supreme interest of the overwhelming majority of the American people. It is precisely because the Communists are the very best defenders of the interests of the American people that eventually our party will be the leading party of the nation. I, as other Communists, love the American people and their glorious revolutionary democratic traditions, their splendid scientific and industrial achievements. And I love, too, our beautiful land, in every corner of which I have lived and worked. I want only the best of everything for our people and this country. I have only contempt, therefore, for the 'foreign agent' charge, and doubly so because it comes from reactionaries who live by exploiting the American people and whose basic principle of operation is to peddle away the national welfare for the sake of their narrow class interests. We Communists revere our country. We are ardent patriots, but not nationalists. We defend the people's interests but we do not try to shove official American (capitalist) interests ahead at the expense of those of other peoples. For that is the road to war and general ruin. We are Marxian internationalists. We realise very well the common interests that the workers and the peoples of the whole world have together. They key to an intelligent internationalism in our day is friendly co-operation between the United States and the Soviet Union. This collaboration is indispensable if world peace is to prevail. On this basic issue we Communists stand four-square, come hell or high water! Our resolute position in this fundamental matter puts us into direct and irreconcilable collision with the imperialists" - William Z. Foster

"Now that the insane Tsar and his soothsayers are relegated to the farm, Lenin is a patriot to the limit, as well as an internationalist, ready to fight for the world" - William Z.

Foster

"Socialism in the United States will, out of necessity, have some American characteristics" - William Z. Foster

"We will incorporate U.S. traditions into the structure of socialism that the working class will create" - William Z. Foster

"One thing is certain: the economic survival of the Black in the South depends on close union with white workers, so as to present a united front against the tremendous growth of monopoly capital in the South today. When we compare African Americans with other groups we are not comparing nations or even cultural groups, since African Americans do not form a nation and are not likely to, if their present increasingly successful fight for political integration succeeds. They will exercise political power but not as a unit, since that would contradict their fight against segregation. They do not even form a complete cultural unit, although by reason of suffering and discrimination, and by historic artistic gifts, such a culture may be deliberately cultivated and in the end will unify the Black with other groups rather than divide them. African American, Russian and Irish art can flourish in the same state side by side. How the political aspect will develop is not clear. The old idea of mass migration of African American to found a foreign state is unlikely to be renewed. The newer idea of an American Black state within the United States is both improbable and undesirable. It contradicts our present effort at complete integration, and also the modern tendency toward fewer rather than more separate political states with state antagonisms, hatreds and war. Cultural units may, on the other hand, develop and grow to the advantage of all" - W.E.B. Du Bois

"The question here concerns the ideology encouraged by the imperialists, which propagates a sham 'obsolescence' of the principle of sovereignty, the 'legitimacy' of limiting state independence, an indifference to natural traditions and contempt for national culture. This ideology alleges that at the present time the idea of motherland is devoid of any meaning. For the financial oligarchy of the U.S.A., cosmopolitism has proved the best way of disguising its struggle for world supremacy and for the doing away with the independence of other states; The unions of monopolists are presented as the embodiment of 'unity of the European peoples' and as the way to overcome 'national limitations'. Small wonder that such propaganda is openly supported and financed by the big monopolies; The favourite thesis of the ideologists of cosmopolitism, especially he Right-wing socialists among them, is the allegation that in the modern world the principle of sovereignty has become an obstacle to the development of the productive forces; The enemies of Marxism assert that by defending the principles of state sovereignty and independence Communists oppose the tendencies of social development and want to preserve the division of the world into states and the disunion of the nations in the international arena; Nor can the danger of war be eliminated by a campaign against sovereignty. In our time wars do not arise as a result of adherence to state independence, as the ideologists of bourgeois cosmopolitism allege, but owing to socio-economic causes connected with the predatory nature of monopoly capital; the propagandists of cosmopolitism claim that the principle of sovereignty is antiquated because it hampers the development of general culture aand impedes the fusion of the peoples into one family; The fact that the proletariat defends the freedom of the nations, their independence and national traditions is an expression of the patriotism of the working class, which is the direct opposite of both the chauvinist and cosmpolitan ideology of the bourgeoisie. The patriotism of the working class springs primarily from the feeling of pride in the contribution that the people or nation concerned has made to the struggle of the oppressed and exploited masses for their liberation from exploitation and oppression. The patriotism of the working class is therefore profoundly progressive and revolutionary. Bourgeois propaganda tries to represent the capitalist class as the bearer of patriotic feelings. They want to slur over the fact that the patriotism of the bourgeoisie is always subordinate to its selfish, narrow class interests, and to disparage the patriotism of the working class and Communists. In this connection, bourgeois propagandists sometimes refer to the passage in the Communist Manifesto which says that 'the working men have no country'. It is perfectly clear, however, that it is not a question of repudiating the fatherland, but of the fact that in a society ruled by capitalists the fatherland is actually usurped by exploiters and is not a good father but a vicious stepfather to the workers. By overthrowing the rule of the exploiting classes the working class creates the conditions for the fullest possible manifestation of its patriotism, for it itself is the true bearer of patriotism in our time; Developing the Marxist point of view regarding the fatherland, Lenin wrote in 1908: 'The fatherland, i.e., the given political, cultural and social environment, is the most powerful factor in the class struggle of the proletariat… The proletariat cannot be indifferent to and unconcerned about the political, social and cultural conditions of its struggle and, consequently, cannot remain indifferent to the fate of its country. But the fate of the country interest it only to the extent that they affect its class struggle, and not in virtue of some bourgeois 'patriotism', quite indecent on the lips of a Social-Democrat; The whole spirit of Marxism, its entire system demands that each proposition should be considered α) only historically, β) only in connection with others and χ) only in connection with the concrete experience of history.'; In what historical situation the slogan of defence of the fatherland is proclaimed, what class proclaims it and for what purposes - these are the things that primarily interest the working class; The Bourgeois ideologists allege that by combating cosmopolitism Marxists disavow the international character of their doctrine and become nationalists. But the authors of such falsifications perpetrate a double forgery. Firstly, they put a sign of equality between the cosmopolitism of the bourgeoisie and the internationalism of the working class, and, secondly, they ascribe to Marxists the nationalist views which are characteristic precisely of bourgeois ideology. The internationalism of the working class is, as already stated, an expression of the community of interests of the workers of all countries in their struggle against their common enemy - capitalism, of the unity of their aim, the abolition of exploitation of man by man... and the unity of their ideology - the ideology of friendship and fraternity of the peoples. In this sense all workers belong to the same 'nation' - the world 'nation' of working people oppressed and exploited in all bourgeois countries by the same force - capital. This does not in any way mean, however, that while belonging to the single international army of working people, the worker ceases to be a Frenchman, Englishman, etc. Quite the contrary. True and not sham patriotism springs naturally from proletarian internationalism. In point of fact, does not faithfulness to the ultimate ideal of the working class imbue the workers with a fervent desire to see their own people free, prosperous, and achieving social progress? Seeking liberation from all forms of oppression and exploitation... The working class wants this not only for itself, but also for all the working people, for the whole nation. Only the achievement of the ultimate aims of the working class, i.e., the overthrow of the power of the exploiters, who impede the progress of the nation... and the building of socialism, can bring every nation real freedom, independence and national greatness. It follows that the most internationalist class - the working class - is at the same time the most patriotic class; The Communist Parties of the capitalist countries hold high the banner of national independence and freedom. Preservation of state sovereignty and realisation of an independent foreign policy are demands that form part of the programme of the Communist movements in France, Italy and other countries" - (Otto Wille Kuusinen, Fundamentals of Marxism-Leninism)

"The internationalism of the Communist Party was expressed by the Communist Timbaud, who was killed at Chateaubriant shouting 'Long Live the German Communist Party!' adding 'Vive la France!'; There is no left or right wing in our party. The Communist Party has never been as united around its Central Committee as it now is in the task that it is accomplishing - together with all patriots - to wrest victory over Hitlerite Germany as quickly as possible" - Maurice Thorez

"I fell in love with my country - its rivers, prairies, forests, mountains, cities and people. No one can take my love of country away from me! I felt then, as I do now, it's a rich, fertile, beautiful land, capable of satisfying all the needs of its people. It could be a paradise on earth if it belonged to the people, not to a small owning class" - Elizabeth Gurley Flynn

"Look at the American Revolution in 1776. That revolution was for what? For land. Why did they want land? Independence. How was it carried out? Bloodshed. Number one, it was based on land, the basis of independence. And the only way they could get it was bloodshed. The French Revolution - what was it based on? The land-less against the landlord. What was it for? Land. How did they get it? Bloodshed. Was no love lost; was no compromise; was no negotiation. I'm telling you, you don't know what a revolution is. 'Cause when you find out what it is, you'll get back in the alley; you'll get out of the way. The Russian Revolution - what was it based on? Land. The land-less against the landlord. How did they bring it about? Bloodshed. You haven't got a revolution that doesn't involve bloodshed. And you're afraid to bleed. I said, you're afraid to bleed" - Malcolm X

"The American dream reminds us that every man is heir to the legacy of worthiness - Martin Luther King Jr.

"When the architects of our republic wrote the magnificent words of the Constitution and the Declaration of

Independence, they were signing a promissory note to which every American was to fall heir" - Martin Luther King Jr.

"I criticise America because I love her. I want her to stand as a moral example to the world; I have a dream that one day this nation will rise up and live out the true meaning of its creed; We hold these truths to be self-evident: that all men are created equal" - Martin Luther King Jr.

"At first, patriotism, not yet Communism, led me to have confidence in Lenin… By studying Marxism-Leninism parallel with participation in practical activities, I gradually came upon the fact that only Socialism and Communism can liberate the oppressed nations and the working people" - Hồ Chí Minh

"All men are created equal; they are endowed by their Creator with certain unalienable Rights; among these are Life, Liberty, and the pursuit of Happiness" - (Hồ Chí Minh, The Vietnamese Constitution, in a direct quote from the American Constitution)

"I would like to tell the American people that the aggressive war now being waged by the U.S. Government in Vietnam not only grossly flouts the national fundamental right of the Vietnamese people, but also runs counter to the aspirations and interests of the American people. This aggressive war has also besmeared the good name of the United States, the country of Washington and Lincoln. I wish to tell the American people about the determination of the entire Vietnamese people to fight the U.S. aggressors till complete victory. But as for the American people, we want to strengthen our relationship of friendship with them" - Hồ Chí Minh

"Our secret weapon is nationalism. To have nationhood, which is a sign of maturity, is greater than any weapons in the world" - Hồ Chí Minh

"I once said, 'We will bury you,' and I got into trouble

with it. Of course we will not bury you with a shovel. Your own [American] working class will bury you" - N.S. Khrushchev

"Something new has happened: For the first time in history our fatherland is guided by a plan that considers only the needs of the people, and aims at building prosperity and reconstructing of our fatherland" - Walter Ulbricht

"The reason that I am here today, from the mouth of the State Department itself, is: I should not be allowed to travel because I have struggled for years for the independence of the colonial peoples of Africa... That is the kind of independence like Sukarno got in Indonesia... The other reason that I am here today, again from the State Department and from the court record of the court of appeals, is that when I am abroad I speak out against the injustices against the Negro people of this land. I sent a message to the Bandung Conference and so forth. That is why I am here... I am not being tried for whether I am a Communist, I am being tried for fighting for the rights of my people, who are still second-class citizens in this United States of America... My mother was a Quaker, and my ancestors baked bread for George Washington's troops when they crossed the Delaware, and my own father was a slave. I stand here struggling for the rights of my people to be full citizens in this country. And they are not. They are not in Mississippi. And they are not in Montgomery, Alabama. And they are not in Washington. They are nowhere, and that is why I am here today. You want to shut up every Negro who has the courage to stand up and fight for the rights of his people, for the rights of workers, and I have been on many a picket line for the steelworkers too. And that is why I am here today" - Paul Robeson

"The demand of Africa and Asia for independence from alien domination and exploitation finds warm support among democratic-minded peoples everywhere. Although the calling of the Bandung Conference evoked bitter words of displeasure from high circles in Washington, the common people of

America have not forgotten that our own country was founded in a revolution of colonies against a foreign tyranny - a revolution proclaiming that all nations have a right to independence under a government of their own choice. To the Negro people of the United States and the Caribbean Islands it was good news... Typical of the Negro people's sentiments are these words from one of our leading weekly newspapers: 'Negro Americans should be interested in the proceedings at Bandung. We have fought this kind of fight for more than 300 years and have a vested interest in the outcome'" - Paul Robeson

"In Russia I felt for the first time like a full human being. No colour prejudice like in Mississippi, no colour prejudice like in Washington. It was the first time I felt like a human being. Where I did not feel the pressure of colour as I feel [it] in this Committee today. [Why do you not stay in Russia?] Because my father was a slave, and my people died to build this country, and I am going to stay here, and have a part of it just like you. And no Fascist-minded people will drive me from it. Is that clear? I am for peace with the Soviet Union, and I am for peace with China, and I am not for peace or friendship with the Fascist Franco, and I am not for peace with Fascist Nazi Germans. I am for peace with decent people" - Paul Robeson

"I say that he is as patriotic an American as there can be, and you gentlemen belong with the Alien and Sedition Acts, and you are the non-patriots, and you are the Un-Americans, and you ought to be ashamed of yourselves" - Paul Robeson

"During the consultations which the Central Committee of the CPSU held on questions of Soviet music, Zhdanov said in part: 'He cannot be an internationalist who does not love and respect his own people.' A bitter struggle is now being pursued in the Soviet Union under this slogan against bourgeois cosmopolitanism in art, philosophy and in science. In the editorial already quoted in No. 2 of the 'Voprossy Filosofii', cosmopolitanism is defined as follows: 'Cosmopolitanism is a reactionary ideology which preaches renunciation of national traditions, disparagement of national individuality in the development of different peoples, rejection of feelings of national honour and national pride.' Of course, we can agree completely with this definition of cosmopolitanism. Cosmopolitanism today is a weapon in the hands of American imperialism, a mean's of spiritual disarmament of a people who are, or are to come, under its domination. Cosmopolitanism proceeds hand in hand with the most unbridled nationalism which belittles, humiliates and rejects all that is foreign, and proclaims everything of its own as 'racially pure' and original; nationalistic cosmopolites or cosmopolitan nationalists are seeking 'proofs' in all corners of the globe and in all fields of human activity of the decisive spiritual influence of their nation upon which to base their exceptional rights to definite territories. Cosmopolitanism as spiritual quislingism is expressed in the slave-like imitation of all that is foreign, in the fettering of the development of national culture, in the servile discrediting of oneself, in reducing the cultural achievements of one's nation to the passive copying of foreign examples. The general laws of social development appear only through the specific forms of development in every individual country. Each nation with its share, with its achievements of material and spiritual culture, participates in the building of universal world culture. Living connections with one's fatherland and nation are, therefore, the pre-requisite for every progressive movement of science, philosophy and art. It is possible to penetrate into the essence of a phenomenon only by making a thorough study of the different specific forms of its manifestation. The generalisation of revolutionary theory becomes fuller and more profound in content, they deepen upon taking concrete form in the specific conditions of time and place, through application in the revolutionary activity of the national parties of the proletariat. Classics of Marxism-Leninism teach that national nihilism is alien to the working class, that the working class cannot and must not be indifferent to its fatherland and to its nation, to the positive traditions of its nation, to the national culture of its country. On the contrary, the working class of every country is the lawful heir to all the great and the significant that has been created in that country for the development of the nation and all of mankind. Engels, in the preface to the first edition of his work 'The Development of Socialism from A Utopia to A Science', stresses: 'We German socialists are proud of having our source not only in Saint Simon, Fourier and Owen, but also in Kant, Fichte, and Hegel.' In his article 'Bellicose Militarism and Anti- Militaristic Tactics of the Social-Democrats', written in 1908, Lenin said: 'The proletariat cannot bear itself with indifference and with equanimity towards the political, social and cultural conditions of its struggle, and, hence, it cannot be indifferent to the fate of its country.' By its profundity, sincerity, and warmth, Lenin's article 'On the National Pride of the Great Russians' is a unique example of deep love for one's fatherland and for one's people for their cultural heritage and for their great progressive traditions. Comrade Stalin, in his works, and especially in his addresses delivered during the Second World War, fired the national consciousness of the Soviet peoples by pointing to their magnificent traditions of struggle for the freedom and independence of their homeland, by calling upon them to be worthy of their great ancestors, thinkers, poets, patriot-generals" - (Boris Ziherl, Communism and Fatherland)

"I call on the workers, peasants, revolutionary intellectuals, enlightened elements of the bourgeoisie and other enlightened persons of all colours in the world, whether white, black, yellow or brown, to unite to oppose the racial discrimination practised by U.S. imperialism and support the American Negroes in their struggle against racial discrimination. In the final analysis, national struggle is a matter of class struggle. Among the whites in the United States, it is only the reactionary ruling circles who oppress the Negro people. They can in no way represent the workers, farmers, revolutionary intellectuals and other enlightened persons who comprise the overwhelming majority of the white people. At present, it is the handful of imperialists headed by the United States, and their supporters, the reactionaries in different countries, who are oppressing, committing agression against and menacing the overwhelmingly majority of nations and peoples of the world. We are in the majority and they are in the minority. At most, they make up less than 10 percent of the 3,000 million population of the world. I am firmly convinced that with the support of more than 90 percent of the people of the world, the American Negroes will be victorious in their just struggle. The evil system of colonialism and imperialism arose and throve with the enslavement of Negroes and the trade in Negroes, and it will surely come to its end" - Mao Zedong

"The U.S. government still has a veil of democracy, but it has been cut down to a tiny patch by the U.S. reactionaries and become very faded, and is not what it used to be in the days of Washington, Jefferson and Lincoln. The reason is that the class struggle has become more intense. When the class struggle becomes still more intense, the veil of U.S. democracy will inevitably be flung to the four winds" - Mao Zedong

"The United States, had first fought a progressive war of independence from British imperialism, and then fought a civil war to establish a free labour market. Washington and Lincoln were progressive men of their time. When the United States first established a republic it was hated and dreaded by all the crowned heads of Europe. That showed that the Americans were then revolutionaries. Now the American people need to struggle for liberation from their own monopoly capitalists" - Mao Zedong

"Society pushed us on to the political stage. Who ever thought of indulging in Marxism previously? I hadn't even heard of it. What I had heard of, and also read of, was Confucius, Napoleon, Washington, Peter the Great, the Meiji Restoration, the three distinguished Italian [patriots] - in other words, all those [heroes] of capitalism. I had also read a biography of Franklin. He came from a poor family; afterwards, he became a writer, and also conducted experiments on electricity" - Mao Zedong

"Washington, Jefferson and others made the revolution against Britain because of British oppression and exploitation of the Americans, and not because of any over-population in America" - Mao Zedong

"Washington [has] a bad 'reputation', and we can ratify him as the 'Communist Party'; Not being able to join the Communist Party is one thing. At that time there was no Communist Party. The revolutionary role played by Washington we should admit that he played a very advanced role at that time and was very progressive. And Lincoln is the same; [The American people] I wish them progress. If I wish them liberation, some of them might not approve of it. I wish those who realise that they have not yet been liberated, and those who have difficulties in life, be liberated; The Americans need to be liberated again. This is their own business. Not liberated from British rule, but liberated from monopoly capital" - Mao Zedong

"The whole world, Britain included dislikes the United States. The masses of the people dislike it; The people are dissatisfied and in some countries so are the authorities. All oppressed nations want independence. Everything is subject to change. The big decadent forces will give way to the small new-born forces. The small forces will change into big forces because the majority of the people demand this change. The U.S. imperialist forces will change from big to small because the American people, too, are dissatisfied with their government" - Mao Zedong

"Now U.S. imperialism is quite powerful, but in reality it

isn't. It is very weak politically because it is divorced from the masses of the people and is disliked by everybody and by the American people too. In appearance it is very powerful but in reality it is nothing to be afraid of, it is a paper tiger. Outwardly a tiger, it is made of paper, unable to withstand the wind and the rain. I believe the United States is nothing but a paper tiger; We have to destroy it piecemeal; If we deal with it step by step and in earnest, we will certainly succeed in the end" - Mao Zedong

"The Japanese nation is a great nation. It will never allow U.S. imperialism to ride on itself for a long time. Over the years, the patriotic united front of the people of all strata of Japan against U.S. imperialist aggression, oppression, and control has continued to expand. This is the most reliable guarantee for the victory of the Japanese people's anti-American patriotic struggle. The Chinese people are convinced that the Japanese people will be able to expel the U.S. imperialists from their homeland" - Mao Zedong

"All reactionaries are paper tigers. In appearance, the reactionaries are terrifying, but in reality, they are not so powerful. From a long-term point of view, it is not the reactionaries but the people who are powerful" - Mao Zedong

"The only ones who crave war and do not want peace are certain monopoly capitalist groups in a handful of imperialist countries that depend on aggression for their profits" - Mao Zedong

"As for people who are politically backward, Communists should not slight or despise them - but should befriend them - unite with them, and convince them and encourage them to go forward" - Mao Zedong

"The attitude of Communists towards any person who has made mistakes in his work should be one of persuasion in order to help him change and start afresh and not one of exclusion, unless he is incorrigible" - Mao Zedong

"...In applying Marxism to China, Chinese Communists must fully and properly integrate the universal truth of Marxism with the concrete practice of the Chinese revolution, or in other words, the universal truth of Marxism must be combined with specific national characteristics and acquire a definite national form if it is to be useful, and in no circumstances can it be applied subjectively as a mere formula" - Mao Zedong

"We must be united both with the party and those not in the party; to be united both domestically and internationally; then, for what will this be unity for? For us all to construct a great socialist country. We can absolutely use the word 'Great' to describe our country. Our party is a great party. Our people is a great people. Our revolution is a great revolution. And our task is of a great task. A country with 600 million, the only one in the world, this is us... that is why in the process of this construction, our ultimate goal is realist and be a great socialist country, to fully change what has been our hundred years of backwardness; hundred of years of being ridiculed; hundred years of being viewed as a sick man; these sorts of poisonous situations. We must as such catch up with the world's most powerful capitalist country, that is, the United States" - Mao Zedong

"The Mongols and Han should co-operate closely and have faith in Marxism. All our minority nations should trust each other, no matter what nationalities they are. They must see on which side truth lies. Marx himself was a Jew, Stalin belonged to a minority nation; and Chiang Kai-shek is a Han, a bad one, whom we strongly oppose. We must not insist that only people of a given province can take charge of the administration of that province. The place of origin of a man is irrelevant - northerner or southerner, this national minority or that minority, [they are all the same]. The questions are whether they have Communism and how much. This point should be explained clearly to our national minorities. To begin with, the Han was not a big race, but a mixture of a great number of races. The Han people have conquered many minority nations in history and have driven them to the highlands. [We] must take a historical view of our nationality question and find out that we either depend on minority nationalism or on Communism. Of course we depend on Communism. We need our regions but not our regionalism" - Mao Zedong

"In some places the relations between nationalities are far from normal. For Communists this is an intolerable situation. We must go to the root and criticise the Han chauvinist ideas which exist to a serious degree among many Party members and cadres, namely, the reactionary ideas of the landlord class and the bourgeoisie, or the ideas characteristic of the Kuomintang, which are manifested in the relations between nationalities. Mistakes in this respect must be corrected at once. Delegations led by comrades who are familiar with our nationality policy and full of sympathy for our minority nationality compatriots still suffering from discrimination should be sent to visit the areas where there are minority nationalities, make a serious effort at investigation and study and help Party and government organisations in the localities discover and solve problems. The visits should not be those of 'looking at flowers on horseback'" - Mao Zedong

"I owe my allegiance to the working class; we want to build a society where our children can live in peace and prosperity, a society where they will control the wealth of this country" - Seamus Costello

"On the question of whether we are nationalists or not I can say the following: we are nationalists to the exact degree necessary to develop a healthy socialist patriotism among our people, and socialist patriotism is in its essence internationalism. Socialism does not require of us that we renounce our love for our socialist country, that we renounce our love for our own people. Socialism does not require of us that we should not make every possible effort to build up our socialist country as quickly as possible, in order that we may so create the best possible living conditions for our working people. Our creative drive in building up our country, that is the creative drive of our workers, our youth, our people's intelligentsia, and all our working peasants and citizens, who are voluntarily contributing their share to the work of construction within the People's Front, - none of these things need, or indeed can, be stigmatised as some sort of nationalist deviation. No, this is socialist patriotism, which in its essence is profoundly international, and for that reason we are proud of it" - Josip Broz Tito

"The notion of patriotism must be understood in a class context - one can be patriotic in defense of a capitalist state or... a workers' state (proletarian patriotism). These are two different things, for when a worker is patriotic in a capitalist state (referring to false patriotism) he is just serving his own oppressor" - Walter Rodney

"The substance of socialist democracy lies in efficient socialist organisation of all society for the sake of every individual, and in the socialist discipline of every individual for the sake of all society" - L.I. Brezhnev

"We, Negro Communists, do not accept the status of 'aliens' to which the Negro Resolution relegates us. We are an integral part of the Negro movement, embodying the great revolutionary traditions of Nat Turner, Frederick Douglass, Harriet Tubman, etc. We do not become 'foreigners' when we become Communists. It is, therefore, not only the right, but the duty of Negro Communists to project forms and methods of struggle consistent with the great revolutionary traditions of the Negro people. As true patriots, we call for a consistent fight against U.S. imperialism as the main enemy of the Negro people. We call for an alliance with the white working class based upon common revolutionary aims. We call for international solidarity with the heroic struggles for national liberation, peace and Socialism which embrace the vast majority of mankind" - Harry Haywood

"In Cambodia, the Cambodian people, Communists and patriots, have risen against the barbarous government of Pol Pot, which was nothing but a group of provocateurs in the service of the imperialist bourgeoisie and of the Chinese revisionists, in particular, which had as its aim to discredit the idea of socialism in the international arena... The anti-popular line of that regime is confirmed, also, by the fact that the Albanian embassy in the Cambodian capital, the embassy of a country which has given the people of Cambodia every possible aid, was kept isolated, indeed, encircled with barbed wire, as if it were in a concentration camp. The other embassies, too, were in a similar situation. The Albanian diplomats have seen with their own eyes that the Cambodian people were treated inhumanly by the clique of Pol Pot and Yeng Sari. Pnom Pen was turned into a deserted city, empty of people, where food was difficult to secure even for the diplomats, where no doctors or even aspirins could be found. We think that the people and patriots of Cambodia waited too long before overthrowing this clique which was completely linked with Beijing and in its service" - Enver Hoxha

"And no man single-handed, can hope to break the bars; it's a thousand like Ned Kelly, who'll hoist the flag of stars" - John Manifold

"It seems paradoxical that the recent avalanche of books and articles portraying the Black condition in the U.S. as that of a colony has been issued by the same monopoly-controlled book and newspaper publishers who use most of the rest of their ideological output to deny the imperialist nature of U.S. state monopoly capitalism. It seems paradoxical but it is not. This development marks a new state of sophistication in the ideological offensive of U.S. imperialism. The colony theory is particularly useful to the monopolists because it appears to be so radical; in fact, it contains the admission that the oppression of Black people in the U.S. is comparable to colonial oppression in Asia, Africa and Latin America. This emphasis on the intensity of Black oppression gives the colony theory its ring of authenticity. But this admission of oppression is not as candid (one might even say benign) as it might seem. By promoting the colony theory, the white ruling class aims to define and determine the direction of the Black liberation movement. In yet another form, the monopolists are striving to prevent Black people themselves from defining the specific features that constitute the special oppression they experience. By analogy, this theory directs attention to those aspects of the Black condition in the U.S. which most closely resemble colonial conditions. These similarities are so powerful that one's attention may be diverted from what is unique in the status of the triply-oppressed Black peoples in colonial or semi-colonial situations, past or present. Via the colony analogy, and variations on this unscientific, anti-Marxist theme, U.S. imperialism's ideologists are trying to influence the Black liberation movement into adopting a self-defeating strategy. While the U.S. 'internal Black colony' theory resembles a winning strategy for an oppressed majority living in a colony, it would mean certain defeat for an oppressed minority - which has indeed been the Black condition for more than 350 years in this part of the world. The supposedly 'revolutionary' (even so-called 'Marxist'!) books on the colony analogy, now in mass circulation, were written by white radicals who have abandoned the struggle against racism, and by Black radicals who seek theoretical short cuts to liberation. By portraying the status of the Black people in the U.S. as a colony, these radicals assist the ruling class' aim of diverting the Black liberation movement from a winning strategy: one that would advance the self-organisation of the Black liberation movement, and simultaneously combine this independent of strength with that of allies - the working class, Black, Brown, Yellow, Red and white, together with all the poor and exploited - in a new formation. This is the basis for an anti-monopoly coalition, the only strategy that opens the way to a future without racism, exploitation, or oppression" - Henry M. Winston

"Without patriotic political education, a soldier is only a potential criminal" - Thomas Sankara

"I ask every Communist individually to set an example, by deeds and without pretense, a real example worthy of a man and a Communist, in restoring order, starting normal life, in resuming work and production, and in laying the foundations of an ordered life; only with the honour thus acquired can we earn the respect of our other compatriots as well" - Janos Kadar

"If colonies cannot decolonise and return to their original existence as nations, then nations no longer exist. Nor, we believe, will they ever exist again. And since there must be nations for revolutionary nationalism or internationalism to make sense, we decided that we would have to call ourselves something new" - Huey P. Newton

"He [a friend of Huey] was inclined to believe you would have been on the side of the colonisers [British]. I'm pleased with the answer, and I agree with [Buckley's support for the American Revolution] the only revolution that is worth fighting is a humane revolution" - Huey P. Newton

"'We Want All Black People When Brought To Trial To Be Tried In Court By A Jury Of Their Peer Group Or People From Their Black Communities, As Defined By The Constitution Of The United States.' Before 1776 America was a British colony. The British government had certain laws and rules that the colonised Americans rejected as not being in their best interests. In spite of the British conviction that Americans had no right to establish their own laws to promote the general welfare of the people living here in America, the colonised immigrant felt he had no choice but to raise the gun to defend his welfare. Simultaneously he made certain laws to ensure his protection from external and internal aggressions, from other governments, and his own agencies. One such form of protection was the Declaration of Independence, which states: '...whenever any government becomes destructive to these ends, it is the right of the people to alter or to abolish it, and to institute a new government, laying its foundations on such principles and organising its powers in such forms as to them shall seem most likely to effect their safety and happiness' Now these same colonised white people, these ex-slaves, robbers and thieves, have denied the colonised black man the right to even speak of abolishing this oppressive system which the white colonised American created. They have carried their madness to the four corners of the earth, and now there is universal rebellion against their continue[d] rule and power" - Huey P. Newton

"Workers! Farmers! Anti-fascists! Spanish Patriots! Confronted with the fascist military uprising, all must rise to their feet, to defend the Republic, to defend the people's freedoms as well as their achievements towards democracy" - Dolores Ibárruri

"It is a lie that I made the people starve. A lie, a lie in my face. This shows how little patriotism there is, how many treasonable offenses were committed... At no point was there such an upswing, so much construction, so much consolidation in the Romanian provinces. I guaranteed that every village has its schools, hospitals and doctors. I have done everything to create a decent and rich life for the people in the country, like in no other country in the world" - Nicolae Ceaușescu

"I may be a German patriot, but if unification comes with McDonalds the class-traitors can keep it" - Erich Honecker

"The emphasis of young radicals on the negative and reactionary side of American tradition is understandable. It is an effort to counteract the brazen hypocrisy and lies with which the ruling class has concealed its own historic role. Its racist oppression of minority peoples, the pilfering of this nation and the plundering of foreign nations, should all be dealt with and exposed. But the ruling class also distorts the history and struggles of the people; it seeks to bury the revolutionary and progressive side of our traditions - the tradition of Black people, the working people, the various ethnic groups, and so forth. It wishes to hide from the people the fact that every gain they have made was because of their own struggle and not because it was given to them. And it is important that the people know about the progressive side of their tradition so that they can reject the caricature of themselves handed to them by their exploiters. To adopt a nihilist position toward one's own people and past is to become a stranger in one's own land. It is to surrender the fight to win the people. It is to mistake those whose minds are poisoned by ideological pollution with the class source of that pollution. If everything in the past of our people had been bad, by what strange logic is one to assume that any good can come from it now or in the future? Such a nihilist position leads only to elitism" - Gil Green

"From the beginning of our policy in regard to the national bourgeoisie was not only to carry out the anti-imperialist, anti-feudal democratic revolution together with them, but also to take them (proletarianisation) along with us to a socialist, Communist society" - Kim Il-sung

"Patriotism is not an empty concept. Education in patriotism cannot be conducted simply by erecting the slogan, 'Let us arm ourselves with the spirit of socialist patriotism!' Educating people in the spirit of patriotism must begin with fostering the idea of caring for every tree planted on the road side, for the chairs and desks in the school… There is no doubt that a person who has formed the habit of cherishing common property from childhood will grow up to be a valuable patriot" - Kim Il-sung

"France is one country, one nation, one people. We protest indignantly against such ridiculous and odious allegations. For us, as for all the citizens of our country, every man and woman of French nationality is French. Every attempt using hazardous criteria which borders on racism in an ill-defined way, seeking to define as not purely French such and such members of the French community, is offensive to the national consciousness. Nobody here can accept that, our Party least of all" - (Georges Marchais, Letter to the Secretariat of the Communist Party of the U.S.S.R., February 1984)

"If a white man wants to lynch me, that's his problem. If he's got the power to lynch me, that's my problem... Racism gets its power from capitalism. Thus, if you're anti-racist, whether you know it or not, you must be anti-capitalist. The power for racism, the power for sexism, comes from capitalism, not an attitude" - Kwame Ture

"Capitalism means that the masses will work, and a few people - who may not labour at all - will benefit from that work. The few will sit down to a banquet, and the masses will eat whatever is left over" - Julius Kambarage Nyerere

"The African is not 'Communistic' in his thinking; he is - if I may coin an expression - 'communitary'" - Julius Kambarage Nyerere

"The working class of each country faces two responsibilities - national and international. How to unite these task has always been a challenge to the revolutionary movements. The main weapon of the enemy is a skillfull use of chauvinism, nationalism, and a false use of patriotism" - Gus Hall

"The difference between most radical left, new left, socialist and quasi socialist parties that say they speak for the working class - and the Communist Party USA is: The Communists mean what they say" - Gus Hall

"To view the U.S. working class as a partner of

monopoly capital in its imperialist exploitation is a slander and a falsehood. The U.S. working class is a victim of the same monopoly capital as are the workers of the U.S. owned plants in other lands. This type of slander is not going to be helpful in getting the U.S. working class to meet its historic responsibilities in the fighting against imperialism. The people on the left who spread this slander are only placing additional obstacles in the path of giving leadership to the working class" - Gus Hall

"There is nothing more criminal, more insane, unpatriotic and Un-American than spending billions for the military, than permitting rich families to plunder and pillage our economy out of hundreds of billions of dollars while tens of millions of Americans live below the official poverty level. The policy of austerity and scarcity creates a crisis for the whole working class, but for working youth it is an absolute catastrophe, a dead-end. Because of this policy, you are not to be allowed to enlist in the future of the United States, except as cannon fodder to kill and be killed for Exxon and Shell" - Gus Hall

"The party which represents the working class has a right to fight. By all standards, that's a legitimate American concept - part of our colonial heritage" - (Samuel A. Darcy, who was expelled from the CPUSA for protesting Earl Browder's leadership)

"My history... describes the inspiring struggle of those who have fought slavery and racism (Frederick Douglass, William Lloyd Garrison, Fannie Lou Hamer, Bob Moses), of the labour organisers who have led strikes for the rights of working people (Big Bill Haywood, Mother Jones, César Chávez), of the socialists and others who have protested war and militarism (Eugene V. Debs, Helen Keller, the Rev. Daniel Berrigan, Cindy Sheehan). My hero is not Theodore Roosevelt, who loved war and congratulated a general after a massacre of Filipino villagers at the turn of the century, but Mark Twain, who denounced the massacre and satirised imperialism. I want young people to understand that ours is a beautiful country, but it has been taken over by men who have no respect for human rights or constitutional liberties. Our people are basically decent and caring, and our highest ideals are expressed in the Declaration of Independence, which says that all of us have an equal right to 'life, liberty, and the pursuit of happiness.' The history of our country, I point out in my book, is a striving, against corporate robber barons and war makers, to make those ideals a reality - and all of us, of whatever age, can find immense satisfaction in becoming part of that" - Howard Zinn

"Dissent is the highest form of patriotism" - Howard Zinn

"The fate of American capitalism lies in the hands of the American workers. The working class must be aware that the current order will remain unhindered so long as the workers plead for higher wages instead of demanding ownership over the means of production and partnership. This should be the objective of workers' strikes" - Muammar Gaddafi

"Nationalism does not conflict with internationalism. Mutual help, support and alliance between countries and nations - this is internationalism. Every country has its borders, and every nation has its identity, and revolution and construction are carried on with the country and nation as a unit. For this reason, internationalism finds its expressions in the relationships between countries and between nations, a prerequisite for which is nationalism. Internationalism divorced from the concepts of nation and nationalism is merely an empty shell. A man who is unconcerned about the destiny of his country and nation cannot be faithful to internationalism. Revolutionaries of each country should be faithful to internationalism by struggling, first of all, for the prosperity of their own coutry and nation" - Kim Jong-il

"Marxism-Leninism is ultimately deeply internationalist and, at the same time, deeply patriotic" - Fidel Castro

"There are few times when the human word would appear to be as limited and deficient as it does today, to express the series of feelings, emotions, and ideas born in the heat of the great display of patriotism we have witnessed this morning, moments of emotions similar to those experienced on other occasions when we have had the chance to meet with large crowds. We consider tonight's event as a victory for Cuba, a victory for Cubans. And the fame of the virtue and the patriotism of our people will grow throughout New York and the prestige of Cuba will grow. As the Apostle said, help the martyr, the martyr who asks for help, who awaits help, who relies on help, who wants to redeem himself with help. Not just today, but every day, not with the patriotism of a single day but with the pure patriotism of an entire lifetime, not just in a moment of fleeting enthusiasm" - Fidel Castro

"The U.S. flag is your flag, you cannot allow the U.S. ruling class to own the flag. The working class of the U.S. must fight for the flag and once socialism is established it is up to the workers to decide what they want to do with flag and the U.S. as it exists - (Fidel Castro, Addressing a group of students who did not want to associate with their flag while people from other countries sat next to theirs)

"The Revolution had therefore set the benchmark against which future generations of Americans - men and women, white and black, rich and poor - would measure their standing. Not only that: in its own time, it proved to be the curtain-raiser on a new epoch of world revolution. For, in the year following ratification of the U.S. Constitution, the people of Paris stormed the Bastille, defeated a military coup, and unleashed the French Revolution" - (Neil Faulkner, Chapter 8: The Second Wave of Bourgeois Revolutions, pp 123, A Marxist History of the World)

"Portraying German history as a line of uninterrupted misery is a reactionary and anti-national concept which serves objectively to destroy national self-respect and the national consciousness of the German people" - Victor Grossman

"Conservatives pawn themselves off as being more patriotic than liberals. Liberals think they are more patriotic than socialists, but we on the left are second to nobody in our patriotism. We want Perestroika, we want fundamental restructuring and democratisation of overseas and domestic policies. We want fundamental restructuring and democratisation of the political process, values, institutions, the economy, and the class power of this country. We real patriots say along with Albert Camus, 'I want to love my country and justice too', and in fact, I believe that the only way you can be a real patriot is to love justice because you can't love, you can't be patriotic to something that's unjust. We want to spend less time trying to save the world with bombers and battleships and more time healing ourselves. This is not a good idea of noble pronouncement; it is a historical necessity. This country does not belong to Ronald Reagan and his billionaire friends, although they act like it does. It belongs to us and sooner or later we will take it back!" - Michael Parenti

"In contrast to the superpatriots, there are the real patriots who care enough about their country they want to improve it. Their patriotism has a social content. They know that democracy is not just the ability to hold elections. Democracy must also serve the needs and interests of the demos, the people. Real patriots educate themselves about the real history of their country and are not satisfied with the flag-waving promotional fluff that passes for history. They find different things in our past to be proud of than do superpatriots, such as the struggle for enfranchisement, the abolitionist movement, the peace movement, the elimination of child labour, and the struggle for collective bargaining, the eight-hour day, occupational safety, and racial justice and gender equality" - Michael Parenti

"If the test of patriotism comes only by reflexively falling into lockstep behind the leader whenever the flag is waved, then what we have is a formula for dictatorship, not democracy... But the American way is to criticise and debate openly, not to accept unthinkingly the doings of government officials of this or any other country" - Michael Parenti

"In the real patriot's pantheon can be found Tom Paine, Harriet Tubman, Frederick Douglass, Mark Twain, Susan B. Anthony, Mother Jones, Big Bill Haywood, John Reed, Eugene Victor Debs, Elizabeth Gurly Flynn, Jeanette Rankin, Rosa Parks, Paul Robeson, A.J. Muste, Harry Bridges, Walter Reuther, Martin Luther King - and the millions in ranks who championed social justice" - Michael Parenti

"Real patriots advocate a freedom of speech and freedom of ideas in the major media that would include dissident Left views as well as the usual right-wing and conventional opinions we are constantly exposed to. Real patriots want some relief from the evasive, fatuous, mealymouthed, know-it-all empire-boosting pundits and conservative or otherwise insipid commentators. They want major media debates on the basic assumptions behind U.S. foreign policy and free-market globalism. hey want to reclaim the nation's airwaves, which belong not to the network bosses but to the people of the United States. Some real patriots want a government that will go directly into not-for-profit production. They want a fair chance given to worker-controlled enterprises and public ownership. If private industry cannot provide for the needs of the people, cannot build homes and hospitals enough for all, then the public sector should do so - not by contracting it out to private profiteers but by direct production as during the New Deal when public workers made tents, cots, and shoes, and canned foods for the destitute - a not-for-profit production that created jobs, served human needs, and expanded individual spending power and the tax base, all done without the parasitic private investors making a penny on it. Real patriots want to open up our political system to new political parties, not just two capitalist globalistic empire-building parties, not just one party that Red-baits and liberal-baits and the other that lives in fear of being Red-baited and liberal-baited. We need to do what numerous other democracies have done and institute proportional representation, ready ballot access to dissident parties, convenient voter-registration conditions, public campaign funding for all candidates, and free TV time for all political parties. Real patriots are not afraid of dramatic changes - if they are in a democratic direction. They want the fundamental democratisation of the political process and the economy of this country. As Mark Twain put it more than a century ago, his loyalty was not to his countries institutions and officeholders as such. His loyalty was to its basic principles of democracy, to the understanding that 'all political power is inherent in the people, and all free governments are founded on their authority and instituted for their benefit; and that they have at all times an undeniable and indefeasible right to alter their form of government in such a manner as they may think expedient'. In sum, real patriots are not enamoured by the trappings of superpatriotism but are interested in the substance of social justice" - Michael Parenti

"Finally, real patriots are internationalists. They feel a special attachment to their own country but not in some competitive way that pits the United States against other powers. They regard the people of all nations as different members of the same human family. In 1936, individuals from many countries and all walks of life joined together to form the International Brigade, which fought in Spain to protect democracy from the fascist forces of Generalissimo Franco. Charles Nusser, a veteran of that great struggle, relates this incident of international patriotism: 'Sam Gonshak and I, both Spanish Civil war veterans were in Guernica on June 1, 1985 [to commemorate the Spanish Civil War]... I will never forget the speech of the organiser of the gathering. He referred to Sam and me as 'Patriots of the World'. There have always been too many patriots in various countries straining to get at the throats of patriots in other countries.' 'Patriots of the World' who happen to live in the United States want to stop destroying others with jet bombers and missiles and US-financed death squads and start healing this nation. This is not just a good and noble ideal, it is a historical necessity. It is the best kind of security. Sooner or later Americans rediscover that they cannot live on flag-waving alone. They begin to drift off into reality, confronted by the economic irrationalities and injustices of a system that provides them with the endless circuses and extravaganzas of superpatriotism, heavy tax burdens, a crushing national debt and military budget, repeated bloodletting in foreign lands, and sad neglect of domestic needs, denying them the bread of prosperity and their birthright as democratic citizens. We need a return to reality. We need to unveil the lies and subterfuges that so advantage the wealthy plutocracy. We need to pursue policies at home and abroad that serve the real needs of humanity. Then we can love our country - and peace and justice too" - Michael Parenti

"I dream that someday the United States will be on the side of the peasants in some civil war. I dream that we will be the ones who will help the poor overthrow the rich, who will talk about land reform and education and health facilities for everyone, and that when the Red Cross or Amnesty International comes to count the bodies and take the testimony of women raped, that our side wont be the heavies" - Michael Parenti

"We are going to create an American liberation front to combat the avaricious businessman, the demagogic politician and the fascist cops who brutalise and terrorise the people" - Bobby Seale

"Socialist patriotism [meant] true love for one's

motherland ...[and]...free[dom] from all forms of chauvinism and racialism" - Mengistu Haile Mariam

"'Down with U.S.A.' means down with the ruling class. It means death to the American politicians currently in power. It means death to the few people running that country; we have nothing against the American nation" - Sayyid Ali Hosseini Khamenei

"All revolutionaries, and all revolutionary organisations eventually have to make a choice between revolution and counter-revolution, if they will not take the lead from the vanguard, then they will have to move to the other side. From now on we will not take theory, but actions as the basis for the coalitions we make. The Young Patriots [A Chicago white working-class youth organisation] are the only revolutionaries we respect that ever came out of the mother country" - (David Hilliard, Aug. 9, 1969 issue of The Black Panther newspaper)

"Revolutionary defeatism means that you oppose the actions of your own government and ruling class in carrying out their wars, which are wars for empire. It means that you welcome any setbacks they suffer in those wars, because that weakens their oppressive hold over masses of people, here and in the world more generally" - Bob Avakian

"We (Russians) are the last power on this planet that is capable of mounting a challenge to the New World Order - the global cosmopolitan dictatorship. We must work against our destroyers, using means as carefully thought out and as goals oriented as theirs are: the unity of all nationalist forces is as necessary to this end as air" - Gennady A. Zyuganov

"Some of the left think that patriotism is in itself proto-fascist. I say no, it means you have a strong trust in your culture and don't need xenophobia; Patriotism is socialism" - Slavoj Žižek

"Patriotism is not a mere slogan. A patriot is one who closely intertwines his/her own ideals with the future of the country, and his/her life with the fate of the nation" - Xi Jinping

"Everything we Chinese Communists do is to better the lives of the Chinese people, renew the Chinese nation, and promote peace and development for humanity - Xi Jinping

"We commemorate Deng Xiaoping by learning from his immense love for the Chinese people. His entire life is an expression of love for the people, which is an inexhaustible source of strength for Chinese Communists... He once said, 'I am a son of the Chinese people. I have a deep love for my people and my country.' It was his love for the people that fostered his love for the Party and the country. That is why he said, 'My life belongs to the party and the country'" - Xi Jinping

"I'm a patriotic American. I love the American people, but I hate the American government. It is the Fourth Reich. It is the equivalence of Nazi Germany today" - Russell 'Texas' Bentley

"Nothing is more precious than the people, as they constitute the foundation of the country, and nothing is more sacred than their interests" - Kim Jong-un

"Slavery is not the remarkable fact of America, but its abolition is" - Chris Cutrone

"I don't want socialism because I want to destroy America. I want socialism because I want to save America" - Caleb T. Maupin

Even the liberal idea of patriotism is not to the government, it is love for the country itself:

"Guard against the impostures of pretended patriotism; The great rule of conduct for us in regard to foreign nations is in extending our commercial relations, to have with them as little political connection as possible" - George Washington

"My ardent desire is, and my aim has been, to comply with all our engagements, foreign and domestic, but to keep the United States free from political connections with every other country; to see that they may be independent of all and under the influence of none" - George Washington

"The duty of a true patriot is to protect his country from its government" - Thomas Paine

"When the people shall have torn to shreds the Constitution of the United States, the Elders of Israel will be found holding it up to the nations of the earth and proclaiming liberty and equal rights to all men, and extending the hand of fellowship to the oppressed of all nations" - John Taylor

"The democracy will cease to exist when you take from those who are willing to work and give to those who would not" - Thomas Jefferson

"Peace, commerce and honest friendship with all nations; entangling alliances with none" - Thomas Jefferson

"Every man who loves peace, every man who loves his country, every man who loves liberty ought to have it ever before his eyes that he may cherish in his heart a due attachment to the Union of America and be able to set a due value on the means of preserving it" - James Madison

"If Congress has a right under the Constitution to issue paper money, it was given them to use by themselves, not to be delegated to individuals or corporations" - Andrew Jackson

"America does not go abroad in search of monsters to destroy. She is the well-wisher to freedom and independence of all. She is the champion and vindicator only of her own" - John Quincy Adams

"[America's] glory is not dominion but liberty. Her march is the march of the mind. She has a spear and a shield: but the motto upon her shield is Freedom, Independence, Peace. This has been her declaration: this has been, as far as her necessary intercourse with the rest of mankind would permit, her practice" - John Quincy Adams

"This nation, under God - shall have a new birth of freedom and that government of the people, by the people, for the people, shall not perish from the earth" - Abraham Lincoln

"I have two great enemies, the Southern Army in front of me, and the financial institution in the rear. Of the two, the one in my rear is my greatest foe" - (Abraham Lincoln, 1865, not long before he was assassinated)

"Labour is prior to, and independent of, capital. Capital is only the fruit of labour, and could never have existed if labour had not first existed. Labour is the superior of capital, and deserves much the higher consideration" - Abraham Lincoln

"The capitalists generally act harmoniously and in concert to fleece the people; and now that they have got into a quarrel with themselves, we are called upon to appropriate the people's money to settle the quarrel" - Abraham Lincoln

"Man still is vile. But such large steps have lately been taken in the true direction, that the patriot has a right to take courage" - Thaddeus Stevens

"Whoever controls the volume of money in our country is absolute master of all industry and commerce... and when you realise that the entire system is very easily controlled, one way or another, by a few powerful men at the top, you will not have to be told how periods of inflation and depression originate" - (James A. Garfield, 1881, not long before he was assassinated)

"America is another name for opportunity; When a whole nation is roaring patriotism at the top of its voice, I am fain to explore the cleanness of its hands and the purity of its heart" - Ralph Waldo Emerson

"The division of the United States into two federations of equal force was decided long before the civil war by the high financial power of Europe. These bankers were afraid that the United States, if they remained in one block and as one nation, would attain economical and financial independence, which would upset their financial domination over the world. The voice of the Rothschilds predominated. They foresaw the tremendous booty if they could substitute two feeble democracies, indebted to the financiers, to the vigorous Republic, confident and self-providing. Therefore they started their emissaries in order to exploit the question of slavery and thus dig an abyss between the two parts of the Republic" - Otto von Bismarck

"Patriotism is supporting your country all the time, and your government when it deserves it" - Mark Twain

"Patriotism means to stand by the country. It does not mean to stand by the president. It is patriotic to serve him insofar as he efficiently serves the country. It is unpatriotic not to oppose him to the exact extent that by inefficiency or otherwise he fails in his duty to stand by the country. It is unpatriotic not to tell the truth about the president or anyone else" - Theodore Roosevelt Jr.

"We must dare to be great; and we must realise that greatness is the fruit of toil and sacrifice and high courage" - Theodore Roosevelt Jr.

"Patriotism is easy to understand in America. It means looking out for yourself by looking out for your country" - Calvin Coolidge

"'m for the poor man - all poor men, black and white, they all gotta have a chance. They gotta have a home, a job, and a decent education for their children. 'Every man a king' - that's my slogan" - Huey P. Long

"True patriotism hates injustice in its own land more than anywhere else" - Clarence Darrow

"We must find practical controls over blind economic forces and blindly selfish men" - Franklin D. Roosevelt

"In the truest sense, freedom cannot be bestowed; it must be achieved" - Franklin D. Roosevelt

"The American Dream is not a dream of motor cars and high wages merely, but a dream of social order in which each man and each woman shall be able to attain to the fullest stature of which they are innately capable regardless of the fortuitous circumstances of one's birth" - James Truslow Adams

"My fellow Americans, ask not what your country can do for you, ask what you can do for your country; One person can make a difference, and everyone should try; A revolution is coming - a revolution which will be peaceful if we are wise enough; Compassionate if we care enough; Successful if we are fortunate enough - but a revolution which is coming whether we will it or not. We can affect its character, we cannot alter its inevitability; Let us not seek the Republican answer, but the right answer. Let us not seek to fix the blame for the past. Let us accept our own responsibility for the future" - John F. Kennedy

"Some have spoken of the American century, I say that the century on which we are entering can be and must be the century of the common man" - Henry A. Wallace

"The difference between patriotism and nationalism is that the patriot is proud of his country for what it does, and the nationalist is proud of his country no matter what it does; the first attitude creates a feeling of responsibility, but the second a feeling of blind arrogance that leads to war" - Sydney J. Harris

"I love America more than any other country in the world and, exactly for this reason, I insist on the right to criticise her perpetually; We can make America what America must become" - James Baldwin

"The problem isn't a lack of money, food, water or land. The problem is that you've given control of these things to a group of greedy psychopaths who care more about maintaining their own power than helping mankind" - Bill Hicks

"I don't like ass-kissers, flag wavers, or team players. I

like people who buck the system. Individualists. I often warn people: Somewhere along the way, someone is going to tell you 'there is no 'I' in team.' What you should tell them is: Maybe not, but there is an 'I' in independence, individuality, and integrity" - George Carlin

"In my generation, Abraham Lincoln was patriotism... What Lincoln represented, as President, was the reaffirmation and the consolidation of the original intent of the founders, an intent which is located in the question of 'life, liberty, and the pursuit of happiness,' in opposition to the Lockean principle of greed. And, the idea that every human being is not only made in the image of God, but society must be ordered in a way which conforms to the implications of that, as I've defined them. Today, that principle is the central issue of all global politics: The fact that the United States, when we were called to service in World War II, went to service with the heritage of Lincoln, and the Union victory in the Civil War..." - Lyndon H. LaRouche Jr.

"My definition of patriotism is to defend your country with the truth no matter the consequences; I saw courage both in the Vietnam War and in the struggle to stop it. I learned that patriotism includes protest, not just military service" - John F. Kerry

"Real patriotism is a willingness to challenge the government when it's wrong" - Ron Paul

"The rich people apparently are leaving America. They're giving up their citizenship. These great lovers of America who made their money in this country - when you ask them to pay their fair share of taxes, they're running abroad. We have 19 year-old kids who died in Iraq and Afghanistan defending this country. They went abroad. Not to escape taxes. They're working class kids who died in wars and now the billionaires want to run abroad to avoid paying their share of taxes. What patriotism! What love of country!" - Bernie Sanders

"When you open your heart to patriotism, there is no room for prejudice. The Bible tells us how good and pleasant it is when God's people live together in unity. We must speak our minds openly, debate our disagreements honestly, but always pursue solidarity" - Donald J. Trump

GLOBALISM:

Globalism is imperialism without borders.

We as Marxist-Leninists use Lenin's definition of imperialism as opposed to the vague general use of the word. (As we do with nation and dictatorship as we have a different ideological framework to liberalism) It is from this that we know that imperialism primarily constitutes an economic form as opposed to a military form, the military is in place to enforce the economic over the exploited third world. Colloquially this is referred to as globalism as it depends on the delivery of materials from all over the third world to the first world by corporations to meet the demands of consumerist society. In Lenin's time imperialism was primarily undertaken by imperialist powers through invasion to acquire resources, but it is for this reason that Lenin's analysis was so acute even for Marxists today is that he correctly identified that the economic was factors were the key element and were at the root of military might. Such to the point that the imperialists when push came to shove ended up laying (mostly due to the threat of their violent overthrow) down their borders. (This was what Kwame Nkrumah referred to as **neo-colonialism**. Michael Hudson would also later coin the term **super imperialism** for the economic system of the unipolar world order. Both of these works are necessary updates to read on from Lenin's analysis of imperialism as while his works are still very relevant he could never have imagined the unipolar world order).

After the British Empire left the vast majority of it's occupied territories following WW2, it was the United States and it's Bretton-Woods system which became the sucessors of the British. Instead of hard borders they put in place loyal comprador bourgeois governments and if they then revolted, the U.S. rigged elections, if that did not work they couped them, and if push came to shove they invaded. This was the relation of the so called peaceful world order where there were no imperial borders of old but instead the U.S. invaded with basically full legal order as for the most part they themselves made the international laws and controlled the so called independent international institutions. In a sense Americanism is anarchism at its peak set forth upon the world. Only a few 'rogues' dared to compete, and anytime a peer competitor emerged, they were crushed even in the case of Japan which was a subservient state in the 80s and was only an ecomonic competitor. Real competitors that were not within the scope of the U.S. empire and the liberal order such as the U.S.S.R., fought a cold war, with many proxies, and when the U.S.S.R. fell, the U.S. reigned supreme. It looked like the unipolar world order would be firmly in place for eternity and that it was "the end of history" to quote Fukiyama.

However today the U.S. and NATO have a real competitor both economic and ideological, in China which threatens not just the unipolar world to the extreme, but also the western powers themselves at home who could buckle under the threat of internal contradictions and fall to a workers revolution. The Belt and Road Initiative gives the third world the ability to fight globalism, neo-colonialism and western debt traps collectively. It is creating win-win conditions and solidarity amongst nations all over the world in a direct response to the imperialism of France, the U.S. and NATO. It is the unleashing of development from the BRI which will lead to the end of the 21st Century being the African century and it is this that the imperialists fear most as it would mean the end of globalism once and for all and would allow the African people to stand on their own two feet and say no to the domination of other peoples upon their land.

Imperial borders might have ended on the African continent once and for all decades ago, but today, imperialism still exists, it exists from the western corporations who outsource to exploit cheaper labour in sweatshops, and the bourgeois comprador governments who uphold them, but it is in the interests of those governments more often than not to oppose this (which historically led to coups of disloyal governments) but it is the BRI which will lead to the final defeat of imperialism and the liberation of the African continent. With the rise of China we are finally moving towards a multipolar world, the end of the unipolar 'rules based world order' is nigh.

Without the contradictions of feudalism capitalism would not have emerged, same for socialism from the contradictions of capitalism and from the contradictions of socialism Communism will be established. The reason Marx was able to analyse this was because of the fact that society had for the first time become truly globalised and industrialisation had paved the way for the establishment of socialism.

Marx was able to know the contradictions of socialism that a Communist party would have to solve and hence know of Communism only because of the industrialisation which created the globalisation first seen in Marx's time. Without that none of Marx's theories would have been created by Marx himself at that time and Communism the stage after socialism would not have been apparent which is why you cannot just say capitalism is the lower stage of socialism because it is the contradictions of the old which lead to the emergence of the new.

The reason that Marx was able to peer 'two stages ahead' is because of that globalisation where for the first time society could be truly analysed on a large scale and with industrialisation there would be the capacity for a Communist party with the apparatus of the state to achieve that.

So from that because of those theories which for the first time allow man to shape his own destiny and move the forces of production beyond in a rational manner that is why socialism can be said to be the lower stage of Communism because in the past due to the lack of global outlook and lack of knowledge it could not be done so with socialism the future is in our (mans) hands.

Without the outlook Marx had (industrial Germany in the mid 1800s), Marx's theories could not have been developed beforehand, and if it was not him someone else would have had, if it was not Marx someone else would have developed what we know as Marxism.

Liberalism is all about the individual and bourgeois values which are upheld by parliamentary laws, whereas Marxism is specifically the vehicle of human progress to a higher stage of development (Communism). The point is that Marxism is what allows mankind to put our destiny in our own hands and move towards Communism the highest stage of human development for the first time to rationally move forward and the other point is that in the past it was simply just impossible for the relations of production to rationally be moved forward without external factors such as enclosure of the commons which were not done for the sake of moving humanity forward but out of countering class struggle and that it would not have been possible to develop Marxism without the globalisation seen in the industrial era because it was in that era that for the first time humanity had the global reach and the knowledge that from that perspective everything could be analysed rationally. So that we can move beyond it, but it would not have been possible without the perspective which globalism allowed to be seen.

Us Marxist-Leninists have the truth on our side. We are consistently right about the plots of the imperialist powers and time and time again it turns out that we were right from the very beginning. We are right about history and do not let it get distorted by those with an interest to lie and slander Communist figures and Communist states. When it comes to the truth, there will always be two opposing narratives, however the truth will always lie closer to one side, this is the simple dialectic of the truth. As the famous quote goes:

"Once you learn a sufficient amount of history you either become a Marxist or a lier"

All those who got involved with the Communist movement were on the right side of history and they died knowing they fought for a better world. Marxism-Leninism is the immortal science that propelled humanity forward allowing us to grasp our destiny in our own hands for the first time. From the first revolutionary success in 1917 brought forth a wave of other successful Communist revolutions, from these revolutions millions were uplifted from poverty and the working class held power across one-third of the world. The Soviet Union may have fell in 1991 however today China, led by the Communist Party of China, is the number one economic power in the world and is leading a socialist and anti-imperialist bloc. A new cold war is on the horizon however this time we will prevail. It is also likely that we are heading into a crash which will rival the Wall Street crash of 1929, just like the 20th century, we will organise large swathes of the working class, and we will win over people of prominence who want to be on the right side of history to our cause. History may very well be repeating itself cyclically in a ripple effect, armed with the truth and the keys to victory we will disarm the lies of the imperialists, win over the masses first in our own countries, and then win!

Remember as Marx said:

"The Communists disdain to conceal their views and aims. They openly declare that their ends can be attained only by the forcible overthrow of all existing social conditions. Let the ruling classes tremble at a Communistic revolution. The proletarians have nothing to lose but their chains. They have a world to win. Working Men of All Countries, Unite!" - Karl Marx

Following the fall of the U.S.S.R., a chain reaction was seen where the United States and NATO and their Capitalist system triumphed over the former Eastern Bloc, socialism fell in it's entirety, in Yugoslavia it took a bloody war and balkanisation to put it down, but put it down they did. That was not the end of it though, Ba'athist socialist regimes were toppled in the noughties across the entire Middle East with the rise of the Arab Spring, a direct result of the Soviet's fall. India fell and to the United States it appeared as if Socialism had all but been annihilated.

However China is still socialist along with the D.P.R.K., Laos, Vietnam and Cuba. If the P.R.C. was to fall it is highly likely a repeat of the fall of socialism in Eastern Europe would be seen, even if you don't think China is socialist today, it is undeniable that it is China that allows these nations to exist and to thrive with their socialist projects today. Comparing China to the Former-U.S.S.R. and it is obvious that China was not looted through complete liberalisation in the same way by the West. The results of the balkanisation and looting the Former-U.S.S.R. endured in the 90's can still be seen to this day. Also if we compare China to India, the success of China also becomes apparent as these two countries in 1949 had similar levels of desolation and poverty, but in every metric today China dwarfs India despite a similar population and land area.

It is ironic that the very radicals of the West (who benefit from imperialism and who have never had a successful revolution) are the very first to denounce a real existing revolutionary state which is dismantling Western economic hegemony right before our eyes. It is also especially ironic that because of the revolution's success in 1949, that China has everything that the Western left have been fighting to achieve for the last hundred years. China has public ownership of the banks, hospitals, schools, prisons, and the key manufacturing of the economy. It has public ownership of all infrastructure which allows it to construct high speed railways, motorways, schools and hospitals as needed. China has not started any wars, sanctioned any countries or couped any other countries and is not imperialist, in fact it offers win-win cooperation and stands in solidarity with the developing world instead. China actually delivers on their promises unlike Western politicians who are full of empty promises and unlike the West where when campaign promises do rarely get completed it gets done long overdue, in China it could be done in months or even years early or even built when needed in an emergency such as the hospitals that were built in ten days in response to the covid pandemic in Wuhan. There is mass public housing for those who need it. All media is controlled by the party itself so as to prevent the spreading of lies by foreign imperialists or internal capitalists. In the West there is massive struggle to get even any of these reforms due to parliament being designed not to allow change through the system itself, and the media which propagates control of the bourgeoisie over the masses through propaganda, lies and manufactured consent. However in China the party already is on the side of the working masses as the party in control of the state is the party of the working class and the gains western leftists have fought for in vain, fight for and will continue to fight for, have already been won for decades.

All socialist countries should be upheld critically and the Western Imperialism against China must be demonised because it's success would be just as catastrophic as the fall of the Soviet Union.

We are living in incredible times, I don't think even nuclear war is out of the question at this point. If there was a nuclear war, for China it would be purely defensive as they have to deal with the physical, inpenetratable U.S. land bases of Taiwan, Okinawa, Jeju and the possibility of a Western invasion into Hong Kong and Xinjiang as well as naval skirmishes in the South China sea and the Korean Strait to protect trade etc. so wouldn't be able to nuke these areas as they are in the perceived Chinese sphere of influence and would be preoccupied to hold the threat over American cities that could be their one way of preventing war.

Whereas NATO/US would hold major leverage in that they could not just drop nukes at any time but also could send in troops to try to wipe out China before they triumph economically, as the lap dog of the West, as the Nazis attempted in WW2 against the Soviets. The propaganda is there and the outrage from it is there for a war in the west, the incentive is there too to distract the people and the military industrial complex needs rejuvenation.

Remember, Biden needs a war as we are entering the worst economic depression in history, the middle of his first term would be the perfect time for him to do so. Due to his low polling and the fact that the media has already successfully manufactured consent.

The Biden Regime is the most aggressive U.S. regime in history. We are seeing a dying empire in it's last days.

Here are a list of coups (attempts) since 2016:

Trump-era (10 Coup Attempts):

Brazil (October 2018) - successful

Gabon (January 2019) - unsuccessful

Venezuela (January 2019) - unsuccessful

Sudan (April 2019) - unsuccessful in the long-term

Ethiopia (June 2019) - unsuccessful

Bolivia (Autumn 2019) - unsuccessful in the long-term

Belarus (Autumn 2020) - unsuccessful

Kyrgyzstan (Autumn 2020) - so far successful

Nagorno-Karabakh (Late 2020) - unsuccessful

Central African Republic (December 2020) - unsuccessful

Biden-era (25 Coup Attempts So Far):

Niger (February 2021) - successful

Jordan (April 2021) - unsuccessful

Ecuador (April 2021) - successful

Chad (April 2021) - successful

Moldova (Summer 2021) - so far successful

Haiti (Summer 2021) - so far successful

Cuba (Summer 2021) - unsuccessful

South Africa (Summer 2021) - unsuccessful

Guinea (September 2021) - successful

Peru (Summer 2021) - unsuccessful

Austria (October 2021) - unsuccessful

Iraq (Autumn 2021) - unsuccessful

Cuba (Late 2021) - unsuccessful

Nicaragua (Late 2021) - unsuccessful

Honduras (Late 2021) - unsuccessful

Gambia (December 2021) - unsuccessful

Kazahstan (January 2022) - unsuccessful

Angola (January 2022) - unsuccessful

Burkina Faso (January 2022) - successful

Guinea-Bissau (February 2022) - unsuccessful

Zimbabwe (February 2022) - unsuccessful

Sri Lanka (March 2022) - unsuccessful

Pakistan (April 2022) - successful

Ivory Coast (April 2022) - unsuccessful

Nepal (April 2022) - unsuccessful

(Up to date as of April 2022)

Most of these coup attempts have failed but we have already seen double the amount of coups in less than 1 year under the Biden Regime than in the entire 4 years of Trump. Us Communists must desire the defeat of the paper tiger, reactionary American government (that is harming the people of the world as well as the people at home) and organise for revolution.

I think to understand the events of today it is necessary to understand the events of the past. The Cultural Revolution in the P.R.C. was a resounding success. It is what prevented the fall of socialism in a repeat of the Eastern Bloc as the bureaucrats were afraid of peasant uprisings. It is what led to the sparking of the Tiananmen Square protests which made the CPC even more scared as the protestors abided by principles learnt from Mao, just as the CPC did in calming it down as the people, the vast majority who had genuine concerns about the countries road, were provided for and their material needs met. The people would be provided for and despite a rocky road only a decade later, the corruption and the path of the country would be re-railed under Xi.

This proves the need of a cultural revolution going forward following any revolution to ensure bureaucrats provide for the people and don't stray from the socialist path and so deeply engrained capitalist and remnant feudalist elements can be driven out and replaced by socialist ones.

This can be seen in today in Nepal, after their recent revolution against the monarchy, where a cultural revolution is being launched by the CPN.
<![if !supportLineBreakNewLine]>
<![endif]>

Now I know that so called 'Maoists' (Gonzaloites, the

real Maoists follow Mao Zedong Thought) will say that Deng was a traitor, but that is categorically false. So Deng was an early adherent to Marxism-Leninism, joining the Chinese Communist Youth League while studying and working abroad in France in 1921, on his return to China in 1923 he joined the Communist Party. In 1926 he went to the Soviet Union's school of Marxism-Leninism and studied with thousands of other comrades, when he returned to China he became the political commissar for the Red Army in rural regions. In 1931 he was demoted from the party for his support of Mao Zedong. He participated in the Long March, and was already considered a revolutionary veteran because his participation he took a leading role in the Hundred Regiments Offensive.

After the revolution Deng presided over the Anti-Rightist Campaign and took on many different roles within the party over years between 1946 and 1978. Took power in 1978 after having been a party member for over 55 years and while he was in his 70s. Implemented a long term plan for an NEP to build up the productive forces.

Despite all this ultras still think Deng was a capitalist roader who implemented a bourgeois coup when in actuality he was a revolutionary to the end who did not do to Mao what Khrushchev did to Stalin, prevented a repeat of liberal, capitalist takeover and fall socialism that was happening in the Former-U.S.S.R. and ultimately kept the revolution alive, allowing the P.R.C. to reach the heights it has today where it is soon to be the number one economic power in the world.

Something to note is that there is no such thing as 'Dengism' as a unique ideology, there is just Marxism-Leninism. Nor is anybody a 'Dengist', unless they are referring to someone who upholds Deng Xiaoping and his legacy, as unlike Marx and Lenin who have 'isms' named after them, Deng did not create a new ideological framework for analysing the world, no he was a Marxist-Leninist. Nor did he advance Marxism-Leninism to a higher stage of development, as Mao

Zedong arguably did with MZT, which is why Deng is not the 6th head of Marxism after Mao (also Deng's theory specifically was applied to the Chinese material conditions and contradictions at hand). What 'Dengism' might refer to, (as a slang term) is SWCC, MZT, DZT and XJPT, which are real ideological advancements of Marxism-Leninism specific to Chinese conditions. Similarly, 'Khrushchevism' which was often used to slander Post-Stalin U.S.S.R. as 'revisionist' does not exist as Khrushchev did not make any advancements to Marxism-Leninism following Stalin and continued the legacy of Stalin in upholding Marxism-Leninism. No one is a 'Khruschevite' unless that phrase is referring to someone who upholds the Khruschev era. 'Stalinism' is often thrown around as a synonym for Marxism-Leninism. While technically 'Stalinism' is not a distinct ideology in any way (as Stalin only made minor advancements to Marxism-Leninism, namely on 'State of the Whole People' and 'Peaceful Coexistence'), it is due to Stalin being the person who synthesised Marxism-Leninism, that it is a synonym. So while technically 'Stalinism' equals Marxism-Leninism, 'Stalinist' solely means someone who upholds Stalin. While on other hand 'Marxist' is not just someone who upholds Marx, but also someone who believes in the theories of Marx, which is Marxism. The same applies to Lenin.

I hope that this post clarifies some things. Watch out for people who unironically use terms like 'Dengism' as they probably have no idea what they are talking about.

Lets take a dogmatic definition of socialism, I will elaborate on the real definition of socialism later:

"Socialism is the transitionary period between Capitalism and Communism.

The criteria for a socialist society are the following:

Dictatorship of the proletariat.

No private ownership over the main means of production.

No exploitation of man to man.

Dying capitalist tendencies and arising Communist tendencies."

Point 1 is met, as Xi elaborates in his book, but by 2001 the state had been what could be refferred to as a degenerated workers state and capitalists were begginning to get some power, Xi could have been Gorbachev but instead he reversed this trend and got elected based on his vow to end this corruption.

Point 2, **The backbone of the economy is state ownership and socialist planning. 24 / 25 of the top revenue companies are state-owned and planned. 70% of the top 500 companies are State-owned. 1, 2**

Point 3, not yet at a fully publically owned economy, but due to point 4 is met.

Point 4, the government has been enacting the 1979 plan of Xiaokang for July 2020, which is a society in which there is no poverty and which everyone can thrive in society and would mark the begginning of a return towards the Maoist era. I had doubts until now but I had heard this date. Looking at recent news they are still on the right path considering they reintroduced the mass-line, and are increasing State Owned Enterprises in just the last month (July 2020 as they said). They are still upholding long term dates and plans on the road towards a fully socialist economy by 2050.

The class nature of the state is very important, for example Saudi Arabia despite 95% state ownership is in fact capitalist, state capitalist, but what matters here is which class the economy serves. In Saudi Arabia Post-WW2 there was an oil boom and the former feudalists shifted the economy to benefit themselves and made the state act like a corporation for the interests of this small ruling minority, Saudi Arabia is capitalist because despite not having the anarchy of production or private ownership dominate, the economy serves a ruling comprador elite rather than the working people who create that wealth.

Compare this to say China which functionally is 'state capitalist' since the reforms of the late 90s and early 00s due to the collapse of the Soviet Union which brought new conditions that forced the acceleration of reform and opening up, however there were also revisionist attempts to dismantle the proletarian structure from revisionists who attempted to exploit this era where China was focusing on laying low and just staying alive, having already experienced a coup attempt. However as China had a dictatorship of the proletariat still intact, they were able to fight back against revisionism within the party where the U.S.S.R. had failed to do so thanks to the cultural revolutions influence, as the CPC still rule and the economy of China serves the people through the PDD (DOTP). China cannot be called capitalist as the anarchy of production does not dominate the economy, private ownership of the means of production is not dominant (although the capitalist mode of production exists to some extent), but it also cannot be called socialist (LSC) and it is because of that you get terms from Xi Jinping such as the 'primary stage of socialism' and 'socialist market economy'. As well as in Xi's New Years address where he said 'socialist modernisation will now begin' because this is explicitly refferring to the period of the U.S.S.R. after the NEP but before it became 'fully' socialist in 1936 when the DOTP had succeeded in abolishing antagonistic classes. Simply put China is socialist and is working towards higher stages of socialist development.

The class nature is key when it comes to capitalism

as it is the DOTB which enforces capital but the bourgeoisie itself is not needed for 'capitalism' to be capitalism as 'market socialism' and coops pushed by 'Vaush' and other radlibs is just capitalism because even though there would be no bourgeoisie, the economy would still serve capital. The issues of anarchy of production and imperialism would not have been addressed. There are capitalist states where what seem like social democrats (to westerners) such as Evo Morales in Bolivia and Maduro in Venezuela, rule through parliaments, but their power does not come solely through parliamentary means itself, because no change can ever come solely from a parliament. Their power comes from the grassroots collectivos and proletarian power on the ground, social democrats here in the west always like to point to them as examples of successful social democracy in action but that couldn't be further from the truth and we saw the failure of the revisionist euro-communists who thought they could muck around in bourgeois parliaments. However these are socialists who are trying to move capitalist states to socialism with what they got, building mass movements without causing a violent reaction of capital internationally and externally. This is also seen in Nicaragua, Angola and Mozambique where revolutions had been won but Communists had been left between a rock and a hard place and had to submit to CIA backed rebels and setup parliaments after the U.S.S.R. fell. Also recently, in Nepal where due to pressure from lack of support in urban areas as well as British Gorka special units, the Maoists had to make peace. They did however succeed in abolishing the monarchy and they still retain power.

In conclusion, it is clear that China is a state led by Marxists, it doesn't matter what you want to call it but it is clear that they are on the road to higher stages of socialism. Western Marxists who have had no revolutionary successes to their name are in no position to criticise or dictate to millions of people who have, what socialism is and isn't. At the very least socialists should provide critical support to China against the imperialist advances of the U.S. and NATO when it comes to the key issues of Taiwan, Hong Kong, Tibet and Xinjiang. That is a baseline for authentic socialists to have. Beyond that, I would of course argue that we should of course correspond with Chinese Marxists themselves and that we cannot allow the successes of China to be claimed by the capitalists without counter, as it is clear that it is the socialist system which has brought China all of it's successes and allowed it uplift itself from the Century of Humiliation.

RUSSIA:

Back in 2020 Left Twitter exploded after a user posted that U.S.S.R. 2 was incoming. Little did they all know that this was far more than just a meme.

To begin I will dispell some common myths, to start, Russia is not imperialist. To suggest so is to side with NATO. Following the collapse of the Soviet Union and throughout the 90's, Russia was subservient to the West, today it is a strong ally of other anti-imperialist states such as Iran, Syria and China. However there has been a power struggle within Russia, for example Medvedev of United Russia wanted to overthrow Libya, while Putin did not, had Putin been in power then the overthrow of Gaddafi could have been prevented. Since Putin returned to the helm, Russia has not capitulated in such ways and has been firmly anti-imperialist. There is no threat, NATO has no reason to exist after the Soviet Union fell, that literally tells you everything you need to know because they have to create the appearance of a military threat that is 'dangerous' so they can justify the military industrial complex, imperialism and geopolitical strategy.

Blaming the Russians is the go to because even though it is obviously fabricated, old Soviet propaganda still permeates from the Cold war era so its an easy scapegoat for the multi-billionaires and billionaires who support the Democrats and want to maintain the status quo, to target against the small business owners and millionaires who want to exploit workers even more and support the Republicans.Yeltsin literally allowed the west to loot the country, everything previously publically owned was sold to the highest bidder, the ultranationalist Putin was the fix to this for the Russian bourgeoisie who had become small fish in a big pond as he cracked down on the liberalisation that was destroying the country and supported the national bourgeois over foreigners, and impoved quality of life for average people after the disaster of the 90s, which is why he has my critical support as the nice appearing chess-master Gary Kasporov would just continue the looting and a Communist revolution does not look to be on the horizon. Another lie about Russia is that it is fascist, in fact every fascist, nazbol and neo-nazi party is banned. Neo-nazi skinheads were cracked down upon hard. Russia is also a country of dozens of ethnicities who are all proud Russians and united around the flag. Chechnya is essentially an independent Islamic emirate within Russia and from the Soviet era all the other ethnic groups such as the Tuvans enjoy a great deal of autonomy.

According to the words of Vladimir Putin himself, since 2020 Russia has been in an NEP. The process of moving towards a socialist state began in 2020 with the establishment of a new NEP. Russia is still capitalist, specifically state capitalist with a strong market sector similar to China but it could be argued that Russia is currently a Dictatorship of the Proletariat:

– DOTP -1 -2 -3 -4 -5 -6 -7 -8 -9 -10 -11

A recent example of Russia being a DOTP was when Putin at the start of the special military operation in Ukraine scolded the bourgeoisie for not falling in line. Russia deals with their bourgeoisie similar to China, with an iron fist.

Putin has called for further state planning:

– Planning -1 -2 -3 -4 -5 -6 -7 -8

Three-quarters of the economy is owned by the state, while there is also strong and vibrant small and medium medium sized firms in a market sector which have been promoted by the state as alternatives to foreign oligopolies.

The leader of the Communist Party of the Russian Federation, Gennady Zyuganov has **high praise** for Putin and has even suggested that he should become leader of the party. This suggestion does not come from an empty vacuum, Putin has actually for the last several years **not been apart** of United Russia and has been **antagonistic** towards the party. He has instead supported Fair Russia (in the last election) who had talks of joining in a coalition with the Communist Party. Putin has also on multiple occasions **praised Communism** and **Communist figures** of the past.

Russia is now **sovereign**, it could be said that this war is Russia's declaration of independence from the globalist system. Since the collapse of the Soviet Union and the declaration of the uni-polar world, Russia has been on the losing side, throughout the 90's Russia was looted by the West, only with the **emergence** of Putin did Russia start to fight back. The very willingness to defy the United States and engage to liberate Ukraine from Neo-Nazi Banderites and NATO (4th Reich) shows that Russia has defiantly broken free completely from the grip of the West. Russia has taken soveriegnty of all sectors previously controlled by the West. Companies that have pulled out have seen **property nationalised**, no longer will profits flow to Wall Street and London from Russia. The sanctions are **accelerating** the process of Russia moving towards socialism. The Russian bourgeoisie who as I stated earlier are under a heavy thumb are under the threat of having their property **returned** to the people. Putin declared the 'oligarchs' are **traitors** who have betrayed the people. Russia has also taken control of it's internet, providing it's own certificates, bypassing the U.S. hegemony of the internet and soft imperialism. Western big-tech companies have been banned, we saw Facebook lift bans on calls to violence against Russian people, and we saw every other mainstream platform quickly fall in line with the agenda of Western imperialism. They were all quickly banned for extremism. This step of independence can be seen as the emergence of the multi-polar world.

Russia is moving towards socialism out of necessity. It has long been said in Russia that there are only two paths that can be taken by the country. Either a return to socialism or capitulation to the West. Socialism is the only way forward if Russia want true sovereignty.

There has been real talk in the last couple of years about a Union State, this would provide a Chechen like arrangement (similar to the U.S.S.R.) for all countries that join, they would effectively be independent but the states would be united around the Union State. The President of Belarus, Alexander Lukashenko recently said in December 2021 that Russia, Belarus and Ukraine would all be united soon. Belarus held a referendum in February 2022, the purpose of which was to make the Belarusian constitution become compatible with the Russian constution. The vote passed strongly with 65% support. The vote was also a litmus test of the popularity of Lukashenko showing that he is still popular. All of this was despite threats by the United States of of cybersecurity attacks and the forming of a 'government in exile' by the opposition on behalf of their Western masters. The passing of the vote opens up the establishment of the Union State as the official successor to the RF. Armenia also expressed a desire to join such a formation. As do Kazakhstan although for the time being their application has been rejected. Unity around the CSTO had been seen in early 2022 with the Central Asian republics all contributing to ridding Kazakhstan of the Western-backed terrorists.

There have been serious talks of a union state uniting the former Soviet States, since 1991 there has been the CIS as well as the CSTO peacekeeping force, which we recently saw prevent a colour revolution succeeding in Kazakhstan. More recently the Shanghai Pact includes, Russia, China and the central asian republics. These countries all have close economic ties.

Three things unite the former Soviet Union - Communism, religion (Orthodox Christianity and Islam) and language (Russian) - principally Communism could be said to be the greatest common denominator, so it is no suprise that the Soviet flag could be seen atop Russian tanks. Given that the breakway Donbass republics, of the Lugansk Peoples Republic (LPR) and the Donetsk Peoples Republic (DPR) (as well as Transnistria) are led by Communists it should be assumed that the ideology of Communism will continue to more and more be brought to the forefront. In fact it was actually the KPRF's bill to recognise the republics, no matter what government was in power in Russia it would have had to intervene militarily in Ukraine. Had the KPRF been in power, they would have intervened all the way back in 2014. It is very likely that more people's republics will be created by the people themselves in Ukraine (in 2014 the Kharkhiv People's Republic was crushed) and as they become more and more important we will see Communism become more relevant. The KPRF are likely to become even more and more popular and we could see the pressure they put on Putin continue. To all Communists who claim that the KPRF are controlled by United Russia, you just have to look at the pressure they put on them (such as with the bill to recognise the Donbass republics) to see that they are a thriving, independent party representative of a broad section of the Russian masses. They are currently the most popular party and I only expect them to become more popular as the Soviet Union becomes closer to being revived.

The Soviet Union still lives on, it is engrained in the Russian civilisation and collective national consciousness. It has left a permanent mark that remains, Russia has for the last two decades taken on the mantle of the main anti-imperialist power, this was supported by the national bourgeoisie. When there was effectively no resistance to the uni-polar world order there was Russia resisting, whether it be in Yugoslavia, Libya, Syria, they have had and are having an objective net positive effect, unlike the West which trys to keep countries poor and divided, Russia on the otherhand has been a force of stability. Russia is a far more collective civilisation and out of all of the Former Soviet Republics it has recovered well from shock therapy, while Turkmenistan, Belarus and Tajikistan never really opened up or privatised in the same way, while Ukraine is a state that still has not surpassed the GDP the country had in 1990 due to all the corruption and looting by foreign powers. What we will see in the next few years as Russia moves towards a socialist system and the union state unites the former Soviet Union is the old returning in new way, the dialectic coming to it's fruition. The sanctions following the Russian intervention in Ukraine have caused Russia to move even closer to (Socialist) China. When the Nordstream 2 pipeline was cancelled by Biden, straight away a new deal was made to redirect the export of gas to China instead, and when sanctions banned the importing of Russian grain into the West, it was China who made a new deal. We are seeing China and Russia develop a strong and resolute alliance. With the fruition of the Union State and the construction of socialism in Russia we will have two strong Socialist superpowers side by side.

Ironically the Western sanctions could cause the collapse of the West themselves rather than Russia as Russia has effectively made themselves immune to their worst effects. All that is left for the West to do is decouple Russia from SWIFT, however that would backfire even more spectacularly than the current sanctions as it would lead to the anti-imperialist bloc creating their own alternative.

Recently we saw Communists in America of the Center

for Political Innovation (CPI) openly celebrate the breakaway republics in the Donbass and state how there is no contradiction between being patriots of their own country (despite the U.S. causing the whole conflict) and supporting the revolutionary movements of the world. American Communists should desire the victory of Russia against Ukraine as any victory of an anti-imperialist state against their own ruling class is a victory not just for Russia but for the American working class. Russia has a long history of supporting the American working class, from the Russians sending ships to prevent the British supplying the confederates to the solidarity and internationalism of the CPSU and CPUSA towards each other for decades.

As Russell Bentley, a proud American fighting on the frontlines of the Donbass against the Ukrainian neo-nazis said:

"I'm a patriotic American. I love the American people, but I hate the American government. It is the Fourth Reich. It is the equivalence of Nazi Germany today" - Russell 'Texas' Bentley

To all the detractors to this post (to which I expect many), Russia unlike most of the Eastern Bloc is erecting statues to Stalin, a majority of Russians see the Soviet Union as the greatest period in Russian history. Majority also regret the collapse, Putin himself states that it was the greatest geopolitical disaster and celebrates the Red Army and victory in WW2 unlike other countries of the Former Eastern Bloc (such as Ukraine, Latvia and other Neo-Nazi infested countries). To conclude we should support Russia on anti-imperialist grounds, have critical support for the government and be supportive of efforts in recent years towards a return to the socialist past, which we now see being accelerated. I have high hopes that in the coming years we will see the emergence of a strong, socialist Union State.

DEFINITION OF SOCIALISM:

I think it would be useful to actually define socialism, this has become almost a buzzword to the Western Left however it does indeed have a real meaning.

When defining something it is important that the definition includes all instances of the use of the word (that have real material basis) at hand. It is also necessary to note that characteristics of a word do not equal a definition as if a word was to meet a checklist criteria to be defined as something then nothing would be definable. In the case of socialism we would get the 'not real socialism' meme from leftcoms and other ultra-leftists, and in the case of capitalism we would get the 'not real capitalism' in the case of some libertarians towards all capitalism currently existing or in a more general sense towards earlier instances of capitalism such as mercantile capitalism that were not as developed as the capitalism of the industrial era today. The point is that everything is in motion and developing and to reduce everything down to a dogmatic definition, a string of words that is **universal**, is an incorrect line of thinking and one which gives precedence to established institutions. As Marx and Engels said:

"The premises from which we begin are not arbitrary ones, not dogmas, but real premises from which abstraction can only be made in the imagination. They are the real individuals, their activity and the material conditions under which they live, both those which they find already existing and those produced by their activity" - Karl Marx

"The thing to be done at any definite given moment of the future, the thing immediately to be done, depends of course entirely on the given historical conditions in which one has to act. But this question is in the clouds and therefore is really the statement of a phantom problem to which the answer can be - the criticism of the question itself" - Karl Marx

"[V]ery anticipation of yet to be proven results seem disrupting to me, and the reader who wants to follow me at all must resolve to ascend from the particular to the general" - Karl Marx

"[Hegel] develops his thinking not out of the object, rather he develops the object in accordance with ready-made thinking put together in the abstract sphere of logic" - Karl Marx

"But had any eighteenth-century Frenchman in the faintest idea, a priori, of the way in which the demands of the French bourgeoisie would be acomplished? The doctrinaire and necessarily fantastic anticipations of the programme of action for a revolution of the future only divert us from the struggle of the present" - Karl Marx

"[Communists] develop new principles for the world out of the world's own principles. We do not say to the world: Cease your struggles, they are foolish; we will give you the true slogan of struggle. We merely show the world what it is fighting for, and consciousness is something that it has to acquire, even if it does not want to. I am therefore not in favour of our hoisting a dogmatic banner. Quite the reverse. We must try to help the dogmatists clarify their ideas" - Karl Marx

"To try to give a definition of property as of an independent relation, a category apart, an abstract and eternal idea, can be nothing but an illusion of metaphysics or jurisprudence" - Karl Marx

"Mr. Bray does not see that this egalitarian reflection,

this corrective ideal that he would like to apply to the world, is itself nothing but the reflection of the actual world, and therefore it is totally impossible to reconstitute society on a basis which is nothing but an embellished shadow of it. In proportion as the shadow becomes embodied again, we perceive that this body, far from being the dreamt transfiguration, is the actual body of existing society" - Karl Marx

"Mr. Proudhon does not directly assert that bourgeois life is an eternal truth for him. He says it indirectly, in that he divinises the categories which express the bourgeois relations under the form of thought" - Karl Marx

"The principles are not the starting-point of the investigation, but its final result; they are not applied to nature and human history, but abstracted from them, it is not nature and the realm of man which conform to these principles, but the principles are only valid in so far as they are in conformity with nature and history" - Friedrich Engels

"Our ideologist may turn and twist as he likes, but the historical reality which he cast out at the door comes in again at the window, and while he thinks he is framing a doctrine of morals and law for all times and for all worlds, he is in fact only fashioning an image of the conservative or revolutionary tendencies of his day. An image which is distorted because it has been torn from its real basis and, like a reflection in a concave mirror, is standing on its head" - Friedrich Engels

"[We should not expect to find] fixed, cut-to-measure, once and for all applicable definitions in Marx's works. It is self-evident that where things and their interrelations are conceived, not as fixed, but as changing, their mental images, the ideas, are likewise subject to change and transformation and they are not encapsulated in rigid definitions, but are developed in their historical or logical process of formation" - Friedrich Engels

"Our definition of life is naturally very inadequate... All definitions are of little value. In order to gain an exhaustive knowledge of what life is, we should have to go through all the forms in which it appears, from the lowest to the highest; To science definitions are worthless because (they are) always inadequate. The only real definition is the development of the thing itself, but this is no longer a definition" - Friedrich Engels

To define socialism we first have to define capitalism. Capitalism is defined by Karl Marx and Friedrich Engels as a system in which the means of production are privately owned and operated to make profits for those who own them. Marx described capitalism as "the anarchy of production". Engels explained:

"For in capitalistic society, the means of production can only function when they have undergone a preliminary transformation into capital" - Friedrich Engels

Mao Zedong, the leader of the Chinese Communist Party, said that:

"[Capitalism is a system of] profits in command" - Mao Zedong

Simply put capitalism is a system where profits are in command, society produces for the sake of profits. Hence from the negation of the negation: Socialism is a rational system where social ends are the primary motivator/determinant of society.

This is the end of the definition anglo box -1 -2 -3.

My way of looking at it is that capitalism being when profits are in command fits every instance of capitalism and socialism being when social ends are dominant fits every instance of socialism to have existed in material reality.

Now I know that some people will point out that Stalin described a socialist society:

"Yes, you are right, we have not yet built Communist

society. It is not so easy to build such a society. You are probably aware of the difference between socialist society and Communist society. In socialist society certain inequalities in property still exist. But in socialist society there is no longer unemployment, no exploitation, no oppression of nationalities. In socialist society everyone is obliged to work, although he does not, in return for his labour receive according to his requirements, but according to the quantity and quality of the work he has performed. That is why wages, and, moreover, unequal, differentiated wages, still exist. Only when we have succeeded in creating a system under which, in return for their labour, people will receive from society, not according to the quantity and quality of the labour they perform, but according to their requirements, will it be possible to say that we have built Communist society" - J.V. Stalin

However, here he is giving a description, and it is not the only description he gave of socialism. The point is that you are not supposed to take the characteristics he describes and see this as the essence of socialism, or ahistorical criteria that define socialism. A description of characteristics is not itself a definition. To summarise the descriptors of socialism he provides, it is each according to his needs to each according to his work, abolition of unemployment, exploitation/the extraction of surplus value/wage labour and oppression of nationalities. These are of course characteristics of a socialist society. However they are not the definition of socialism itself. The definition I have outlined of socialism is a "system where social ends are the primary motivator/determinant of society" is hence correct.

Now when it comes to the topic of Chinese Socialism. In the west it is the normal view that China is capitalist, state capitalist to be exact. However the ruling Chinese Party, the CPC, completely disagree with this assessment and have actively been engaged in the construction of their own socialism since 1949. The Chinese understanding of

Marxism is among the least dogmatic, China is in real time innovating and discovering what socialism is and means:

"But the idea of 'Socialism with Chinese Characteristics' means that socialism does not really have a fundamental developmental model, and instead consists of a handful of basic principles and ideas. These principles and ideas must be continually explored and developed in practice following the advance of time. 'Socialism with Chinese Characteristics' is not adding Chinese characteristics to an already defined 'socialist framework.' Rather, it uses China's lived experience to explore and define what, in the final analysis, 'socialism' is. For this reason, 'socialism' is not ossified dogma, but instead an open concept awaiting exploration and definition. China is not blindly following socialist ideas and institutions produced by the Western experience of socialism, but rather is charting the socialist developmental path on the basis of a greater self-confidence, taking the project of the modernisation of socialist construction to its third phase. For this reason, the report of the Eighteenth National Congress correctly talked about 'self-confidence in the path,' 'self-confidence in the theory,' and 'self-confidence in the institutions' involved in the construction of Socialism with Chinese Characteristics" - Jiang Shigong

Even when it comes to dogmatic definitions of Socialism: I have proven that China is still socialist according to them when you bend the rules of these dogmatic criteria to actually apply to material reality.

BOURGEOIS SOCIALISM:

However when it comes to the question of socialism today, the burning question of the inevitability of socialism must be addressed. It is the monopolisation of capital inherent (capital accumulation) of the capitalist system as well as the conditions that arise from that monopolisation (socialisation of production) which make inevitable the development of socialism, this is how us Marxists know that socialism is inevitable, and in just the same way it is the contradictions that arise in socialism which make Communism inevitable. So from this it is no wonder that capitalists would try and remain in power with some kind of bourgeois socialism as the processes they themselves created from their own system necessitate the development of socialism. Profit (while still a still a significant determinant in smaller firms) no longer dominates society, there is no anarchy of production. Social control (social end) and holding onto their power is far more important to the capitalist elite.

Engels himself referred to bourgeois socialists (which he distinguished from us Communists) as one type of socialist in the 'The Principles of Communism':

"[Bourgeois Socialists:] The second category consists of adherents of present-day society who have been frightened for its future by the evils to which it necessarily gives rise. What they want, therefore, is to maintain this society while getting rid of the evils which are an inherent part of it. To this end, some propose mere welfare measures - while others come forward with grandiose systems of reform which, under the pretense of re-organising society, are in fact intended to preserve the foundations, and hence the life, of existing society. Communists must unremittingly struggle against these bourgeois socialists because they work for the enemies of Communists and protect the society which Communists aim to overthrow" - Friedrich Engels

As did Marx in 'The Communist Manifesto':

"A part of the bourgeoisie is desirous of redressing social grievances in order to secure the continued existence of bourgeois society. To this section belong economists, philanthropists, humanitarians, improvers of the condition of the working class, organisers of charity, members of societies for the prevention of cruelty to animals, temperance fanatics, hole-and-corner reformers of every imaginable kind. This form of socialism has, moreover, been worked out into complete systems; The Socialistic bourgeois want all the advantages of modern social conditions without the struggles and dangers necessarily resulting therefrom. They desire the existing state of society, minus its revolutionary and disintegrating elements. They wish for a bourgeoisie without a proletariat. The bourgeoisie naturally conceives the world in which it is supreme to be the best; and bourgeois Socialism develops this comfortable conception into various more or less complete systems. In requiring the proletariat to carry out such a system, and thereby to march straightway into the social New Jerusalem, it but requires in reality, that the proletariat should remain within the bounds of existing society, but should cast away all its hateful ideas concerning the bourgeoisie. A second, and more practical, but less systematic, form of this Socialism sought to depreciate every revolutionary movement in the eyes of the working class by showing that no mere political reform, but only a change in the material conditions of existence, in economical relations, could be of any advantage to them. By changes in the material conditions of existence, this form of Socialism, however, by no means understands abolition of the bourgeois relations of production, an abolition that can be affected only by a revolution, but administrative reforms, based on the continued existence of these relations; reforms, therefore, that in no respect affect the relations between capital and labour, but, at the best, lessen the cost, and simplify the administrative work, of bourgeois government; It is summed up in the phrase: the bourgeois is a bourgeois - for the benefit of the working class" - Karl Marx

Martin Luther King Jr. also referred to the concept of socialism for the rich:

"We all too often have socialism for the rich and rugged free market capitalism for the poor" - Martin Luther King Jr.

It is up to the Communist party to seize power and scientifically (serve social ends) guide this process of socialisation in the interests of the proletariat (gear society towards the implemention of serving the working masses), as either way we are heading into some kind of bourgeois socialism (or arguably have been for a long time since the Wall Street Crash due to the falling rate of profit).

As Lenin said:

"Capitalism in its imperialist stage leads directly to the most comprehensive socialisation of production; it, so to speak, drags the capitalists, against their will and consciousness, into some sort of a new social order, a transitional one from complete free competition to complete socialisation" - V.I. Lenin

The foremost proof of this (and beginning of this process) was the end of the gold standard in 1931 by the Bank of England. This was done due to Great Depression that occured from the Wall Street Crash of 1929, which caused the bank to nearly run out of gold. Gold was the direct measure of value as understood by Marx as all commodities were tied to it:

"[Measure of Value] The first phase of circulation is, as it were, a theoretical phases preparatory to real circulation. Commodities, which exist as use-values, must first of all assume a form in which they appear to one another nominally as exchange-values, as definite quantities of materialised universal labour-time. The first necessary move in this process is, as we have seen, that the commodities set apart a specific commodity, say, gold, which becomes the direct reification of universal labour-time or the universal equivalent; gold is converted into money by commodities" - Karl Marx

Marx himself stated that as soon as labour in it's direct form has ceased to be the creation of wealth, that exchange value breaks down. I will explain this in further detail later:

"As soon as labour in the direct form has ceased to be the great well-spring of wealth, labour time ceases and must cease to be its measure, and hence exchange value [must cease to be the measure] of use value. The surplus labour of the mass has ceased to be the condition for the development of general wealth, just as the non-labour of the few, for the development of the general powers of the human head. With that, production based on exchange value breaks down" - Karl Marx

Marx also recognised that gold was the one true universal commodity. In order for money to serve as the universal measure of value, it has to contain intrinsic value, i.e. it has to itself be a commodity imbued with a definite magnitude of labour. Marx stated that it would be impossible for the capitalist class to get around this:

"Money - the common form into which all commodities as exchange values are transformed, i.e. the universal commodity - must itself exist as a particular commodity alongside the others, since what is required is not only that they can be measured against it in the head, but that they can be changed and exchanged for it in the actual exchange process. The contradiction which thereby enters, to be developed elsewhere. Money does not arise by convention, any more than the state does. It arises out of exchange, and arises naturally out of exchange; it is a product of the same; Gold becomes the measure of value because the exchange-value of all commodities is measured in gold, is expressed in the relation of a definite quantity of gold and a definite quantity of commodity containing equal amounts of laobur-time. To begin with, gold becomes the universal equivalent, or money, only because it thus functions as the measure of value and as such its own value is measured directly in all commodity equivalents; Their golden equivalent reflects the universal character of the labour-time contained in them" - Karl Marx

"But it should never be forgotten, that money, in the first place, in the form of precious metals, remains the basis from which the credit system naturally can never detach itself; Secondly, that the credit system presupposes the monopoly of social means of production by private persons; capitalist production forever strives to overcome this metallic barrier, the material and fantastic barrier of wealth and its movements, in proportion as the credit system develops, but forever breaks its head on this same barrier" - Karl Marx

This is also further elaborated on in 'An Introduction to Karl Marx's Capital':

"In Capital, Marx assumes that money always has to be linked to a particular commodity. During Marx's time, gold played the role of this 'money commodity.' But even back then it was hardly the case that pieces of gold were widely used in everyday commerce; small sums were paid with silver or copper coins, larger sums with 'banknotes.' Banknotes were originally issued by individual banks, which promised to honour the notes in gold. Ultimately, banknotes were only issued by state central banks, which also promisesd to honour the notes in gold. As a rule, the central banks of individual countries were not allowed to print an arbitrary amount of banknotes, but rather had to ensure that the banknotes were covered by a proportionate amount of gold reserves. Gold was hardly circulated, but the paper money in circulation acted as a representative of gold. At the end of the Second World War, at a conference in Bretton Woods, New Hampshire, an international currency system was agreed upon that was still based upon a gold standard. But only the U.S. dollar was covered by gold, thirty-five dollars corresponding to an ounce of gold. All other currencies had a fixed exchange rate to the dollar. However, the obligation to honour dollars in gold was not valid for private individuals, only for state central banks. At the end of the 1960s, it had become clear that the massive amount of dollars in circulation had rendered the coupling of the dollar to gold a fiction. At the beginning of the 1970s, the gold standard was formally abolished, as were fixed currency exchange rates. Since then, there is no longer any commodity that functions at a national or international level as a money commodity. Now money is essentially the paper money issued by the state central banks, and there is nothing for which this paper money can be redeemed. Of course, one can still buy gold with this paper money, but now gold is just another commodity like silver or iron, and no longer plays the special role of a money commodity, neither legally nor by default. Marx could not imagine a capitalist system existing without a money commodity, but the existence of such a commodity is in no way a necessary consequence of his analysis of the commodity and money. Within the framework of the analysis of the commodity form, he developed the form-determinations of the general equivalent, and the analysis of the exchange process yields the result that commodity owners do in fact have to relate their commodities to a general equivalent. But that the general equivalent must be a specific commodity was not proven by Marx, merely assumed. That which serves as a general equivalent (whether an actual physical commodity or merely paper money) cannot be determined at the level of simple commodity circulation (for a more extensive analysis, see Heinrich 1999, 233). Only when the capitalist credit system is taken into consideration does it become clear that the existence of a money commodity is merely a historically transitional state of affairs, but does not correspond to 'the capitalist mode of production, in its ideal average' that Marx sought to analyse" - (Michael Heinrich, An Introduction to Karl Marx's Capital)

Where it is stated that "Marx could not imagine a capitalist system existing without a money commodity". The collapse of the exchange value means the collapse of the countervailing tendency for the rate of profit, Marx talks about this in Capital Volume 3. Clearly you do not understand the LTV if you think otherwise. Surplus value is not guiding the economy. Capitalists make more money off of ground rent, which Marx predicted would be the last bit of surplus value left. the prerequisite of exchange value is commodity money.

Marx explains the collapse of exchange value via absolute overproduction of capital. Commodities can still be sold, but capitalists would not make a profit by selling them. Production based on exchange value has become incompatible with production for profit; which is to say, the capitalist cannot make a profit selling commodities at their values. How can surplus value be said to drive the economy when products are no longer profitable? Hence the M-C-M' circuit no longer applies. Price has drastically fallen below value… so much so that it cannot be said wage labour is the primary driver of the economy. This is why Marx introduced a theory of absolute overproduction of capital, and why capitalists become national capitalists. Both Marx and Engels said "the expropriators expropriate themselves…". Clearly something fundamental occurs in the production of commodity's, however Commodity-Money does not exist today. Meaning the value of money is socially and politically determined, not rooted in a universal commodity. What we have since 1971 is Fiat currency. Fiat has no value in a Marxist sense because the more that is printed the less valuable it becomes as it is not tied to a universal commodity.

The point is the money made from surplus today, is not commodity money or even money as Marx defined it, it is government credit being redistributed through speculative market signals. Financial profits are nothing more than redistributed government credit, backed not by any 'real profits' or even production, but information signals that themselves direct production. Marx explicitly outlined how, as a prerequisite for general commodity production, abstract labour and universal exchange, there has to be a universal commodity that crystalises a definite magnitude of labour value. The need to 'socialise' production by using the state so as to fulfill 'social' interests of any kind, was precisely why Marx said socialism was inevitable, and arising out of capitalist production itself.

The idea that socialism was not inevitable is revisionism. Capital transformed into an alien, occult object of socialist planning, sustained by institutions and U.S. military violence, not economics.

MMT is the Hitlerite theory of economics, made by theorists of the American Empire which is trying to save its economy through the raw power of state violence (war). Mao discovered there is still class antagonism under socialism. Socialism is not the fulfillment of your ideological, moral and psychological aspirations. It is a mode of production. The question is why does there remain a class antagonism? That was Mao's question:

"In China, although in the main socialist transformation has been completed with respect to the system of ownership, and although the large-scale and turbulent class struggles of the masses characteristic of the previous revolutionary periods have in the main come to an end, there are still remnants of the overthrown landlord and comprador classes, there is still a bourgeoisie, and the remolding of the petty-bourgeoisie has only just started. The class struggle is by no means over. The class struggle between the proletariat and the bourgeoisie, the class struggle between the different political forces, and the class struggle in the ideological held between the proletariat and the bourgeoisie will continue to be long and tortuous and at times will even become very acute. The proletariat seeks to transform the world according to its own world outlook, and so does the bourgeoisie. In this respect, the question of which will win out, socialism or capitalism, is still not really settled" - Mao Zedong

'Socialism' is not heaven on earth, it is a mode of production, production for social ends. I can see dogmatic responses to this which hold onto dogma of Marxism specific to another era:

"...Volume One of Marx's Capital gives a detailed description of the condition of the British working class for about 1865, i.e. the time when Britain's industrial prosperity had reached its peak. I would therefore have had to repeat what Marx says. It will be hardly necessary to point out that the general theoretical standpoint of this book - philosophical, economical, political, - does not exactly coincide with my standpoint of today" - Friedrich Engels

Which Mao further elaborates on with his opposition to dogmatism and book worship:

"The dogmatists do not observe this principle; they do not understand that conditions differ in different kinds of revolution and so do not understand that different methods should be used to resolve different contradictions; on the contrary, they invariably adopt what they imagine to be an unalterable formula and arbitrarily apply it everywhere, which only causes setbacks to the revolution or makes a sorry mess of what was originally well done" - Mao Zedong

Marx, Engels and Lenin all spent significant time debating fellow 'socialists' because of an adherence to dogmatism:

"Marx and myself have fought harder all one's life long against the alleged socialists than against anyone else (for we only regarded the bourgeoisie as a class and hardly ever involved ourselves in conflicts with individual bourgeois)" - Friedrich Engels

"But what the workers' cause needs is the unity of Marxists, not unity between Marxists, and opponents and distorters of Marxism" - V.I. Lenin

Now I know that is controversial, but to put it simply, the capitalism from Marx's day is long dead due to its innate contradictions. We now live in a socialistic centrally planned economy for the elites. We call ourselves Communists because we want a Communist party that can implement a planned economy for society. Yes, I know socialism is synonymous with the state explicitly calling itself socialist, establishing common ownership of the means of production by directly attaching them to some political power (or co-operative) that directly controls them, etc. This view of 'socialism' does not recognise socialism as an actual mode of production. It only conceives socialism as a political, not economic force. Stalin explicitly rejected this notion in Economic Problems of Socialism in the U.S.S.R.:

"Some comrades deny the objective character of laws of science, and of laws of political economy particularly, under socialism. They deny that the laws of political economy reflect law-governed processes which operate independently of the will of man. They believe that in view of the specific role assigned to the Soviet state by history, the Soviet state and its leaders can abolish existing laws of political economy and can 'form,' 'create,' new laws; These comrades are profoundly mistaken. It is evident that they confuse laws of science, which reflect objective processes in nature or society, processes which take place independently of the will of man, with the laws which are issued by governments, which are made by the will of man, and which have only juridical validity. But they must not be confused; It is said that some of the economic laws operating in our country under socialism, including the law of value, have been 'transformed,' or even 'radically transformed,' on the basis of planned economy. That is likewise untrue. Laws cannot be 'transformed,' still less 'radically' transformed. If they can be transformed, then they can be abolished and replaced by other laws. The thesis that laws can be 'transformed' is a relic of the incorrect formula that laws can be 'abolished' or 'formed.' Although the formula that economic laws can be transformed has already been current in our country for a long time, it must be abandoned for the sake of accuracy. The sphere of action of this or that economic law may be restricted, its destructive action - that is, of course, if it is liable to be destructive - may be averted, but it cannot be 'transformed' or 'abolished'" - J.V. Stalin

Do not think of socialism as an ideal but an objective mode of production. I am saying that the capitalism of the 19th and 20th century gradually evolved through the course of history. The cycle of capitalist crisis eventually led to an increasing socialisation of production. We can observe this not only in 1929 but in 1947, 1972, 2004, and 2008 and even today as we speak. So the contradictions of capitalism led to the transformation of itself. It is only that the political and ideological superstructure has not replicated this fundamental change in the relations of production:

"Man, who moved from the simple and coarse Communism of primitive times, returns to a complex and scientific Communism; capitalist civilisation elaborates the elements, having removed the personal character from private property; Capitalist civilisation, which begins to put together the economic form of Communism, also brings into the social and political field, the institutions and customs of it. Universal suffrage, which the savages-men and women-used to choose their sachems and their military leaders, after having been suppressed, was put back in force by the bourgeoisie, who limited it to one sex, but boast of it as the sole source of public powers. It presupposes, at least in appearance that equality and freedom of citizens, which really existed in the bosom of primitive Communism. The dwellings of the Communist tribes were common; common also were the meals, and the education of the children. Communal school children are educated in common at the expense of the municipality; they are likewise fed together, at common expense, in socialist municipalities. The civilised, on the other hand, are poisoned and robbed in common in the inns and quartered together in the six - or seven-story houses, of the big cities. So far, universal suffrage has been a deception; if the houses are nothing but rooms where people get sad and fever-generating centers, if the other institutions having a Communist form are backwards, i.e., directed against those who are forced to endure them, he is that these institutions were introduced into bourgeois society only to give profit to the capitalists; however, in spite of their imperfections and all the drawbacks they draw with them, they weaken and erase the individualistic feelings of the civilised, and adapt them to the customs and mores of Communism" - Paul Lafargue

All that socialism boils down to is the sublation of production for profits sake to transform into production for social ends. That has already happened. The Socialism of the United States is a kind of Socialism for the rich. We as Communists want a socialism for the people. Socialism won the cold war. What remains now is a socialist civil war between the West and China.

Further proof of this comes from Michael Hudson. In his work 'Super Imperialism' he states that through the institutions of the IMF and the World Bank that the Western elite effectively plan the economies of the third world for the benefit of themselves. The states of today are planned by the bourgeoisie for their own benefit directly, profit is no longer the primary determinant of society. Since the end of the Vietnam War, imperialism has moved from capital exports to primarily keeping third-world countries indebted, old metrics of determining imperialist powers such as net-capital exports, no longer apply as even the United States, the foremost imperialist power in the world since the establishment of Bretton Woods, has net capital imports. The imperialism of the 21th Century is based in America's ability to borrow, not invest. What changed was that in 1971 the gold/dollar convertability was terminated (and Bretton Woods), instead it was replaced by the petrodollar (Fiat), which pegged all petroleum exports (and essentially all trade as a result, due to the importance of energy to the economy) to the U.S. dollar. This process took two years to complete, and was the beginning of neoliberalism, where before the pioneers of bourgeois socialism wanted to implement some social-reforms at home to keep the first-world in check, others wanted to self-imperialise the country at home. It was not just privatisation but it was privatisation for the benefit of the capitalist elite who were subsidised by the government to complete the tasks previously performed by the state, planning actually increased it just became more alienated. It also has to be said that the anarchy of production does not exist to the dominating degree it once did, and as Lenin stated, imperialism was the highest stage of capitalism, a transitional phase between capitalism and what came next, we have passed to that new social order and it is socialism, albeit bourgeois socialism. James Connolly spoke all the way back in 1916 as living in the "last days of capitalism". Rosa Luxemburg stated that it would either be "barbarism or socialism".

Since the aftermath of the Wall Street Crash the system we live under has been synarchy, bourgeois socialism or simply put barbarism. None of this would be possible if not for the bourgeois-socialists to implement it. For example, Andrew Carnegie, who made his fortune in the steel industry, and today would have wealth valued at $310 billion by today's standards, proclaimed himself in favour of socialistic doctrines. As did John D. Rockefeller who was stated to 'sound more like Marx than our classical image of a capitalist'. Henry Ford was stated by Kojeve "as the one great authentic Marxist of the twentieth century". Elon Musk also proclaims himself to be a socialist, which obviously at first seems contradictory given that he is a monopoly capitalist, however given what has just been elaborated as well as all of the government subsidies his companies benefit from, it is of no suprise.

This has been a gradual process which actually was completed in 1971 with the diminishing of profit and the start of the neoliberal era which effectively brings imperialism home to the developed countries. There is no free market, for example BlackRock manage assets worth over a total of $21 Trillion with it's Aladdin portfolio management tool, it effectively is planning these assets on a rational level. BlackRock seeks complete control, 'surplus value', in the Marxist sense, only matters to BlackRock insofar as it is a measure of their general investment success, as represented by the return to investors. What is more important to a BlackRock executive, how much 'profit' they receive as a return on investment, or the general confidence in their brand? Inspiring confidence is how acquisitions are made in this day and age. They are interested in ground rent, not surplus value, so they will prioritise their image of good management over profit, since what matters is owning everything. Amazon is also known for it's internal planning and has been unprofitable since it's founding and is heavily subsidised by the government while effectively being an oligopoly of ecommerce. Also companies cannot just do what they want, they have to go along with government sanctions even if that means loss, as social ends of the capitalist elite dominate.

Economically the system is (bourgeois) socialist but it is politically capitalist (as in led by the bourgeoisie), whereas China is both economically and politically socialist (as it is led by the proletariat and is ruled by a Communist system). What we need is to seize power for our class (proletariat) and scientifically address the contradictions of our society, while gearing society towards the well-being of the people as opposed to a few parasites on top.

Socialism is an objective mode of production, detractors of this piece who hold socialism as an ideal are debunked by the dialectical materialist outlook of Marxism which recognises that matter is constantly in motion:

"The new productive forces have already outgrown the capitalistic mode of using them. And this conflict between productive forces and modes of production is not a conflict engendered in the mind of man, like that between original sin and divine justice. In exists, in fact, objectively, outside us, independently of the will and actions even of the men that have brought it on. Modern socialism is nothing but the reflex, in thought, of this conflict in fact; its ideal reflection in the minds, first of the class directly suffering under it, the working class" - Friedrich Engels

"Needless to say, of course, all boundaries in nature and in society are conventional and changeable, and it would be absurd to argue, for example, about the particular year or decade in which imperialism 'definitely' became established" - V.I. Lenin

In this bourgeois socialism the fundamental contradiction of the capitalist mode of production still dominates, carries on from the old system:

"The contradiction between socialised production and capitalistic appropriation manifested itself as the antagonism of proletariat and bourgeoisie; With this recognition, at last, of the real nature of the productive forces of today, the social anarchy of production gives place to a social regulation of production upon a definite plan, according to the needs of the community and of each individual. Then the capitalist mode of appropriation, in which the product enslaves first the producer and then the appropriator, is replaced by the mode of appropriation of the products that is based upon the nature of the modern means of production: upon the one hand, direct social appropriation, as means to the maintenance and extension of production - on the other, direct individual appropriation, as means of subsistence and of enjoyment" - Friedrich Engels

Today no organisation represents this system more than the WEF. We cannot let the **Great Reset Agenda** of the WEF and **Club of Rome** (which are at the forefront of bourgeois socialism) win out. The proponents of this agenda are the elite of the elite, the Wall Street and City of London elite. These **parasites** want us to own nothing and be renters of the capitalist class in every aspect of life. They want complete control over us. They do not care about the consequences of what a nuclear war would entail and see overpopulation as the greatest threat to their existence. This **malthusian** agenda sees us merely as ants to be squashed, they see us as in the way of their continued existence as they recognise that even with all of the propaganda and attempts at dumbing down the masses with overdoses of dopamine, that they cannot hold back the angst of class antagonism. The Great Reset is a recognition of bourgeois socialism, it seeks the ending of democracy, ending of property rights for us commoners to the gain of the bourgeoisie, overall increasing state intervention and authoritarianism to serve the neoliberal cartels. The interesting thing is that they are doing it openly, and (almost) everyone just accepts it under the guise of 'emergency measures'. Thing that would have been unacceptable and obviously seen as aggression of the elites and the powers that may be, are now seen as completely acceptable, even by the left. For a long time the establishment had to hide the fact that it is building capital's socialism, but it was necessary because people intrinsically understood that this is very bad for them, but now it is becoming more and more open and the Great Reset is the proof of that.

"It reproduces a new financial aristocracy, a new variety of parasites in the shape of promoters, speculators and simply nominal directors a whole system of swindling and cheating by means of corporation promotion, stock issuance, and stock speculation. It is private production without the control of private property... Success and failure both lead here to a centralisation of capital, and thus to expropriation on the most enormous scale. Expropriation extends here from the direct producers to the smaller and the medium-sized capitalists themselves. It is the point of departure for the capitalist mode of production; its accomplishment is the goal of this production. In the last instance, it aims at the expropriation of the means of production from all individuals" - Karl Marx

"[Petty-bourgeois socialism] This school of socialism dissected with great acuteness the contradictions in the conditions of modern production. It laid bare the hypocritical apologies of economists. It proved, incontrovertibly, the disastrous effects of machinery and division of labour; the concentration of capital and land in a few hands; overproduction and crises; it pointed out the inevitable ruin of the petty-bourgeois and peasant, the misery of the proletariat, the anarchy in production, the crying inequalities in the distribution of wealth, the industrial war of extermination between nations, the dissolution of old moral bonds, of the old family relations, of the old nationalities. In its positive aims, however, this form of socialism aspires either to restoring the old means of production and of exchange, and with them the old property relations, and the old society, or to cramping the modern means of production and of exchange within the framework of the old property relations that have been, and were bound to be, exploded by those means. In either case, it is both reactionary and Utopian. Its last words are: corporate guilds for manufacture; patriarchal relations in agriculture. Ultimately, when stubborn historical facts had dispersed all intoxicating effects of self-deception, this form of socialism ended in a miserable fit of the blues" - Karl Marx

We need to overcome this bourgeois socialist system and establish proletarian socialism (Communism) and scientifically guide society towards social ends for our class. There is no going back to capitalism, we have already eclipsed it economically, it is time to end this barbarism and to put power in the hands of the people themselves, not back into the hands of smaller capitalists who will just repeat the same process all over again. We must advance forward to proletarian political power!

"With the seizing of the means of production by society production of commodities is done away with, and, simultaneously, the mastery of the product over the producer. Anarchy in social production is replaced by systematic, definite organisation. The struggle for individual existence disappears. Then for the first time man, in a certain sense, is finally marked off from the rest of the animal kingdom, and emerges from mere animal conditions of existence into really human ones. The whole sphere of the conditions of life which environ man, and which have hitherto ruled man, now comes under the dominion and control of man who for the first time becomes the real, conscious lord of nature because he has now become master of his own social organisation. The laws of his own social action, hitherto standing face to face with man as laws of nature foreign to, and dominating him, will then be used with full understanding, and so mastered by him. Man's own social organisation, hitherto confronting him as a necessity imposed by nature and history, now becomes the result of his own free action. The extraneous objective forces that have hitherto governed history pass under the control of man himself. Only from that time will man himself, with full consciousness, make his own history - only from that time will the social causes set in movement by him have, in the main and in a constantly growing measure, the results intended by him. It is the humanity's leap from the kingdom of necessity to the kingdom of freedom" - Friedrich Engels

"We propose that production be made to serve the needs of those who work, rather than to serve the needs of a few parasites" - Moissaye J. Olgin

NAZBOL:

The terms 'nazbol' and 'red-fash' or 'red-brown' gets thrown around a lot lately, even by self-professed 'Communists'. The people who use these terms tend to be liberals who slander Communists and want to associate us with the horrors and brutality of fascism, while at the same time denouncing our history as such. This is in great contrast to the brutality that the Soviet had to endure and their heroic sacrifice in defeating the Nazis. While at the same time there are also 'Communists' who use this term to slander real Communists.

However while all this is a recent trend on the internet. (With some clowns actually identifying with and filling in the blanks of a meme ideology). In real life the real meaning (it's real material application) of the term nazbol could not be further from that of the internet. In Russia the nazbol party was not actually a meme fusion of Nazism and Communism, in reality it's ideology was actually a strange fusion of anarchism, liberalism and some fascist elements with nationalist characteristics and it's membership was comprised almost exclusively of hippies. It rejected racism with the fascist elements being that it wanted Russia to unite the former U.S.S.R. through conquest (remember that this was the 90's in the fallout of the U.S.S.R.'s collapse) and that it was a party that emphasised Russian ethnicity over other ethnic groups.

While these terms might originally have been used on the internet as memes to mock both Communism and fascism at the same time, it has also more recently began to be used by radical-liberals online deceptively to suggest that Communists are similar to fascists. Making out that both are 'totalitarian' (which is a term invented by the CIA and has been used to suggest that anyone who opposes the established liberal/globalist world order is fascist). According to these radical-liberals, anyone who opposes the unfettered imperialism of the United States is a 'nazbol' and any state that dares stand in their way is 'red-fash' or 'red-brown'.

Radlibs such as 'Vaush' (who ironically are social-fascists, social-imperialists and even outright imperialists for their support of U.S. imperialist narratives time and time again) try to claim that Russia, China (and other anti-imperialist states) are 'red-brown' states, this whole argument is an imperialist argument that sets the precedent for US imperialism in Eastern Europe and elsewhere on 'humanitarian' grounds coming from the left. Ironically in Russia all nationalist parties are banned, this includes Nazi groups and nazbol parties, while parties that suck up to the west such as liberal parties are also banned with their leaders going to jail. An example of both would be Alexei Navalny who has a history of using slurs and even violence against minority groups. What is even more ironic is that despite all this Navalny is still pushed by the west and despite all their media fawning over him he enjoys absolutely zero popular support in Russia.

The term 'red-brown alliance' was used to dismiss the peaceful protestors of the 1993 Russian constitutional crisis who opposed the rigging of the election against the Communists, and other parties who opposed the austerity of Yeltsin (who was backed the CIA). The police used violence against the protestors killing 147 people. Yeltsin refered to the protestors as a 'red-brown alliance'. What made this whole situation even worse is that even internationally some

Communist parties (such as the CPUSA) used this term and denounced the protestors.

The term is also used to refer to anyone who holds 'social conservative' views, radlibs were calling Pedro Castillo a 'nazbol' prior to his election as President of Peru, for his previous opposition to gay marriage. All this is despite the fact that historically Communists have been for the most part conservative with regard what we now call 'social issues' (prior to the neo-liberal era this term referred to issues such as housing and healthcare). The reason that the western left does this is so that they can completely dismiss mass movmements in the third-world as 'reactionary' and beneath them. They focus on social issues in the west so as to distract from their economic failings and failure to reach the masses as a result and so they can push their 'humanitarian' and 'woke' imperialism on the world under the guise of the left. Ironically these third-world movements are often more progressive on these issues than the western left themselves. Here is a good article which debunks lies from American leftists on this matter.

The people who use this term also use the term so as to protect the ruling class. Whenever we talk about the DoTB (normalised as the 'Deep State') or the bourgeoisie (normalised as the 'Elites') they cry 'nazbol' and assume that we are talking about a certain ethnicity, Jewish people, as they have already due to the use of this term equated us with Nazis. However what is ironic is that they are themselves anti-semetic because they are making the assumption that the elite and the establishment are composed solely of Jews or otherwise that there is no elite, when this could not be further from the truth. They show their true colours and expose themselves for who and what they are.

"Furthermore, [radlib] voices tend to argue that anything resembling Lenin's analysis of capitalism in its imperialist stage is somehow anti-semitic. [Radlibs] will often claim that references to bankers, international bankers, or globalism is merely a coded repackaging of Nazi conspiracy theories about Jewish global domination. This allegation is absurd, and would render not just all adherents of Marxism-Leninism, but also many liberal critics of globalisation such as Noam Chomsky, Arundhati Roy, and Naomi Klein to be Nazi propagandists" - Caleb T. Maupin

I have demonstrated the complete hypocrisy and malicious intent of those who use this term. It is clear that these are terms that we should avoid as they are used to slander and divide our movement. Given that fascism is the psychosis (breakdown) of liberalism, it should be of no suprise that that the fascism of the future will come from radlibs. We have seen recently their support of big tech censorship ('conservatives' are right-liberals while 'liberals' are left-liberals, the point is that radlibs are the avant-garde of liberalism) with them even becoming the footsoldiers (similar spiritually as to how the lumpen were the footsoldiers of Bonparte despite him serving finance capital primarily) of the Silicon Valley cartel crackdown on anti-imperialist voices. We have also seen their recent support for the neo-Nazi Azov Battalion in Ukraine (as well as other CIA backed counter-gangs elsewhere). As the U.S. empire continues to breakdown and the quality of life decreases at home and society collapses, we can expect them to become the footsoldiers of imperialism, reaction and further authoritarianism at home, and in a last ditched attempt to hold onto their quality of life and empire, who knows what they could do?

As Mao said:

"It is good if we are attacked by the enemy... It demonstrates that we have not only drawn a clear line of demarcation between the enemy and ourselves but also achieved a great deal in our work" - Mao Zedong

Remember that the bourgeoisie will mercilessly attack and slander those individuals who expose their agenda, look at what happened to Julian Assange.

With regard the work of Caleb Maupin I have a great post debunking all of the lies and slander directed towards him.

Remember what Caleb said:

"There will will never be a socialism that the New York Times approves of" - Caleb T. Maupin

This applies as well to individuals who are anti-establishment and do good work in opposing the status quo and building a mass movement.

Back in 2018, Caleb Maupin attended a Conference by the name of 'The Alternatives to Globalisation' which is held every year, of which the key theme of the year was 'The Strategies of the Multipolar World'. Also in attendance was the 'Ho Chi Minh Communist Youth Union', the youth wing of the Communist Party of Vietnam, along with the PSUV of Venezuela, the Islamic Republican party of Iran and several other anti-imperialist parties and organisations. Caleb was in attendance due to his employment at Russia Today (RT) and was there to offer his viewpoints which he wanted to put out there, rather than them (our viewpoints) not getting heard, because if we don't get out there and present our viewpoints they simply won't be seen.

At the conference he gave a speech which I am sure you would agree with if you listened to. In it he focused on anti-imperialism, the need to fight the ruling order as well as the need for populism in the American Communist movement. It was not a debate, Caleb merely gave his viewpoint while the other speakers sat beside him (two of which were Fourth Positionists, and one who was a fascist, as they were also invited as they claim their viewpoint opposes liberalism and globalism) while an audience below them listened on. This was not Caleb agreeing with them or pandering to them, it was Caleb offering his viewpoint and presenting it in his speech. He also mentioned how he often got called a 'Duginist' despite never before reading Dugin's works, which ended up leading him to read Dugin's 'Fourth Political Theory' and from this he realised he did not agree with Dugin, but not that he completely dismissed Dugin. He saw some good in the idea of the 'Multipolar World' and the opposition his idea of 'Eurasianism' poses to U.S. imperialism:

"In principle, Eurasia and our space, the heartland Russia, remain the staging area of a new anti-bourgeois, anti-American revolution. The new Eurasian empire will be constructedon the fundamental principle of the common enemy: the rejection of Atlanticism, strategic control of the U.S., and the refusal to allow liberal values to dominate us. This common civilisational impulse will be the basis of a political and strategic union" - Alexander Dugin

"The philosophers Locke and Kant described the project of 'civil society' in which nation-states were to be abolished. Some individuals could theoretically do without them. This is how the philosophy of cosmopolitanism arose, involving the abolition of nation-states and (as an ideal) the creation of a World Government. This was the birth of globalism albeit in theory" - Alexander Dugin

"There is another, 'hidden', 'secret' or 'implicit' unipolarity, that is globalism, multilateralism, and the so-called 'No Polarity' promoted by the chief of the Council on Foreign Relations. We roughly call this 'globalisation.' Globalisation means that all systems, societies, peoples and countries in the world will accept the Western way of progress, development, human rights, democracy, and liberalism. And when this happens, there will be no great differences between the United States, Russia, China, or Africa. Everyone will be 'equal.' But in what sense? Everybody will become Americans,

Western, and everybody must like liberal democracy and human rights. This is a special kind of globalism. It is not a dialogue between countries, cultures, and civilisations. For example, Russia has proposed Russian values, and China has proposed a Chinese identity. But there should not be any collective identity in this concept of globalisation. Everybody should be equal precisely because everyone should only be statistical individuals - no cultures, no religions, no ethnic roots" - Alexander Dugin

(Just as a sidenote I have not read Dugin, and I am sure it is the same for the vast majority of people here, so take what I say with a grain of salt, but from everything I have heard and I am aware of) I do not agree with Dugin at all (except in opposition to U.S. imperialism), but it is clear to me that Dugin is presented as a scary, bearded, hairy Russian boogeyman by radlibs. To them he is a 'Rasputin-like' figure who they can project all of their Russophobia onto. This is despite the fact that none of them have read any of Dugin's work (which Caleb did and from this he realised he disagreed with Dugin). Dugin is someone that we should read, so that we can debunk him, due to his prominence in Post-Soviet states. As Mao Zedong said:

"Oppose book worship; Seek truth from facts; No investigation, no right to speak" - Mao Zedong

"All erroneous ideas, all poisonous weeds, all ghosts and monsters, must be subjected to criticism; in no circumstance should they be allowed to spread unchecked" - Mao Zedong

"If you don't study the negative stuff, you won't be able to refute it. Neither Marx nor Engels nor Lenin was like that. They made great efforts to learn and study all sorts of things, contemporary and past, and taught other people to do likewise" - Mao Zedong

Dugin is just a Russian conservative, (in the past he was everything from liberal, to fascist, to nazbol) I do not get why us as Communists have to rally around the lies and slanders of radical-liberals. We should oppose them and oppose the 'Fourth Political Theory' as well, but we should not make a mountain out of a molehill and we should not spread lies, especially lies about a theorist (however bad) in an anti-imperialist country who has nothing to do with the west except opposition to it's imperialism.

Caleb Maupin is a prominent figure in Communist circles, however he is also a heavily slandered figure who is regarded as controversial due to Breadtube going after him with slanders to the point he wrote a book about them titled 'Breadtube Serves Imperialism'. Unfortunately I also see Communists going after him. The CPUSA recently posted an article where they completely slander Maupin which was disappointing to see (here is a good response which completely debunks this slander).

Caleb Maupin is my foremost insight into the American situation. He has helped win me over to the right side. He is right on all of the topics discussed in this book. I see him as the ideological leader of the renaissance of Communism in America. His Think-Tank, the Center for Political Innovation is putting the CPUSA to shame, as the old law of leadership goes, when an inept old leadership has held

on to power, eventually the young, rising leader who gets results elsewhere will get his day in the sun and I guarantee you that when he does Caleb will make hay.

Caleb Maupin's anti-imperialist work is so important. He went to Yemen to deliver aid on an Iranian ship as if a ship has an American on board the American-Saudi led alliance could not strike the ship. He risked his life to provide aid to a war torn people fighting for their lives. He consistently opposes U.S. imperialism and is one of the only journalists with a track record of exposing the imperialist war machine. He is also someone who consistently defends China and for me personally was the person who showed me the light when it came to supporting China. He also happens to work for anti-imperialist media which oppose the imperialism of his own country, he works for the Russian RT and the Iranian Press TV media organisations. He often gets called anti-American for this yet he is a proud socialist and hence a patriot so there is no contradiction. He is outspoken about both his anti-imperialism, and his patriotism for his country and wants to see a Communist America.

Domestically Caleb has also done great work. He was actively involved with Occupy Wall Street and would donate Plasma to survive in those years where he was a leader of the movement. He also witnessed police brutality against black youths, recorded it and prevented the victims from going to jail by exposing the footage, if not for his footage the victims would have wrongfully gone to jail. Several years ago he founded an organisation called 'Students and Youth for a New America' (SYNA). This organisation has been active on college campuses and from it he has developed a milieu of activists such as Mason Steiner from RedScareTV, Dakotah Lily, Ramiro Sebastián Fúnez and Nick Maniace to name a few.

He also recently founded the 'Center for Political Innovation' (CPI) which is a think tank and the idea is to not be a party but to have members from every Communist Party in America and to ensure that the movement moves in the right direction and gets out of the movement itself and to the masses. The vanguard of this organisation is the 'John Brown Volunteers' (JBV) which evangelises the good word of our cause to the masses on the streets and runs food programs to feed the poor. Amid all this less than 3 months ago, the foreign minister of Nicaragua visited the U.S., however he was attacked by protestors while in a New York church, the JBV rushed over and defended him. Caleb later got a shoutout from Nicholas Maduro and was invited to expose U.S. meddling in the Nicaraguan elections.

Now to address all of the slander:

Here is a copypasta which addresses all of the slander directed towards Maupin.

Here is a video which addresses everything.

With regards the accusations of transphobia (which is solely based off of association of association and supposedly not talking about these issues enough, which is ridiculous) thrown at him, here is him protesting for trans rights years before it was hip and trendy.

Here is a page which highlights the activist work of Maupin over the years.

Here is a good post detailing the usefulness of Maupin's analysis in the American and even international context. His important contributions are his slogan of "Out of the movement and to the masses" which I think is really needed as the American Communist movement is stuck in the protest cage and should instead be engaged in the ongoing strike wave and reaching the masses. As well as the slogan of "A government of action to fight for working families". He promotes 'Bill of Rights Socialism' which was the line of W.Z. Foster and still today of the CPUSA, and he promotes '21st Century Socialism', firmly supporting actual existing socialism in the world today. He is an ardent student of past American progressives, continuing the revolutionary struggle and teaching this history which has all but been forgotten to the masses. He upheld the correct line of Socialist Patriotism even while American Communists had all but ignored the calls to be patriotic from international comrades time and time again and engaged in reckless flag burning instead. He also noticed the need for professionalism among the movement after attending an International Communist Youth Congress and saw that comrades from all around the world were dressed professionally, and engaged directly with the masses.

Unlike the Infrared Collective,

Caleb is NOT trying to takeover the CPUSA.

Here is a good meme relating to Maupin.

It is clear that Caleb Maupin is someone that should be highly regarded, he is loved by international Communists. His YouTube channel and his livestreams are a useful resource and he is very good at bringing people into our movement. He does good work and deserves respect. He does not deserve the treatment he gets, he constantly gets abuse and death treats, even from self declared 'Communists' and that is a pure disgrace. I hope that this post clarifies misconceptions for those who genuinely were misinformed about this man who I hope continues to spread the good word of socialism to the masses.

SOCIALIST BILLIONAIRES:

Some people have an incorrect idea that Caleb Maupin wants socialist billionaires.

The so called 'socialist billionaires' argument is a strawman of Caleb calling Chinese billionaires 'socialist billionaires' (As in billionaires under a socialist system who are not actually in power). Compared with Caleb calling anti-wealth, degrowth and the 'abolish billionaires' slogan bad in a debate with Jason Unruhe from a year ago. This was confusion from that, he never actually said 'socialist billionaires' is what he wanted in the context of the 'abolish billionaires' argument except for when he was talking about a society close to Communism hundreds of years in the future where being a billionaire (As in someone who owns over a billion in value, remember that billionaire itself is not a class, it is the bourgeoisie, being a billionaire does not necessarily have to imply being a capitalist, but of course all billionaires today are capitalists) could be possible without exploitation as there would be so much wealth and abundance that a stateless, classless, moneyless society would be possible. This is also known as higher stage Communism. What he is not saying is that billionaires in a capitalist society are good, no in fact it is the exact opposite. He is simply pointing out the fact that it is not the wealth itself that is bad, it is how they got that wealth, as in through exploitation (stealing of surplus value) of workers.

It is human nature to innovate, it is because of human

ingenuinity and how we can work together that we have been able to advance. Ants have been making their ant hills the same way since forever but us humans have been able to innovate and reach higher stages of development and advance our society.

Consider that even a thousand years ago the richest kings would have had lived under worse material conditions than the average person today who enjoys far higher living conditions and life expectancy, this is the advancement of the productive forces and it is fundamental to Marxism which you would know if you read 'Critique of the Gotha Program'. The problem is that average people incorrectly think that Communists want 'everyone to be equal' when this could not be further from the truth, we want everyone to have a solid societal base from which they can thrive allowing themselves to be unleashed to their full potential for the benefit of society, we do not want some moralistic fantasy of full equality. This is the reason he is pointing this out, however even though that is a caricature of actual Communists spread from the establishment, there are still some people who call themselves Communists and live up to that caricature and every other caricature invented by the right, living up to it, and in the process diminishing our message and drowning it out which is then what is shone down upon by the media and the cycle continues where average people believe all the McCarthyist caricatures.

It is Marxism which gives us the tools to put behind the barbarism of the past and move forward, Marxism came to light because of the stage of history Marx was present in, the globalism of the age which made it possible for the first time to analyse human history from a complete perspective and it was this analysis which allowed Marx to know that Communism was inevitable even though it was 'two stages' of human development ahead.

Caleb Maupin explains his argument here:

Carlos from 'Midwestern Marx' offers his insight here:

Socialism is not 'redistribution', all systems redistribute wealth. It is a caricatural understanding of socialism, as well as one adopted by liberals who co-opt the radical aesthetic and fit into that very caricature, which make people associate socialism with poverty. When in fact socialism is about achieving vast material abundance. It is for this reason that we MUST fight against this notion as what we say, the slogans we use and what we focus on matters. When it comes to wealth, we must focus on how that wealth is created and why that is bad, not that the wealth itself is bad and that must show in our messaging as well as our slogans.

We must focus on building a new, as opposed to focusing on tearing everything down. We must be optimistic, only then can we win the masses and be victorious!

SWAC:

Socialism with American characteristics or SwAC, refers to the idea of building socialism in America. It's origins come from a play on the term SwCC coined by Deng Xiaoping to refer to the construction of socialism in China (Which itself came from Mao Zedong saying that socialism in China needs to have Chinese characteristics). Although it might be a term, it is not something new as leaders of the CPUSA have been saying this for decades most notably William Z. Foster:

"Socialism in the United States will, out of necessity, have some American characteristics" - William Z. Foster

"We will incorporate U.S. traditions into the structure of socialism that the working class will create" - William Z. Foster

When it comes to the debate around the use of this term (Which was a hot topic a few months back particularly in relation to Caleb Maupin). I definitely side with the people who use it, because I think that the view of SwAC the people who oppose it hold comes from a slander/misinterpretation of what SwCC means in relation to China (usually MLM/Third Worldist). This translates into their view of SwAC, so again like the misconception around the 'socialist billionaires' debate, their view comes from a misconception that it goes back to China, except with SwAC it is related to China because it is a play on SwCC, whereas the billionaires argument was not related to China at all.

The main misconceptions around this term is that the term is mutually exclusive with self-determination of the native peoples however this could not be further from the truth. I do not see them as incompatible the way they do, SwAC will address the question of native tribes nationality in a way the current liberal bourgeois establishment cannot. The issue of the loss of native land is a fundamental issue and the treatment of the native peoples that continues today is a contradiction in America hence SwAC would have to fundamentally deal with that contradiction. It is assumed that it would by the name as the point of SwAC is the construction of socialism in America and the negation of the contradictions of the old system.

Everyone who believes in SwAC thinks it will involve coming to terms with the effects of colonialism and slavery that persist to this day, but in order to do with we have to abandon the ultra-left rhetoric and aesthetics. In my opinion, we have to build off of the actual positive, progressive aspects of American history and culture, which many self proclaimed 'Marxists' do not accept as being real despite America being a reality for hundreds of millions of people who live it day to day.

SwAC is not a system of thought or ideas, it is literally just a slogan for a call to action. Socialism always arises in countries that appear to be too backwards, SwAC means that socialism can only arise out of the national movement and cannot be imported or some kind of non-determinate abstract socialism, it must arise from the ground and soil of America itself, from the people of America.

The point of the phrasing 'characteristics' from the term is to call Marxists to innovatively analyse America from a Marxist perspective. America has many characteristics: historical racial oppression and systemic inequality, rural-urban divide, deindustrialised working class, etc. It has the positive and it has the negative, however we do not let the negative negate the postive as we are looking at this from a Marxist viewpoint one predicated on the current material conditions, not one of a depraved calvinist 'burn it all down' approach. We seek to build a new from the old order, to 'sublate' it as Marx said, not abolish and reject everything from the past. We can only build atop what is already existing.

Personally I think all criticisms come more from misconceptions around the phrasing rather than the substance of the term and I hope to see American comrades work towards building socialism (U.S.S.A. or whatever it would be called wouldn't matter, what matters is that it would be socialist) in the decades to come.

So now that it is clear that such revolutionary leaders as W.Z. Foster have formulated and supported SwAC, it is clear that there should be no dispute on this line.

Just in case anyone doubts William Z. Foster, he was the leader of the CPUSA for decades, following his ouster (and before) of the revisionist Earl Browder from the party. He led the Communist party for decades during it's heyday. He came from a union background and under his leadership the Communist party was at the forefront of the labour struggle and the civil rights movement. The party had membership in the hundreds of thousands and it was a significant force in American politics. He popularised 'Bill of Rights Socialism' and wrote about how socialism would come to America via the popular front movement of varying different anti-establishment movements and classes in his books 'The Twilight of World Capitalism' and 'Towards Soviet America'. If there is anyone who today the CPUSA should be looking towards as inspiration from the past, it is W.Z. Foster.

Mao Zedong himself was impressed by W.Z. Foster:

"We are glad to learn that the special convention of the Communist Political Association of the United States has resolved to repudiate Browder's revisionist, that is, capitulationist line, has re-established Marxist leadership and revived the Communist Party of the United States. We hereby extend to you our warm congratulations on this great victory of the working class and the Marxist movement in the

United States. Browder's whole revisionist-capitulationist line (which is fully expressed in his book Teheran) in essence reflects the influence of reactionary U.S. capitalist groups on the U.S. workers' movement. These groups are now doing their utmost to extend their influence in China too; they are supporting the erroneous policy of the reactionary clique inside the Kuomintang, a policy which is against the interests of the nation and the people, and are thereby confronting the Chinese people with the grave danger of civil war and jeopardising the interests of the peoples of our two great countries, China and the United States. Beyond all doubt the victory of the U.S. working class and its vanguard, the Communist Party of the United States, over Browder's revisionist-capitulationist line will contribute signally to the great cause in which the Chinese and American peoples are engaged the cause of carrying on the war against Japan and of building a peaceful and democratic world after the war" - (Mao Zedong, Comrade William Z. Foster and the National Committee of the Communist Party of the United States of America)

This should never have been a matter that needed addressing as it is something that should have been obvious. I hope that you found this elaboration useful. If you are American make sure to join the CPUSA and carry the banner forward to victory!

REVOLUTION:

To preface: I think that people completely misunderstand the nature of revolution. All successful revolutions have only turned violent in self defence against the forces of reaction, no revolutionary wants violence but in the struggle to seize power where the ruling class have a tight control, violence is bound to happen.

There have actually been peaceful revolutions as a matter of fact (Such as in Somalia and the Eastern Bloc) and advocating for violence has never worked except with petty-bourgeois classes who have some stake in the system but are poor such as the peasantry.

Once a movement becomes violent without it being in self defence and without the approval of the masses it over time just ends up as left adventurist terrorism and the end result is the selling of drugs. Revolutions do not happen by a few rogues with nothing to lose wielding guns (Except for national liberation movements where all it takes is a spark to light a fire), revolutions happen when the masses come together and organise on the streets and march to seize power, because they have just had enough. Defenceless revolutions and revolutions without a mass organisation have in the past happened but the people should be armed in self defence and there should be a mass Communist party organising logistics and being with the people.

When the masses are behind something you cannot lose, it could even be peaceful because if the state fires on peaceful marchers then the law has broken loose and the states legitimacy vanishes (it no longer has a monopoly on violence).

A revolution is not some glorified fantasy where you let loose all your rage with the system and seek to abolish and destroy everything, it is about building a new and serving the people, more likely than not it would be in some united front with petty-bourgeois elements and even the national bourgeois (As W.Z. Foster has written in detail about in the case of America). Even Marx and Lenin believed peaceful revolution was possible especially in the developed countries and Lenin thought the Russian revolution would be peaceful until March 1917.

For example, the Russian revolution only turned violent in self-defence as the forces of reaction led by the Kerensky government fired upon the peaceful general strike led by the Bolsheviks which was mobilising the working masses for change and to seize power. It was this act of the government which saw the legitimacy of the law and the state break down and showed the gov for what it was. It was from this in self defence that the Bolsheviks fought back and won the civil war, (over white forces that emerged from the breakdown of the Kerensky regime) and established the U.S.S.R.

Similarly in China, initially the Communists were allied with the KMT, as both shared the legacy of Sun Yat-sen. The Communists were even encouraged to join the KMT because it was the pre-eminent force of progress in China as they overthrew the monarchy in the Xinhai revolution which awoke the Chinese people and paved the way for them to arise from the Century of Humiliation. However after Chiang Kai-shek took over the KMT took a turn and ended up supporting landlords and warlords as opposed to the masses. It was only when the KMT massacred Communists in 1927, (as they knew they were becoming a threat) did the Communists fight back in self defence, and they still were able to ally with them against a common enemy (the Japanese imperialists) later. Mao Zedong also developed revolutionary political innovations. He noticed that the peasants were already up in arms but due to Soviet dogma, which regarded the peasants as backward, they were reluctant to organise them. However Mao realised that they needed to be mobilised as most people were peasants at the time (only a minority were proletarian) and that looking down on the masses would get the Communists nowhere and if they did not organise them then the reactionaries would. He was expelled from the CPC Central Committee in 1927 for his organising of the peasantry. However he continued his own organising from his base of power in Jiangxi and the party eventually ended up adopting his tactics as they worked.

A revolution in America will come from building up a mass movement and creating a coalition of workers, farmers and small business owners centered around the working class against the capitalist ruling class and the capitalist oligopolies. There are divides among the bourgeoisie and there can be a coalition of lower levels of capitalism who feel they are at odds with the upper levels (As stated by William Z. Foster in 'The Twilight of World Capitalism'). Revolutions do not come from thin air, nor are they astro-turfed by us, no they come from the objective contradictions in society. Revolutionary zeal is crystallised in the masses who either know that there is something wrong with the system (social revolution) but cannot formulate why, or else they develop false consciousness. It is up to us Communists to guide this phenomena towards a proletarian revolution as the alternative is a fascist putsch, if we don't reach the masses fascism will take hold.

A revolution is not inherently violent, it is wreckers such as ultra-leftists, left adventurists or simply put terrorists who start violence within the movement and they should be opposed. Historically all revolutions have only turned violent when violence was forced down upon them, it is funny that so called 'reformist' socialists say they want want a mass movement to put pressure on the government but that is literally what the CPUSA did in the 30's with the F.D.R.

government (such as winning massive gains for the working class, stopping a fascist coup and being a major force in getting the U.S. to intervene against Nazi Germany) and the reason they were not able to go further was because they did not have a mass movement big enough that would have been able to make a coalition with other groups to build a movement of the people which could have brought about change peacefully. As the majority would have been on their side and everyone but the very top levels of capital (as socialism would benefit the vast majority of people and most people are completely dissatisfied with the current system and ruling regime) and those they pay to put down the protestors would support the movement and even then they can be changed and see that the mass coalition of people peacefully demanding change are right as it us through our coalition that a new government that actually represents the people would be elected which can bring in the changes desperately needed right now in America and start actually addressing issues.

The point is that our guns are in self defence against this bourgeois system which exploits us, we would prefer a peaceful resolution although it is unlikely, although everything should be done before we go on the revolutionary offensive. There is no revolution without first being actively engaged with and winning over the hearts and minds of the masses, and once the bourgeois state fires upon us it loses all legitimacy and it is open game for us to go on the revolutionary offensive and for our proletarian organs to replace the bourgeois apparatus.

There is a false binary of either parliamentary reformism and nothing else or go straight on the offensive against the bourgeois state. What I am talking about is arming ourselves to be ready for the moment we strike, I am not talking about parliamentary reform at all, this has nothing to do with bourgeois parliaments at all. I am talking about building our own proletarian grassroots bases of power and institutions within our own communities and once we have won over the masses going out and tearing down the bourgeois institutions that oppress us and replacing them with our own. I am talking about general strikes and marching to seize power. Hopefully it can be peaceful, the question is whether they fire upon us or not and whether or not the military will defect to us or not.

In the Latvian revolution of 1939 (following the Molotov-Ribbentrop pact), the people (in the major cities as well as towns and rural areas) marched on the bourgeois institutions of power and occupied them and workers got rid of their bosses, police stopped listening to orders and the Communists managed to establish a Soviet Republic before the Red Army even entered. In the Somalian revolution the Communists had infiltrated the army, the Communist movement was limited mostly to the cities but there were general strikes of workers and they similarly marched on the bourgeois seats of power, the military then defected and took over power, straight away proletarian institutions were established, the Communist party took power and representatives from China and the Soviet Union came in.

As a class, it is the working class themselves who are the revolutionary subject because they work and toil and if they organise and come together they can halt production. Whereas the professionals such as teachers and engineers not doing something will not result in gains for us (nor should we be focusing on their organising as there was an actual working class strike wave that got ignored in Winter 2021) because they are trying to maintain their professional status when they organise (usually tends to not have a working class nature, but we need to make it such and organise them to ally with the working class). While if we look at the petty-bourgeoisie (and peasantry) if they organise it is just for individual benefit even if they are really poor (which the majority are as they are a dying class, but they do need to be mobilised as well). While the lumpen is almost impossible to organise as a whole because they are the criminal elements at the bottom of society. As this is a 'dog eat dog world', this manifests most harshly at the bottom because they are the people in society who are oppressed by their position to society under which they go unnoticed and lurk in the shadows of society. This reflects on their worldview and the lumpen as a class are highly individualised, atomised and are act 'dog eat dog' towards everyone else in their position unless in an organised gang, or in rare cases, enlightened lumpen (can be organised) who are in the minority (but have no influence over the class). It is the working class, the proletariat who are the revolutionary subjects, who made the revolutions of the 20th century and will make the revolutions of the 21st century!

The capitalist class WILL use violence to stop the revolution. The only way to effectively counter violence is violence. Revolutionaries do not want violence, but they must be prepared to defend the revolution from the assaults of counter-revolutionary forces. Violence in revolutions must be used as self-defense when necessary. Excesses of violence must be avoided, the kind arising from anger, disgust and hatred. Torture, no quarter, physical/psychological/verbal/sexual abuse/harassment of POWs, deliberate use of lethal force against unarmed civilian populations, deliberate use of weapons of mass destruction, deliberate targetting of basic infrastructure such as water treatment facilities, power plants, farms, crop lands, food banks, hospitals and schools, posing as humanitarian aid workers and medical professionals to trick the enemy, deliberately devastating the enemy's local ecosystem, deliberate killing of children and extrajudicial executions should be strictly forbidden and those guilty should be tried in the revolution's own courts for war crimes or crimes against humanity.

Finally with regard the so called 'reformists' who oppose us. Ironically, us Marxist-Leninists do reform better than the reformists, while building up a revolutionary movement as we are actually genuine. Fundamentally we abide by the Communist principle of taking up the gun to put down the gun.

We must focus on building a new, as opposed to focusing on tearing everything down. We must be optimistic, only then can we win the masses and be victorious!

QUOTES ON REVOLUTION:

"We must announce to the governments: We know you are the armed power which is directed against the proletarians; we will against you in peaceful way where it is possible, and with arms if it should become necessary" - Karl Marx

"You know that the institutions, mores, and traditions of various countries must be taken into consideration, and we do not deny that there are countries - such as America, England, and if I were more familiar with your institutions, I would perhaps also add Holland - where the workers can attain their goal by peaceful means. This being the case, we must also recognise the fact that in most countries on the Continent the lever of our revolution must be force; it is force to which we must some day appeal in order to erect the rule of labour" - Karl Marx

"The objective in the case under consideration is the emancipation of the working class and the revolution (transformation) of society implicit therein. An historical development can remain 'peaceful' only for so long as its progress is not forcibly obstructed by those wielding social power at the time. If in England, for instance, or the United States, the working class were to gain a majority in Parliament or Congress, they could, by lawful means, rid themselves of such laws and institutions as impeded their development, though they could only do so insofar as society had reached a sufficiently mature development. However, the 'peaceful' movement might be transformed into a 'forcible' one by resistance on the part of those interested in restoring the former state of affairs; if (as in the American Civil War and French Revolution) they are put down by force, it is as rebels against 'lawful' force" - Karl Marx

"Any attempt to disarm the workers must be frustrated, by force if necessary" - Karl Marx

"The workers' party must never be the tagtail of any bourgeois party; it must be independent and have its goal and its own policy. The political freedoms, the right of assembly and association, and the freedom of the press - those are our weapons. Are we to sit back and abstain while somebody tries to rob us of them? It is said that a political act on our part implies that we accept the existing state of affairs. On the contrary, so long as this state of affairs offers us the means of protesting against it, our use of these means of protesting it, our use of these means does not signify that we recognise the prevailing order" - Karl Marx

"(Marx) led to the conclusion that, at least in Europe, England is the only country where the inevitable social revolution might be effected entirely by peaceful and legal means. He certainly never forgot to add that he hardly expected the English ruling classes to submit, without a 'pro-slavery rebellion', to this peaceful and legal revolution" - Friedrich Engels

[As you wish to prepare for community of property by the enlightening and uniting of the proletariat, then you reject revolution?] "We are convinced not only of the uselessness but even of the harmfulness of all conspiracies. We are also aware that revolutions are not made deliberately and arbitrarily but that everywhere and at all times they are the necessary consequence of all circumstances which are not in any way whatever dependent either on the will or on the leadership of individual parties or of whole classes. But we also see that the development of the proletariat in almost all countries of the world is forcibly repressed by the possessing classes that thus a revolution is being forcibly worked for by the opponents of Communism. If, in the end, the oppressed proletariat is thus driven into a revolution, then we will defend the cause of the proletariat just as well by our deeds as now by our words" - Friedrich Engels

"We shall not achieve socialism without a struggle. But we are ready to fight, we have started it and we shall finish it with the aid of the apparatus called the Soviets" - V.I. Lenin

"The working class would, of course, prefer to take power peacefully (we have already stated that this seizure of power can be carried out only by the organised working class which has passed through the school of the class struggle), but to renounce the revolutionary seizure of power would be madness on the part of the proletariat, both from the theoretical and the practical-political points of view; it would mean nothing but a disgraceful retreat in face of the bourgeoisie and all other propertied classes. It is very probable - even most probable - that the bourgeoisie will not make peaceful concessions to the proletariat and at the decisive moment will resort to violence for the defence of its privileges. In that case, no other way will be left to the proletariat for the achievement of its aim but that of revolution. This is the reason the programme of 'working-class socialism' speaks of the winning of political power in general without defining the method, for the choice of method depends on a future which we can not precisely determine. But, we repeat, to limit the activities of the proletariat under any circumstances to peaceful 'democratisation' alone is arbitrarily to narrow and vulgarise the concept of working-class socialism" - V.I. Lenin

"The second sentence is, in the first place, historically wrong. We Bolsheviks participated in the most counterrevolutionary parliaments, and experience has shown that this participation was not only useful but indispensable to the party of the revolutionary proletariat, after the first bourgeois revolution in Russia (1905), so as to pave the way for the second bourgeois revolution (February 1917), and then for the socialist revolution (October 1917). In the second place, this sentence is amazingly illogical. If a parliament becomes an organ and a 'centre' (in reality it never has been and never can be a 'centre', but that is by the way) of counter-revolution, while the workers are building up the instruments of their power in the form of the Soviets, then it follows that the workers must prepare - ideologically, politically and technically - for the struggle of the Soviets against parliament, for the dispersal of parliament by the Soviets. But it does not at all follow that this dispersal is hindered, or is not facilitated, by the presence of a Soviet opposition within the counter-revolutionary parliament. In the course of our victorious struggle against Denikin and Kolchak, we never found that the existence of a Soviet and proletarian opposition in their camp was immaterial to our victories. We know perfectly well that the dispersal of the Constituent Assembly on January 5, 1918 was not hampered but was actually facilitated by the fact that, within the counter-revolutionary Constituent Assembly which was about to be dispersed, there was a consistent Bolshevik, as well as an inconsistent, Left Socialist-Revolutionary Soviet opposition. The authors of the theses are engaged in muddled thinking; they have forgotten the experience of many, if not all, revolutions, which shows the great usefulness, during a revolution, of a combination of mass action outside a reactionary parliament with an opposition sympathetic to (or, better still, directly supporting) the revolution within it" - V.I. Lenin

"Bourgeois states are most varied in form, but their essence is the same: all these states, whatever their form, in the final analysis are inevitably the dictatorship of the bourgeoisie. The transition from capitalism to Communism is certainly bound to yield a tremendous abundance and variety of political forms, but the essence will inevitably be the same: the dictatorship of the proletariat" - V.I. Lenin

"In a country where the bourgeoisie will not offer such furious resistance, the tasks of the Soviet government will be easier; it will be able to operate without the violence, without the bloodshed that was forced upon us by the Kerenskys and the imperialists. We shall reach our goal even by this, more difficult, road. Russia may have to make greater sacrifices than other countries; this is not surprising considering the chaos that we inherited. Other countries will travel by a different, more humane road, but at the end of it lies the same Soviet power" - V.I. Lenin

"In Russia, the dictatorship of the proletariat must inevitably differ in certain particulars from what it would be in the advanced countries, owing to the very great backwardness and petty-bourgeois character of our country. But the basic forces - and the basic forms of social economy - are the same in Russia as in any capitalist country, so that the peculiarities can apply only to what is of lesser importance" - V.I. Lenin

"The history of revolutions in particular, is always richer in content, more varied, more multiform, more lively and ingenious than is imagined by even the best parties, the most class-conscious vanguards of the most advanced classes" - V.I. Lenin

"You are wrong if you think that the Communists are enamoured of violence. They would be very pleased to drop violent methods if the ruling class agreed to give way to the working class. But the experience of history speaks against such an assumption" - J.V. Stalin

[Does this, your statement, mean that the Soviet Union has to any degree abandoned its plans and intentions for bringing about world revolution?] "We never had such plans and intentions; This is the product of a misunderstanding; No, a comical one. Or, perhaps, tragicomic. You see, we

Marxists believe that a revolution will also take place in other countries. But it will take place only when the revolutionaries in those countries think it possible, or necessary. The export of revolution is nonsense. Every country will make its own revolution if it wants to, and if it does not want to, there willbe no revolution. For example, our country wanted to make a revolution and made it, and now we are building a new, classless society. But to assert that we want to make a revolution in other countries, to interfere in their lives, means saying what is untrue, and what we have never advocated" - J.V. Stalin

"Communists do not in the least idealise the methods of violence. But they, the Communists, do not want to be taken by suprise, they cannot count on the old world voluntarily departing from the stage, they see the old system is violently defending itself, and that is why the Communists say to the working class: Answer violence with violence; do all you can to prevent the old dying order from crushing you, do not permit it to put manacles on your hands, on the hands which you will overthrow the old system" - J.V. Stalin

"The draft of the programme correctly puts forward the task of utilising the traditional English institutions (Parliament) in the struggle for socialism. It is well known that the English Communists are being accused that they will establish Soviet Power in England. Hence it is imperative that in the draft of the programme it should be very clearly and definitely stated that the English Communists are not going to delegitimise Parliament, that England shall come to socialism through its own path and not through Soviet Power, but through Peoples' Democracy that would be guided by people's power and not by capitalists" - (J.V. Stalin, letter to CPGB leader Harry Pollitt on the draft of the party's British Road to Socialism, September 28th 1950)

"There is no reason to doubt that in the future that Soviet Union will be true to its policy - the policy of peace and security, the policy of the equality and friendship of the peoples" - J.V. Stalin

"The peaceful coexistence of capitalism and Communism is quite possible if there is a mutual desire to cooperate, with a willingness to fulfill the obligations assumed, while respecting the principle of equality and non-interference in the internal affairs of other states" - J.V. Stalin

"[The] peoples [of the world]... no longer wish to live in the old way. [They want to] carry on an active struggle against the forces of reaction, against instigators of a new war. The peoples of the world do not wish a repetition of the calamities of war. They fight persistently for the strengthening of peace and security. In the vanguard of the struggle for peace and security marches the Soviet Union" - J.V. Stalin

"They, these aggressive forces, control the reactionary governments and direct them. But at the same time they are afraid of their peoples who do not want a new war and stand for the maintenance of peace. Therefore they are trying to use the reactionary governments in order to enmesh their peoples with lies, to deceive them, and to depict the new war as defensive and the peaceful policy of the peace-loving countries as aggressive. They are trying to deceive their peoples in order to impose on them their aggressive plans and to draw them into a war. Precisely for this reason they are afraid of the campaign in defence of peace, fearing it can expose the aggressive intentions of the reactionary governments. Precisely for this reason they turned down the proposal of the Soviet Union for the conclusion of a Peace Pact, for the reduction of armaments, for banning the atomic weapon, fearing that the adoption of these proposals would undermine the aggressive measures of the reactionary governments and make the armaments of the reactionary governments and make the armaments race unnecessary. What will be the end of this struggle between the aggressive and the peace-loving forces? Peace will be preserved and consolidated if the peoples will take the cause of preserving peace into their own hands and will defend it to the end. War may become inevitable if the warmongers succeed in entangling the masses of the people in lies, in deceiving them and drawing them into a new world war. That is why the wide campaign for the maintenance of peace as a means of exposing the criminal and machinations of the warmongers is now of a first-state importance. As for the Soviet Union, it will continue in the future as well firmly to pursue the policy of averting war and maintaining peace" - J.V. Stalin

"Alexander Werth: Do you believe that with the further progress of the Soviet Union towards Communism the possibilities of peaceful co-operation with the outside world will not decrease as far as the Soviet Union is concerned? Is 'Communism in one country' possible? Stalin: I do not doubt that the possibilities of peaceful co-operation, far from decreasing, may even grow. 'Communism in one country' is perfectly possible, especially in a country like the Soviet Union" - (J.V. Stalin interview with Alexander Werth, September 24th 1946)

"The U.S. and U.S.S.R. systems are different but we didn't wage war against each other and the U.S.S.R. does not propose to. If during the war they could co-operate, why can't they today in peace, given the wish to co-operate?" - J.V. Stalin

"Let us not mutually criticise our systems. Everyone has the right to follow the system he wants to maintain. Which one is better will be said by history. We should respect the systems chosen by the people, and whether the system is good or bad is the business of the American people. To co-operate, one does not need the same systems. One should respecct the other system when approved by the people. Only on this basis can we secure co-operation. Only if we criticise, it will lead us too far. As for Marx and Engels, they were unable to foresee what would happen forty years after their death. But we should adhere to mutual respect to people. Some call the Soviet system totalitarian. Other people call the American system monopoly capitalism. If we start calling each other names with the words monopolist and totalitarian, it will lead to no co-operation. We must start the historical fact that there are two systems approved by the people. Only on that basis is co-operation possible. If we distract each other with criticism, that is propaganda" - J.V. Stalin

"In order for the people to put the United States firmly on the path towards peace, democracy, and general well-being the power of the monopolists who dominate our country must be curbed and finally broken, anda the people themselves must take political charge, under the leadership of the working class. The struggle for socialism grows inevitably out of the everyday fight of the workers and their allies, especially against the present menaces of economic chaos, fascism, and war. In all good time the American people, on the basis of their existing conditions, will decide how and in what forms they will introduce socialism. They way our party foresees the possible development of the future is along the following general lines: First, we propose the regular election of a democratic coalition government, based on a broad united front combination of workers, small farmers, Negroes, professionals, small business groups, and other democratic elements who are ready to fight against monopoly, economic breakdown, fascism, and war. This type of united front government could well have behind it an overwhelming majority of the people, as it has in other lands. It goes without saying that the election of such a democratic government could only be brought about in the face of powerful and very surely violent opposition from organised reaction. The whole history of the American class struggle, which is full of examples of employer violence in strikes and in other mass struggles, teaches this lesson with unmistakable clarity. The bitter attacks made against the Progressive Party, led by Henry Wallace, during the 1948 elections, gave a sure indication of the frenzy and desperation with which the capitalists would confront a people's united front combination that was strong enough to actually threaten their control of Congress and the Presidency. Obviously, it would be an extremely difficult proposition to elect a truly democratic government in the face of this strong, violent, and reactionary opposition. Second, our party contends that such an anti-fascist, anti-war, democratic coalition government, once in power, would be compelled either to move to the Left or to die. With state power in its hands, it would be forced to pass over from the more or less defensive program upon which it was elected to an offensive policy. Confronted with the sabotage and open resistance of big business, it would have no other alternative than this, if it hoped to realise any of the progressive legislation of its program and to ensure its staying in power. A people's government would be forced to proceed directly to curb and undermine the power of the monopolies by adopting far-reaching policies of nationalisation of the banks and major industries, the break-up of big landholdings, the beginnings of a planned economy, the elimination of reactionary elements from the control of the army, schools, and industry, as well as various other measures to weaken monopoly and to strengthen the working class as the leading progressive force in the nation. Third, a democratic, anti-fascist, anti-war government, under the violent attacks of the capitalists and in its efforts to find solutions to the burning economic and political problems, if it were to survive, would necessarily move leftward, towards socialism, much as the People's Democracies of Eastern and Central Europe are now doing. Some liberals believe that a united front coalition government in this country would introduce a regime of 'progressive capitalism,' but this is a naive and dangerous illusion. Any people's government in our times, in order to be progressive (or even to live), inevitably must move towards socialism. American socialism, beyond question, will have its own specific forms and methods, but basically it will be the same as socialism in other countries, with monopoly capital completely defeated, the industries and natural resources in the hands of the people, production for general use instead of for profit, and the working class the leader of the whole people. Only in this way will this country and the world be finally freed of the dangers of poverty, economic chaos, fascist slavery, and murderous war. These steps could be taken legally by a people's government, notwithstanding the opposition of the capitalists, however violent. To promote the election of a progressive, coalition government of this type which, by force of circumstances, would move to the Left and, eventually, to socialism, on the general pattern of the European People's Democracies, is obviously not to advocate a program of force and violence, the enemies of the Communist Party to the contrary notwithstanding. The charge by the Department of Justice that our party advocates the forcible overthrow of the government is a brazen conscious lie. The plain fact of the matter is that the Communist movement in this country as well as abroad, since the Seventh World Congress in 1935, has been going along on the practical working theory that in this period, because of the broad mass struggle against fascism and war, it had become possible in a whole number of democratic countries, including the United States, legally to elect democratic governments which could, by curbing and defeating capitalist violence, orient themselves in the direction of building socialism. Is it possible to elect such a democratic coalition, anti-monopoly government in the United States, the stronghold of world capitalism? It is a sinister fact that civil rights in this country, notably since the end of the war, have been seriously whittled away; but the United States is by no means at the stage of fascism. Nor do we Communists consider American fascism to be inevitable. The big popular upsurge in the recent presidential elections was a dramatic justification of our faith in the democratic strength of the American people. It showed a profound anti-fascist, anti-war sentiment among the masses. In the event of an economic crisis or a war, this mass democratic upsurge would be vastly greater and more clear-sighted. Our party's political line is thus based upon the assumption that it is possible, under present political conditions in the United States, for the broad masses of the people, militantly led by the trade unions and a strong mass political party, to elect a coalition, anti-monopoly government. How long this possibility may last in the face of the fascist trends in this country is problematical. But if we should get fascism, if the United States were to be reduced to the level of fascist Spain, then the Communists will also know how to reshape their policies to meet that kind of situation. It may well be asked, what resistance will American capitalism be able to make when the great masses of the people finally decide, as they surely will, to establish socialism? Today American capitalism is strong; but it is not as strong as it appears to be, nor has it got a permanent lien on its present strength. Now, it is true, Wall Street is the world bully and is busy trying to organise civil wars in various countries and to arm itself and other capitalist countries for another world war. But what will its power of resistance to socialism be when, as may be likely, the vast bulk of the rest of the world has 'gone socialist,' when its own foreign markets have largely dried up, when it is undermined by economic crises, when it may have just about wrecked itself by its projected world war, and when its working class has developed a Marxist-Leninist ideology and sets out to bring about socialism? It may well turn out that it will be far easier for the American working class, in the midst of a socialist world, to establish socialism in this country than now appears to be the case, with American capitalism at the peak of its strength. Who can foretell these things? Certainly we Marxist-Leninists do not indulge in such prophecy. In connection with the fight for eventual socialism, there are three basic, general considerations to be borne in mind: First, the question is not that the Social-Democrats want to bring about socialism in a legal manner, while the Communists want to establish it by violence. Such a placing of the question is utter nonsense. The true issue is that the Social-Democrats do not fight for socialism at all, their line leading only to the buttressing of capitalism; whereas, the Communists do fight for socialism, and in their relentless struggle against capitalist resistance they adapt their strategy and tactics to the given situation. Second, the question also is not whether the capitalists will or will not use violence to prevent the establishment of socialism. Of course, they will use violence, hereas well as elsewhere; it would be silly to think otherwise. Lenin taught us that long ago. Are not the capitalists, even at this very moment, attempting to organise another world war in their effort to murder world socialism? The real question, therefore, is how to confront the capitalists with such gigantic masses of people in broad, democratic political movements that they will be relatively isolated and thus unable to organise effective violence against the cause of the progress. This is the purpose of the Communist united front, anti-fascist policy. Third, the question, finally, is not whether or not there will be socialism in the United States and the rest of the world. History has already settled that matter. Socialism will come, eventually, regardless of all the violent efforts of the capitalists to stop it. The real issue is to bring about socialism with the minimum of capitalist violence and at the earliest date. The Communist line is the way of peaceful advanced and social progress; the policy of the capitalists leads to mass suffering, political enslavement, and devastating war" - (William Z. Foster, The Twilight of World Capitalism)

"Those who make peaceful revolution impossible will make violent revolution inevitable" - John F. Kennedy

"I don't favour violence. If we could bring about recognition and respect of our people by peaceful means, well and good. Everybody would like to reach his objectives peacefully" - Malcolm X

"Sometimes you have to pick the gun up to put the gun down" - Malcolm X

"No revolutionary wants violence, if the ruling class were to lay down their arms tomorrow there would be no need for violence" - Ernesto 'Che' Guevara

"Looking at the earth from afar you realise it is too small for conflict and just big enough for co-operation" - Yuri Gagarin

"Our enemies like to depict us Leninists as advocates of violence always and everywhere. True, we recognise the need recognise the need for the revolutionary transformation of capitalist society into socialist society. It is this that distinguishes the revolutionary Marxists from the reformists, the opportunists. There is no doubt that in a number of capitalist countries the violent overthrow of the dictatorship of the bourgeoisie and the sharp aggravation of class struggle connected with this are inevitable. But the forms of social revolution vary. It is not true that we regard violence and civil war as the only way to remake society. It will be recalled that in the conditions that arose in April 1917 Lenin granted the possibility that the Russian Revolution might develop peacefully" - N.S. Khrushchev

"Liberation wars will continue to exist as long as imperialism exists, as long as colonialism exists. These are revolutionary wars. Such wars are not only admissible but inevitable since the colonialists do not grant independence voluntarily... We recognise such wars, we help and will help the people striving for their independence... These uprisings must not be identified with wars among states, with local wars, since in these uprisings the people are fighting for implementation of their right for self-determination, for independence social and national development" - N.S. Khrushchev

"The stated provisions of the Marxist-Leninist theory are they also overturn the notorious formulation of the question of 'ex-port of the revolution'. It is Marxism, in contrast to all bourgeois ideological concepts, proved that revolutions occur do not occur by order, not because of the desires of individuals, but due to the natural course of the historical process. 'Of course,' Lenin pointed out, 'there are people who think that a revolution can be born in a foreign country by order, by co-announcement. These people are either madmen or provocateurs… We know that they cannot be made either by order or by agreement that they grow when tens of millions of people come to the conclusion that it is impossible to live like this any longer" - N.S. Khruschev

"To strengthen the cause of peace in the entire world it would be of great importance to establish strong friendly relations between the two major powers of the world, the Soviet Union and the United States of America. We believe that if the basis of relations between the U.S.S.R. and the U.S.A. was based on the known five principles of peaceful coexistence, it would be truly a remarkable value for all of humanity and it would certainly be healthy to the people of America, no less than the peoples of the Soviet Union and all other nations. The principles are mutual respect for territorial integrity and sovereignty, non-aggression, non-interference in each other's internal affairs, equality and mutual benefit, peaceful coexistence and economic cooperation are now shared and supported by two dozen states" - N.S. Khrushchev

"In advocating peaceful coexistence, we of course have no intention of saying that there are no contradictions between socialism and capitalism, that complete 'harmony' can be established between them, or that it is possible to reconcile the Communist and bourgeois ideologies. Such a viewpoint would be tantamount to retreating from Marxism-Leninism. The ideological differences are irreconcilable and will continue so" - N.S. Khrushchev

"When we talk about that in the competition between the two systems, capitalism and socialism, wins the socialist system, then that does not mean at all that victory will be achieved through armed interference by the socialist countries in the internal affairs of the capitalist countries" - N.S. Khrushchev

"The system under which some states sell arms to others is not for our invention. France, Britain and the United States have long since been supplying arms to very many countries, and particularly to the countries whose governments take the most hostile attitude towards the Soviet Union. Therefore we have nothing else to do but to act in the same way. We sell arms to countries which ask us to do so and want to be friendly with us. Apparently they buy arms because they fear the countries which you supply with arms. Thus we are doing only the same thing which you have been doing for a long time. If the Western powers want to come to agreement on this score, we are willing to do so. We said this as far back as 1955 in London and made a statement to this effect. The Soviet Union is prepared to reach agreement that no country should sell its arms to any other country" - N.S. Khrushchev

"Our enemies like to depict us Leninists as advocates of violence always and everywhere. True, we recognise the need recognise the need for the revolutionary transformation of capitalist society into socialist society. It is this that distinguishes the revolutionary Marxists from the reformists, the opportunists. There is no doubt that in a number of capitalist countries the violent overthrow of the dictatorship of the bourgeoisie and the sharp aggravation of class struggle connected with this are inevitable. But the forms of social revolution vary. It is not true that we regard violence and civil war as the only way to remake society. It will be recalled that in the conditions that arose in April 1917 Lenin granted the possibility that the Russian Revolution might develop peacefully... Leninism teaches us that the ruling class will not surrender their power voluntarily. And the greater or lesser degree of intensity which the struggle may assume, the use or the non-use of violence in the transition to socialism, depends on the resistance of the exploiters, on whether the exploiting class itself resorts to violence, rather than the proletariat. In this connection the question arises of whether it is possible to go over to socialism by using parliamentary means. No such course was open to the Russian bolsheviks... Since then, however, the historical situation has undergone radical changes which make possible a new approach to the question. The forces of socialism and democracy have grown immeasurably throughout the world, and capitalism has become much weaker... In these circumstances the working class, by ralling around itself the working peasantry, the intelligentsia, all patriotic forces, and resolutely repulsing the opportunist elements who are incapable of giving up the policy of compromise with the capitalists and landlords, is in a position to defeat the reactionary forces opposed to the interests of the people, to capture a stable majority in parliament, and transform the latter from an organ of bourgeois democracy into a genuine instrument of the people's will... In the countries where capitalism is still strong and has a huge military and police apparatus at its disposal, the reactionary forces will, of course, inevitably offer serious resistance. There the transition to socialism will be attended by a sharp class, revolutionary struggle. Whatever the form of transition to socialism, the decisive and indispensible factor is the political leadership of the working class headed by its vanguard. Without this there can be no transition to socialism" - N.S. Khrushchev

"It is quite often said in the West that peaceful coexistence is nothing but a tactical move of the socialist states. There is not a grain of truth in such allegations. Our desire for peace and peaceful coexistence is not prompted by any time-serving or tactical considerations. It springs from the very nature of socialist society..." - N.S. Khrushchev

"We shall use peaceful means and not use any other type of method" - Zhou Enlai

"The people's democratic dictatorship needs the leadership of the working class. For it is only the working class that is most far-sighted, most selfless and most thoroughly revolutionary. The entire history of revolution proves that without the leadership of the working class revolution fails and that with the leadership of the working class revolution triumphs" - Mao Zedong

"Revolution is not a dinner party, or writing essay, or painting picture or doing embroidery; it can't be so refined... so temperate, kind, courteous, restrained and magnanimous. A revolution is an insurrection, an act of violence by which one class overthrows another" - Mao Zedong

"Every Communist must grasp the truth: Political power grows out of the barrel of a gun" - Mao Zedong

"In 1954 the Chinese Government initiated the celebrated Five Principles of peaceful coexistence. They are mutual respect for territorial integrity and sovereignty, mutual non-aggression, non-interference in each other's internal affairs, equality and mutual benefit, and peaceful coexistence. Together with other Asian and African countries, we formulated the Ten Principles on the basis of the Five Principles at the Bandung Conference of 1955" - Mao Zedong

"Mao being interviewed in 1938 by Haldore Hanson, a foreign correspondent: 'You mean to say,' I commented, 'that the Chinese Communist party is willing to support a democratic government after this war and does not intend to renew its struggle against the landlords?' Mao nodded. 'How then, I asked, do you hope to achieve Communism? How can you build a socialist republic?' Mao said he hoped that the change from Democracy to Socialism would be 'evolutionary, not revolutionary. The chief weapon would be education, not an execution ax.' 'But there is no historical precedent for a peaceful introduction of Socialism,' I protested. Mao smiled and added, 'We are trying to make history, not to imitate it'"

- (Hanson, Humane Endeavour: The Story of the China War, 1939, p. 310)

"We believe it would be a fatal mistake to commit ground troops; If our troops went in, the situation in your country would not improve. On the contrary, it would get worse. Our troops would have to struggle not only with an external aggressor, but with a significant part of your own people. And the people would never forgive such things" - Alexei Kosygin

"We must fight actively and persistently for peace and detente... [with] a calm and clear confirmation of our course towards detente and towards the development of good, mutually beneficial relations with the United States" - L.I. Brezhnev

"Some bourgeois leaders raise a howl over the solidarity of Soviet Communists, the Soviet people, with the struggle of other peoples for freedom and progress. This is either naivete or a deliberate befuddling of minds. Detente and peaceful coexistence have to do with interstate relations. This means above all that conflicts between countries are not to be settled by war, by the use or threat of force. Detente cannot abolish or alter the laws of class struggle. No one should expect that detente will cause Communists to reconcile themselves with capitalist exploitation or that monopolists will become revolutionists. On the other hand, strict observance of the principle of non-interference in the affairs of other states and respect for their independence and sovereignty is one of the essential conditions of detente. We make no secret of the fact that we see detente as the way to create more favorable conditions for peaceful socialist and Communist construction. This only confirms that socialism and peace are indissoluble. As for the ultra-leftist assertion that peaceful coexistence is the next thing to 'helping capitalism' and 'freezing the socio-political status quo', our reply is this: every revolution is above all a natural result of the given society's internal development.

Life itself has refuted the inventions about 'freezing of the status quo'. Suffice it to recall the far-reaching revolutionary changes in the world in recent years" - L.I. Brezhnev

"Socialist emulation spells out innovation by the people. Underlying it are the people's high level of consciousness and initiative. It is this initiative that helps to reveal and tap the potentialities of production, and enhance efficiency and quality. But in practice - there's no hiding it - socialist commitments are sometimes not worked out from below but handed down from above, from higher bodies. This is prejudicial to the very spirit of labour emulation. In it the emphasis should be on upwardly revised plans and other similar initiatives going from below to the top: worker-team-factory-industry. Only then should these initiatives be dovetailed with the state plan. This accords with the nature of socialist emulation and with the planned character of our economy" - L.I. Brezhnev

"We hold the truth itself to be revolutionary and we stand firm by its side" - Maurice Bishop

"Many would-be revolutionaries work under the fallacious illusion that the vanguard party is to be a secret organisation that the power structure knows nothing about, and the masses know nothing about, except for occasional letters that come to their homes by night. Underground parties cannot distribute leaflets announcing an underground meeting. These are contradictions and inconsistencies of the so-called revolutionaries. The so-called revolutionaries are in fact afraid of the very danger that they are advocating for the people. These so-called revolutionaries want the people to say what they themselves are afraid to say, and the people to do what they themselves are afraid to do. This makes the so-called revolutionary a coward and a hypocrite. If these imposters would investigate the history of revolution, they would see that the vanguard group always starts out above ground and is later driven underground by the aggressor.

The Cuban Revolution exemplifies this fact; when Fidel Castro started to resist the butcher Batista and the American running dogs, he started by speaking on the campus of the University of Havana in public. He was later driven to the hills. His impact upon the dispossessed people of Cuba was very great and received with much respect. When he went into secrecy, Cuban people searched him out. People went to the hills to find him and his band of twelve. Castro handled the revolutionary struggle correctly. If the Chinese Revolution is investigated, it will be seen that the Communist Party was quiet on the surface so that they would be able to muster support from the masses. There are many areas one can read about to learn the correct approach, such as the revolution in Kenya, the Algerian Revolution, Fanon's The Wretched of the Earth, the Russian Revolution, the works of Chairman Mao Zedong, and a host of others" - Huey P. Newton

"The gun itself is not necessarily revolutionary because the fascists carry guns, in fact they have more guns. A lot of so-called revolutionaries simply do not understand the statement by Chairman Mao that 'Political power grows out of the barrel of a gun.' They thought Chairman Mao said political power is the gun, but the emphasis is on 'grows.' The culmination of political power is the ownership and control of the land and the institutions thereon so that we can then get rid of the gun. That is why Chairman Mao makes the statement that 'We are advocates of the abolition of war, we do not want war; but war can only be abolished through war, and in order to get rid of the gun, it is necessary to take up the gun.' He is always speaking of getting rid of it. If he did not look at it in those terms, then he surely would not be revolutionary. In other words, the gun by all revolutionary principles is a tool to be used in our strategy; it is not an end in itself. This was a part of the original vision of the Black Panther Party" - Huey P. Newton

"The nature of the panther is that he never attacks. But if

anyone attacks or backs into a corner, the panther comes up to wipe that agressor or that attacker out" - Huey P. Newton

"There's no reason for the establishment to fear me. But it has every right to fear the people collectively - I am one with the people" - Huey P. Newton

"We also know that for a time following the Russian February Revolution, in view of the specific conditions of the time, Lenin did adopt the policy of peaceful development of the revolution. He considered it 'an extraordinarily rare opportunity in the history of revolutions' and grasped tight hold of it. The bourgeois Provisional Government and the White Guards, however, destroyed this possibility of peaceful development of the revolution and drenched the streets of Petrograd in the blood of the workers and soldiers marching in a peaceful mass demonstration in July. Lenin, therefore, pointed out: The peaceful course of development has been rendered impossible. A non-peaceful and most painful course has begun. We know too that when there was a widespread and ardent desire for peace among the people throughout the country after the conclusion of the Chinese War of Resistance to Japanese Aggression, our Party conducted peace negotiations with the Kuomintang, seeking to institute social and political reforms in China by peaceful means, and in 1946 an agreement on achieving internal peace was reached with the Kuomintang. The Kuomintang reactionaries, however, defying the will of the whole people, tore up this agreement and, with the support of U.S. imperialism, launched a civil war on a nationwide scale. This left the Chinese people with no option but to wage a revolutionary war. As we never relaxed our vigilance or gave up the people's armed forces in our struggle for peaceful reform but were fully prepared, the people were not cowed by the war, but those who launched the war were made to-eat their own bitter fruit. It would be in the best interests of the people if the proletariat could attain power and carry out the transition to socialism by peaceful means. It would be wrong not to make use of such a possibility when it occurs. Whenever an opportunity for 'peaceful development of the revolution' presents itself, Communists must firmly seize it, as Lenin did, so as to realise the aim of socialist revolution. However, this sort of opportunity is always, in Lenin's words, 'an extraordinarily rare opportunity in the history of revolutions.' When in a given country a certain local political power is already encircled by revolutionary forces or when in the world a certain capitalist country is already encircled by socialism - in such cases, there might be a greater possibility of opportunities for the peaceful development of the revolution. But even then, the peaceful development of the revolution should never be regarded as the only possibility and it is therefore necessary to be prepared at the same time for the other possibility, i.e., non-peaceful development of the revolution. For instance, after the liberation of the Chinese mainland, although certain areas ruled by slave-owners and serf-owners were already surrounded by the absolutely predominant people's revolutionary forces, yet, as an old Chinese saying goes, 'Cornered beasts will still fight,' a handful of the most reactionary slave-owners and serf-owners there still gave a last kick, rejecting peaceful reforms and launching armed rebellions. Only after these rebellions were quelled was it possible to carry out the reform of the social systems; It can thus be seen that the proletariat is compelled to resort to the means of armed revolution. Marxists have always been willing to bring about the transition to socialism by the peaceful way. As long as the peaceful way is there to adopt, Marxist-Leninists will never give it up. But the aim of the bourgeoisie is precisely to block this way when it possesses a powerful, militarist-bureaucratic machine of oppression; It is necessary to take part in parliamentary struggles, but not place a blind faith in the bourgeois parliamentary system. Why? Because so long as the militarist-bureaucratic state machine of the bourgeoisie remains intact, parliament is nothing but an adornment for the bourgeois dictatorship even if the working-class party commands a majority in parliament or becomes the biggest party in it. Moreover, so long as such a state machine remains intact, the bourgeoisie is fully able at any time, in accordance with the needs of its own interests, either to dissolve parliament when necessary, or to use various open and underhand tricks to turn a working-class party which is the biggest party in parliament into a minority, or to reduce its seats in parliament, even when it has polled more votes than before in an election. It is, therefore, difficult to imagine that changes will take place in the dictatorship of the bourgeoisie itself as a result of votes in parliament and it is just as difficult to imagine that the proletariat can adopt measures in parliament for a peaceful transition to socialism just because it has won a certain number of votes in parliament. The experience in a series of capitalist countries long ago proved this point fully and the experience in various European and Asian countries since World War II has provided fresh proof of it" - (Lu Dingyi, Long live Leninism!)

"Once he [Stalin] asked Vassily and myself who we wanted to be when we grew up. Vassily said we shall become officers and go to the capitalist countries and help the proletariat to break free from the bourgeoisie. Stalin replied to this: 'Are you sure you will be welcome? First, make it attractive here in the U.S.S.R., so that all the world appreciates how we live. Then, probably, you will be asked for help. But you will surely have to fight for our motherland. We have many enemies'" - (Artyom Sergeyev, adopted son of Stalin)

"It's hard to believe. That such a peaceful country wants war. And Brezhnev. I never thought he was such a quiet and calm person. It is difficult to imagine that he can be the person who would start a war. I have not seen a hitchhiker on the road. And I have not seen a single beggar on the streets of Soviet Russia. I had never felt so safe. No risk of being robbed. I was told that there is no freedom of religion in the Soviet Union. But Muslims, Christians and Jews worship freely here. I think the relationship between our people is bad just because of false propaganda" - Muhammad Ali

"Revolutionaries didn't choose armed struggle as the best path, it's the path oppressors imposed [on] to people" - Fidel Castro

"In Nicaragua, an entire people is fighting for its independence. I would condemn revolutionary violence if I thought that a non-violent way existed" - Rev. Miguel D'Escoto

"[He quotes Stalin in saying] 'to achieve socialism in a new way, without the dictatorship of the proletariat; the situation has radically changed with respect to our revolution, what's needed is to apply different methods and forms [...]. You shouldn't fear accusations of opportunism. This isn't opportunism, but the application of Marxism to the current situation.' [And to Tito] 'in our time socialism is possible even under the English monarchy. The revolution is no longer necessary everywhere [...]. Yes, socialism is even possible under an English king.' [For his part, the historian who recorded these declarations adds:] 'As these observations show, Stalin was actively rethinking the universal validity of the Soviet model of revolution and socialism'" - (Domenico Losudro, Stalin: The History and Critique of a Black Legend)

"See, people with power understand exactly one thing: violence" - Noam Chomsky

"We reject Left adventurism and like all responsible revolutionary organisers we advocate a peaceful, democratic transition to socialism. We recognise that as capitalism enters a crisis, the ruling class often move to abolish democratic rights in order to preserve their power. We recognise the people's right to defend their organisations and communities in such a context. However, we are absolutely clear that we want peace and stability, not chaos. It is capitalism that is destroying the United States of America, and socialism will rescue it, rebuilding the country of new foundations, overcoming the legacy of colonialism, slavery, and many other crimes that hang over this society as a curse" - Caleb T. Maupin

"Every great revolution in history has been an act of self-defence by people who would have preferred a peaceful resolution" - Caleb T. Maupin

MORALITY:

"Communists do not oppose egoism to selflessness or selflessness to egoism, nor do they express this contradiction theoretically either in its sentimental or in its highflown ideological form; they rather demonstrate its material source, with which it disappears of itself. The Communists do not preach morality at all. They do not put to people the moral demand: love one another, do not be egoists, etc.; on the contrary, they are very well aware that egoism, just as much selflessness, is in definite circumstances a necessary form of the self-assertion of individuals. Hence, the Communists by no means want to do away with the 'private individual' for the sake of the 'general', selfless man. That is a statement of the imagination" - Karl Marx

"I have, which will surprise you not a little, been speculating; in English stocks, which are springing up like mushrooms this year; and are forced up to quite an unreasonable level and then, for the most part, collapse. In this way, I have made over £400" - Karl Marx

"...Now that the complexity of the political situation affords greater scope, I shall begin all over again. It's a type of operation that makes demands on one's time, [but] it's worthwhile running some risk in order to relieve the enemy of his money" - Karl Marx

"The minor panic in the money market appears to be over, consols [a type of government bond] and railway shares are again rising merrily, money is easier... I don't believe that the crisis will this time be preceded by a rage for speculation; crucial ill-tidings from overstocked markets must surely come soon. Massive shipments continue to leave for China and India; Calcutta is decidedly overstocked; I don't believe prosperity will continue beyond October" - Friedrich Engels

"Firstly, he saves himself the trouble of explaining the various forms of distribution which have hitherto existed, their differences and their causes; taken in the lump, they are simply of no account–they rest on oppression, on force. We shall have to deal with this before long. Secondly, he thereby transfers the whole theory of distribution from the sphere of economics to that of morality and law, that is, from the sphere of established material facts to that of more or less vacillating opinions and sentiments. He therefore no longer has any need to investigate or to prove things; he can go on declaiming to his heart's content and demand that the distribution of the products of labour should be regulated, not in accordance with its real causes, but in accordance with what seems ethical and just to him, Herr Dühring" - Friedrich Engels

"From a scientific standpoint, this appeal to morality and justice does not help us an inch further; moral indignation, however justifiable, cannot serve economic science as an argument, but only as a symptom" - Friedrich Engels

"The moment anyone started to talk to Marx about morality, he would roar with laughter" - Karl Vörlander

"I am closely following the situation in Russia. I try to get testimonies from eyewitnesses, not from newspapers that lie non-stop. I approve of the Russian revolution because it proclaimed the principle of honesty on one-sixth of the earth's surface. The Soviet Union is facing incredible temptations, but the state is ready to overcome them. The Russians were lucky - they have socialism and Stalin. Happy people with a wise leader. I envy the Russians and pity my compatriots who are ruled by three random people (after the assassination of Alexander, a three-member governorship took over the role of king). Only under the leadership of a wise and strong leader are the people capable of feats. If I could go back half a century, I wouldn't think for a second, I would go to Moscow and send Bechelor and Edison to hell. In my small library, I keep a collection of texts about the October Revolution, which was given to me by Skvirski (Soviet Ambassador to the United States). I often return to the collection and think with sympathy about the country I cannot visit. Age has many advantages, but also two disadvantages - poor health and thinking in the spirit: 'I will never succeed in this.' If I had children or grandchildren, I would probably, for their happiness, decide to go to the U.S.S.R. To go alone, at this age, I will not. I remember saying to Skvirski on one occasion: 'There is no point in transporting old bones across the ocean. You need to move while you are young so that the new homeland can benefit as much as possible. My departure to the U.S.S.R. would be just a burden for you'" - Nikola Tesla

"Capitalism is the extraordinary belief that the nastiest of men for the nastiest of motives will somehow work for the benefit of all" - John M. Keynes

"[On the industrialisation of the Soviet economy] The result is impressive" - John M. Keynes

"It is said that in that 'will' Comrade Lenin suggested to the congress that in view of Stalin's 'rudeness' it should consider the question of putting another comrade in Stalin's place as General Secretary. That is quite true. Yes, comrades, I am rude to those who grossly and perfidiously wreck and split the Party. I have never concealed this and do not conceal it now. Perhaps some mildness is needed in the treatment of splitters, but I am a bad hand at that. At the very first meeting of the plenum of the Central Committee after the Thirteenth Congress I asked the plenum of the Central Committee to release me from my duties as General Secretary. The congress itself discussed this question. It was discussed by each delegation separately, and all the delegations unanimously, including Trotsky, Kamenev and Zinoviev, obliged Stalin to remain at his post. What could I do? Desert my post? That is not in my nature; I have never deserted any post, and I have no right to do so, for that would be desertion. As I have already said before, I am not a free agent, and when the Party imposes an obligation upon me, I must obey" - J.V. Stalin

"I know that after my death a pile of rubbish will be heaped on my grave, but the wind of History will sooner or later sweep it away without mercy" - (J.V. Stalin, to V. Molotov, 1943)

"What would happen if capital succeeded in smashing the Republic of Soviets? There would set in an era of the blackest reaction in all the capitalist and colonial countries, the working class and the oppressed peoples would be seized by the throat, the positions of international Communism would be lost" - J.V. Stalin

"Either place yourself at the mercy of capital, eke out a wretched existence as of old and sink lower and lower, or adopt a new weapon - this is the alternative imperialism puts before the vast masses of the proletariat. Imperialism brings the working class to revolution" - J.V. Stalin

"It is difficult for me to imagine what 'personal liberty' is enjoyed by an unemployed person, who goes about hungry, and cannot find employment. Real liberty can exist only where exploitation has been abolished, where there is no oppression of some by others, where there is no unemployment and poverty, where a man is not haunted by the fear of being tomorrow deprived of work, of home and of bread. Only in such a society is real, and not paper, personal and every other liberty possible" - J.V. Stalin

"This crippling of individuals I consider the worst evil of capitalism. Our whole education system suffers from this evil. An exaggerated competitive attitude is inculcated into the student, who is trained to worship acquisitive success as a preparation for his future career. I am convinced there is only one way to eliminate these grave evils, namely through the establishment of a socialist economy, accompanied by an educational system which would be oriented toward social goals" - Albert Einstein

"The Russians have proved that their only aim is really the improvement of the lot of the Russian people; There are increasing signs the Russian trials are not faked, but that there is a plot among those who look upon Stalin as a stupid reactionary who has betrayed the ideas of the revolution" - Albert Einstein

"Anyone who loves freedom owes such a debt to the Red Army that it can never be repaid" - Ernest Hemingway

"It was here that in 1919 he brought Nadya Alleluiev, the daughter of his old friend of early Bolshevik days, and now grown into a beautiful woman. He was at this time forty and she seventeen, but for her he was still the same hero who had once come from afar and taken refuge in her parents' home. This was Stalin's great love affair. He was by nature monogamous. Those in search of sexual scandal in his life will search in vain. I recall Radek speaking to me of Stalin's reaction to the vagaries and often abominable aberrations in the sexual life of modern civilisation. Several illustrated German books dealing with the subject lay on Radek's table, which was as usual piled with volumes newly arrived from Europe and America. Stalin was just about to leave Radek's room when he noticed these books and began thumbing over their pages. Turning to Radek he asked: 'Are there really people in Europe who do these kinds of things?' 'Yes, of course,' answered Radek. 'Stalin,' Radek said to me, 'looked utterly disgusted, shrugged his shoulders, and walked away without saying another word.' To Stalin they reflected a diseased way of life, and he was a normal healthy man in his reactions to disease whether of the mind or of the body" - J.T. Murphy

"I think there are two swords: one is Lenin and the other is Stalin" - Mao Zedong

"Communism is not love. Communism is the hammer we use to destroy the class enemy" - Mao Zedong

"First, Stalin is disowned, now, little by little, it gets to prosecute socialism, the October Revolution, and in no time they will also want to prosecute Lenin and Marx" - Lazar Kaganovich

"With the revolution progressing and getting into its stride our view on and attitude towards the role of the young people and students changed radically. We defined the young people and students as constituting the fully-fledged main force of the revolution, thus breaking away from the old viewpoint according to which the motive force of the revolution had been defined with the main emphasis on the workers and peasants. This is proved to be correct by the course of the youth and student movement... the old theory which did not regard students even as a social stratum does not conform with the actual situation in our country" - Kim Il-sung

THE LUMPEN:

"Thus in the field of private property, morality teaches that theft is to be condemned; While Communists do not believe in the sacredness of private property, they do not approve of stealing; It is true that Communists by no means recognise the inviolability of private property; the nationalisation of factories is an expropriation of the bourgeoisie; the working class appropriates "the property of others", trangresses the right of private property, undertakes a 'despotic intervention in the right of property' But Communists condemn stealing, for the reason that individual thefts by each worker from the capitalists, for his own advantage, would not result in common struggle, but would make the worker a petty bourgeois. Horse-thieves and swindlers will not fight in the class struggle, even though they may be offspring of the proletariat. If many members of the proletariat should become thieves, the class would break down and be condemned; Therefore Communists condemn stealing, not in order to protect private property, but in order to maintain the integrity of their class, to protect it from 'demoralisation' and 'disintegration', without which protection the proletariat can never be transformed into the next following stage. We are therefore dealing witth a class standard in the conduct of the proletariat. It is obvious that the rules we have considered are determined by the economic conditions of society" - Karl Marx

"One could just as well have said that only in society can useless and even socially harmful labour become a branch of gainful occupation, that only in society can one live by being idle, etc., etc. - in short, once could just as well have copied the whole of Rousseau" - Karl Marx

"Observation has persuaded me that you are not very industrious by nature, despite spasmodic feverish activity and good intentions. In these circumstances, you will need external support if you are to set out in life with my daughter. I know nothing of your family. Although they may enjoy a comfortable living, that does not in itself mean that they would be disposed to make sacrifices for you. I do not even know with what favour they regard your proposed alliance. I repeat that I must have positive clarification on all these matters. Moreover, as an avowed realist, you cannot, of course, expect that I should behave as an idealist in respect of my daughter's future" - Karl Marx

"Alongside decayed roués with dubious means of subsistence and of dubious origin, alongside ruined and adventurous offshoots of the bourgeoisie, were vagabonds, discharged soldiers, discharged jailbirds, escaped galley slaves, swindlers, mountebanks, lazzaroni, pickpockets, tricksters, gamblers, maquereaux [pimps], brothel keepers, porters, literati, organ grinders, ragpickers, knife grinders, tinkers, beggars - in short, the whole indefinite, disintegrated mass, thrown hither and thither, which the French call la bohème; from this kindred element Bonaparte formed the core of the Society of December 10. A 'benevolent society' - insofar as, like Bonaparte, all its members felt the need of benefiting themselves at the expense of the labouring nation. This Bonaparte, who constitutes himself chief of the lumpenproletariat, who here alone rediscovers in mass form the interests which he personally pursues, who recognises in this scum, offal, refuse of all classes the only class upon which he can base himself unconditionally, is the real Bonaparte, the Bonaparte sans phrase. An old, crafty roué, he conceives the historical life of the nations and their performances of state as comedy in the most vulgar sense, as a masquerade in which the grand costumes, words, and postures merely serve to mask the pettiest knavery" - Karl Marx

"The 'dangerous class,' the lumpenproletariat, the social scum, that passively rotting mass thrown off by the lowest layers of the old society, may, here and there, be swept into the movement by a proletarian revolution; its conditions of life, however, prepare it far more for the part of a bribed tool of reactionary intrigue" - Karl Marx

"The same relation holds for all services which workers exchange directly for the money of other persons, and which are consumed by these persons. This is consumption of revenue, which, as such, always falls within simple circulation; it is not consumption of capital. Since one of the contracting parties does not confront the other as a capitalist, this performance of a service cannot fall under the category of productive labour. From wh*re to pope, there is a mass of such rabble. But the honest and 'working' lumpenproletariat belongs here as well; e.g. the great mob of porters etc. who render service in seaport cities etc" - Karl Marx

"The lumpenproletariat, this scum of the decaying elements of all classes, which establishes headquarters in all the big cities, is the worst of all possible allies. It is an absolutely venal, an absolutely brazen crew. If the French workers, in the course of the Revolution, inscribed on the houses: Mort aux voleurs! (Death to the thieves!) and even shot down many, they did it, not out of enthusiasm for property, but because they rightly considered it necessary to hold that band at arm's length. Every leader of the workers who utilises these gutter-proletarians as guards or supports, proves himself by this action alone a traitor to the movement" - Friedrich Engels

"Rosa acted and felt as a Communist when in an article she championed the cause of the prostitutes who were imprisoned for any transgression of police regulations in carrying on their dreary trade. They are, unfortunately, doubly sacrificed by bourgeois society. First, by its accursed property system, and, secondly, by its accursed moral hypocrisy. That is obvious. Only he who is brutal or short-sighted can forget it. But still, that is not at all the same thing as considering prostitutes - how shall I put it? - to be a special revolutionary militant section, as organising them and publishing a factory paper for them. Aren't there really any other working women in Germany to organise, for whom a paper can be issued, who must be drawn into your struggles? The other is only a diseased excrescence. It reminds me of the literary fashion of painting every prostitute as a sweet Madonna. The origin of that was healthy, too: social sympathy, rebellion against the virtuous hypocrisy of the respectable bourgeois. But the healthy part became corrupted and degenerate" - V.I. Lenin

"For example. In the eighties of the last century a great controversy flared up among the Russian revolutionary intelligentsia. The Narodniks asserted that the main force that could undertake the task of 'emancipating Russia' was the petty-bourgeoisie, rural and urban. Why? - the Marxists asked them. Because, answered the Narodniks, the rural and urban petty-bourgeoisie now constitute the majority and, moreover, they are poor, they live in poverty. To this the Marxists replied: It is true that the rural and urban petty-bourgeoisie now constitute the majority and are really poor, but is that the point? The petty-bourgeoisie has long constituted the majority, but up to now it has displayed no initiative in the struggle for 'freedom' without the assistance of the proletariat. Why? Because the petty-bourgeoisie as a class is not growing; on the contrary, it is disintegrating day by day and breaking up into bourgeois and proletarians. On the other hand, nor is poverty of decisive importance here, of course: 'tramps' are poorer than the petty-bourgeoisie, but nobody will say that they can undertake the task of 'emancipating Russia.' As you see, the point is not which class today constitutes the majority, or which class is poorer, but which class is gaining strength and which is decaying" - J.V. Stalin

"We felt we knew what we wanted to do, because Huey had already run it down to the central group of the SSAC that we had to arm ourselves. This was before we organised the Black Panther Party, maybe eleven months before. Huey had run it down, to Douglas Allen, to Isaac Moore, to Kenny Freeman, and to Ernest Allen, that what we needed to do was involve the black community. Huey understood the meaning of what Fanon was saying about organising the lumpen proletariat first, because Fanon explicitly pointed out that if you didn't organise the lumpen proletariat, if the organisation didn't relate to the lumpen proletariat and give a base for organising the brother who's pimping, the brother who's hustling, the unemployed, the downtrodden, the brother who's robbing banks, who's not politically conscious 'that's what lumpen proletariat means' that if you didn't relate to these cats, the power structure would organise these cats against you" - Bobby Seale

WOMENS ISSUES:

"So the phraseology, [Marx distanced himself from what he defined as the 'vulgar-democratic phraseology' of Atlantic liberalism: the Manchester School of free trade and Laissez-faire and Henry Carey's American school of Political Economoy. According to Marx, Atlantic liberalism raised the abolitionist flag of free labour against slavery only under the pressure of the 'slave movement' and the workers' struggle] to which such scribbling is restricted at least distinguishes itself from the vulgar, democratic phraseology; Victoria Woodhull, who for years has had an eye on the presidency; she is president of the spiritists, preaches free love, has a banking business etc.; agitated especially for the women's franchise; [Section 12's 'Appeal'] Among other things in it there was talk of personal liberty, social liberty (free love), dress regulation, women's franchise, universal language, etc.; [should be expelled from the International Workingmen's Association because] they give precedence to the women's question over the question of labour and take exception to the assumption that the I.W.A. is a workingmen's organisation.Both these sisters, millionairesses, advocates of women's emanipation and especially 'free love', resolutely joined the International. Section No. 9 was set up under the leadership of Miss Claflin, Section No. 12 under that of Mrs. Woodhull; new sections soon followed in the most diverse parts of America, all set up by adherents of the two sisters. According to the currently valid arrangements, every section had the right to send a delegate to the Central Committee, which met in New York. The consequence was that, very soon, this federal council, which had originally been made up of German, Irish and French workers, was swamped by a whole host of bourgeois American adventurers of all sorts and of both sexes. The workers were pushed into the background; victory for the two speculating sisters seemed assured. Then section No. 12 took central stage and explained to the founders of the American International what it was really all about" - Karl Marx

"In the approach to woman as the spoil and handmaid of communal lust is expressed the infinite degradation in which man exists for himself, for the secret of this approach has its unambiguous, decisive, plain and undisguised expression in the relation of man to woman and in the manner in which the direct and natural species-relationship is conceived. The direct, natural, and necessary relation of person to person is the relation of man to woman. In this natural species-relationship man's relation to nature is immediately his relation to man, just as his relation to man is immediately his relation to nature - his own natural destination. In this relationship, therefore, is sensuously manifested, reduced to an observable fact, the extent to which the human essence has become nature to man, or to which nature to him has become the human essence of man. From this relationship one can therefore judge man's whole level of development. From the character of this relationship follows how much man as a species-being, as man, has come to be himself and to comprehend himself; the relation of man to woman is the most natural relation of human being to human being. It therefore reveals the extent to which man's natural behaviour has become human, or the extent to which the human essence in him has become a natural essence - the extent to which his human nature has come to be natural to him. This relationship also reveals the extent to which man's need has become a human need; the extent to which, therefore, the other person as a person has become for him a need - the extent to which he in his individual existence is at the same time a social being" - Karl Marx

"Our bourgeois, not content with having wives and daughters of their proletarians at their disposal, not to speak of common prostitutes, take the greatest pleasure in seducing each other's wives. Bourgeois marriage is, in reality, a system of wives in common and thus, at the most, what the Communists might possibly be reproached with is that they desire to introduce, in substitution for a hypocritcally concealed, an openly legalised community of women. For the rest, it is self-evident that the abolition of the present system of production must bring with it the abolition of the community of women springing from that system, i.e., of prostitution both public and private" - Karl Marx

"Just as woman passes from marriage to general prostitution, [Prostitution is only a specific expression of the general prostitution of the labourer, and since it is a relationship in which falls not the prostitute alone, but also the one who prostitutes - and by the latter's abomination is still greater - the capitalist, etc., also comes under this head] so the entire world of wealth (that is, of man's objective substance) passes from the relationship of exclusive marriage with the owner of private property to a state of universal prostitution with the community" - Karl Marx

"The bourgeoisie has torn away from the family its sentimental veil, and has reduced the family relation into a mere money relation" - Karl Marx

"The bourgeois clap-trap about the family and education, about the hallowed co-relation of parents and child, becomes all the more disgusting, the more, by action of Modern Industry, all the family ties among the proletarians are torn asunder, and their children transformed into simple articles of commerce and instruments of labour" - Karl Marx

"Abolition [Aufhebung] of the family! Even the most radical flare up at this infamous proposal of the Communists. On what foundation is the present family, the bourgeois family, based? On capital, on private gain. In its completely developed form, this family exists only among the bourgeoisie. But this state of things finds its complement in the practical absence of the family among the proletarians, and in public prostitution. The bourgeois family will vanish as a matter of course when its complement vanishes, and both will vanish with the vanishing of capital" - Karl Marx

"...It is self-evident that the abolition of the present system of production must bring with it the abolition of the community of women springing from that system, i.e., of prostitution both public and private" - Karl Marx

"...However impressive the people of this epoch appear to us, they are completely undifferentiated from one another; as Marx says, they are still attached to the navel string of the primitive community. The power of this primitive community had to be broken, and it was broken. But it was broken by influences which from the very start appear as a degradation, a fall from the simple moral greatness of the old gentile society. The lowest interests - base greed, brutal appetites, sordid avarice, selfish robbery of the common wealth - inaugurate the new, civilised, class society. It is by the vilest means - theft, violence, fraud, treason - that the old gentile society is undermined and overthrown. And the society itself during all the 2500 years of its existence has never been anything else but the development of the small minority at the expense of the great exploited and oppressed majority; today it is so more than ever before" - Friedrich Engels

"What we can now conjecture about the way in which sexual relations will be ordered after the impending overthrow of capitalist production is mainly of a negative character, limited for the most part to what will disappear. But what will there be new? That will be answered when a new generation has grown up: a generation of men who never in their lives have known what it is to buy a woman's surrender with money or any other social instrument of power; a generation of women who have never known what it is to give themselves to a man from any other considerations than real love, or to refuse to give themselves to their lover from fear of the economic consequences. When these people are in the world, they will care precious little what anybody today thinks they ought to do; they will make their own practice and their corresponding public opinion about the practice of each individual - and that will be the end of it" - Friedrich Engels

"The equality of woman thereby achieved will tend in infinitely greater measure to make men really monogamous than to make women polyandrous" - Friedrich Engels

"Thus in the Greek constitution of the heroic age, we see the old gentile order as still a living force. But we also see the beginnings of its disintegration: father right, with transmission of the property to the children by which accumulation of wealth within the family was favoured and the family itself became a power against the gens; reaction of the inequality of wealth on the constitution by the formation of the first rudiments of hereditary nobility and monarchy; slavery at first only of prisoners of war but already preparing the way for the enslavement of fellow members of the tribe and even of the gens; the old wars between tribe and tribe already degenerating into systematic pillage by land and sea for the acquisition of cattle, slaves and treasure, and becoming a regular source of wealth; in short the riches praised and respected as the highest good and the old gentile order misused to justify the violent seizure of riches. Only one thing was wanting: an institution which not only secured the newly acquired riches of individuals against the Communistic traditions of the gentile order, which not only sanctified the private property formerly so little valued and declared this sanctification to be the highest purpose of all human society; but an institution which set the seal of general social recognition on each new method of acquiring property and thus amassing wealth at continually increasing speed; an institution which perpetuated not only this growing cleavage of society into classes but also the right of the possessing class to exploit the non-possessing, and the rule of the former over the latter. And this institution came. The state was invented" - Friedrich Engels

"We are now approaching a social revolution in which the economic foundations of monogamy as they have existed hitherto will disappear just as surely as those of its complement - prostitution. Monogamy arose from the concentration of considerable wealth in the hands of a single individual - a man - and from the need to bequeath this wealth to the children of that man and of no other. For this purpose, the monogamy of the woman was required, not that of the man, so this monogamy of the woman did not in any way interfere with open or concealed polygamy on the part of the man. But by transforming by far the greater portion, at any rate, of permanent, heritable wealth - the means of production - into social property, the coming social revolution will reduce to a minimum all this anxiety about bequeathing and inheriting. Having arisen from economic causes, will monogamy then disappear when these causes disappear? One might answer, not without reason: far from disappearing, it will, on the contrary, be realised completely. For with the transformation of the means of production into social property there will disappear also wage-labour, the proletariat, and therefore the necessity for a certain - statistical calculable - number of women to surrender themselves for money. Prostitution disappears; monogamy, instead of collapsing, at last becomes a reality - also for men" - Friedrich Engels

"With the rise of the inequality of property - already at the upper stage of barbarism, therefore - wage-labour appears sporadically side by side with slave labour, and at the same time, as its necessary correlate, the professional prostitution of free women side by side with the forced surrender of the slave. Thus the heritage which group marriage has bequeathed to civilisations is double-edged, just as everything civilisations brings forth is double edged, double tongued, divided against itself, contradictory: here monogamy, there hetaerism with its most extreme form, prostitution. For hetaerism is as much a social institution as any other; it continues the old sexual freedom - to the advantage of men" - Friedrich Engels

"[What will be the influence of Communist society on the family?] It will transform the relations between the sexes into a purely private matter which concerns only the persons involved and into which society has no occasion to intervene. It can do this since it does away with private property and educates children on a communal basis, and in this way removes the two bases of traditional marriage - the dependence rooted in private property, of the women on the man, and of the children on the parents. And here is the answer to the outcry of the highly moral philistines against the 'community of women.' Community of women is a condition which belongs entirely to bourgeois society and which today finds its complete expression in prostitution. But prostitution is based on private property and falls with it. Thus, Communist society, instead of introducing community of women, in fact abolishes it" - Friedrich Engels

"...So long as wage-slavery exists, inevitably prostitution too will exist. All the oppressed and exploited classes throughout the history of human societies have already been forced... to give up to their oppressors, first, their unpaid labour and, second, their women as concubines for the 'masters'" - V.I. Lenin

"We have begun to learn and are rapidly learning to fight - and to fight not as individuals, as the best of our fathers fought, not for the slogans of bourgeois speechifiers that are alien to us in spirit, but for our slogans, the slogans of our class. We are fighting better than our fathers did. Our children will fight better than we do, and they will be victorious. The working class is not perishing, it is growing, becoming stronger, gaining courage, consolidating itself, educating itself and becoming steeled in battle. We are pessimists as far as serfdom, capitalism and petty, production are concerned, but we are ardent optimists in what concerns the working-class movement and its aims. We are already laying the foundation of a new edifice and our children will complete its construction. That is the reason - the only reason - why we are unconditionally the enemies of neomalthusianism, suited only to unfeeling and egotistic petty-bourgeois couples, who whisper in scared voices: 'God grant we manage somehow by ourselves. So much the better if we have no children.' It goes without saying that this does not by any means prevent us from demanding the unconditional annulment of all laws against abortions or against the distribution of medical literature on contraceptive measures, etc. Such laws are nothing but the hypocrisy of the ruling classes. These laws do not heal the ulcers of capitalism, they merely turn them into malignant ulcers that are especially painful for the oppressed masses. Freedom for medical propaganda and the protection of the elementary democratic rights of citizens, men and women, are one thing. The social theory of neomalthusianism is quite another. Class-conscious workers will always conduct the most ruthless struggle against attempts to impose that reactionary and cowardly theory on the most progressive and strongest class in modern society, the class that is the best prepared for great changes" - V.I. Lenin

"The capitalist exploitation of the proletarian work force through its starvation wages, sees to it that there is a large supply of prostitutes which corresponds to the demand by the men" - Clara Zetkin

"Bourgeois professors are not ashamed to declare in print that prostitutes are not slaves, that they voluntarily chose this road! This is disgusting hypocrisy, which claims that nothing prevents a worker from leaving a factory where it is impossible to breathe from dust, poisonous fumes, and the heat. He 'voluntarily' stays to work on it, 'voluntarily' works for 16-18 hours" (- Nadezhda Krupskaya, 'The female worker', 1899)

"But the red flag, the horrible red flag, what does that mean? Not that the streets should run with gore, but that the same red blood courses through the veins of the whole human race. It meant the brotherhood of man. When the red flag floats over the world the idle shall be called to work. There will be an end of prostitution for women, of slavery for man, of hunger for children" - Lucy Parsons

"Prostitution destroys the equality, solidarity and comradeship of the two halves of the working class. A man who buys the favours of a woman does not see her as a comrade or as a person with equal rights... The contempt he has for the prostitute, whose favour he has bought, affects his attitude to all women" - Alexandra Kollontai

"While for the feminists the achievement of equal rights with men in the framework of the contemporary capitalist world represents a sufficiently concrete end in itself, equal rights at the present time are, for the proletarian women, only a means of advancing the struggle against the economic slavery of the working class" - Alexandra Kollontai

"However apparently radical the demands of the feminists, one must not lose sight of the fact that the feminists cannot, on account of their class position, fight for the fundamental transformation of the contemporary economic and social structure of society without which the liberation of women cannot be complete; The feminists see men as the main enemy, for men have unjustly seized all rights and privelages for themselves, leaving women only chains and duties. For them a victory is won when a prerogative previously enjoyed exclusively by the male sex is conceded to the 'fair sex'. Proletarian women have a different attitude. They do not see men as the enemy and the oppressor; on the contrary, they think of men as their comrades, who share with them the drudgery of the daily round and fight with them for a better future. The woman and her male comrade are enslaved by the same social conditions; the same hated chains of capitalism oppress their will and deprive them of the joys and charms of life. It is true that several aspects of the contemporary system lie with double weight upon women, as it is also true that the conditions of hired labour sometimes turn working women into competitors and rivals to men. But in these unfavourable situations, the working class knows who is guilty" - Alexandra Kollontai

"Besides the large-scale development of motherhood protection, the task of labour [in] Russia is to strengthen in women the healthy instinct of motherhood, to make motherhood and labour for the collective compatible and thus do away with the need for abortion. This is the approach of the labour republic to the question of abortion, which still faces women in the bourgeois countries in all its magnitude; Abortion exists and flourishes everywhere, and no laws or punitive measures have succeeded in rooting it out. A way round the law is always found. But 'secret help' only cripples women; they become a burden on the labour government, and the size of the labour force is reduced. Abortion when carried out under proper medical conditions, is less harmful and dangerous, and the woman can get back to work quicker. Soviet power realises that the need for abortion will disappear on the one hand when Russia has a broad and developed network of institutions protecting motherhood and providing social education, and on the other hand when women understand that childbirth is a social obligation; Soviet power has therefore allowed abortion to be performed openly and in clinical conditions" - Alexandra Kollontai

"[What must every working woman do?] How are all these demands to be won? What action must be taken? Every working-class woman, every woman who reads this pamphlet, must throw off her indifference and begin to support the working-class movement, which is fighting for these demands and is shaping the old world into a better future where mothers will no longer weep bitter tears and where the cross of maternity will become a great joy and a great pride. We must say to ourselves, 'There is strength in unity'; the more of us working women join the working-class movement, the greater will be our strength and the quicker we will get what we want. Our happiness and the life and future of our children are at stake" - Alexandra Kollontai

"Women hold up half the sky" - Mao Zedong

"The specific character of [women's] oppression cannot be explained away by equating different situations through superficial and childish simplifications[:] It is true that both the woman and the male worker are condemned to silence by their exploitation. But under the current system, the worker's wife is also condemned to silence by her worker-husband. In other words, in addition to the class exploitation common to both of them, women must confront a particular set of relations that exist between them and men, relations of conflict and violence that use physical differences as their pretext" - Thomas Sankara

"Thus, someone who owns property and has a secure job cannot actually experience what it means to be a sex-worker because her prime vocation is not one where she is forced to sell her body as an economic necessity. Sex labour in a context of class privilege is an activity, a game, where one's material reality produces a different set of options: you can always stop, you have a far greater margin of choice (your clientelle are more like dating options on Craigslist but with reimbursement attached), and by-and-large you are not a sex-worker because this is simply compensated dating - it is not the material institution of prostitution defined by labourers who have no other choice but to sell their labour in this institution. You are not part of this institution's army of labour; you are not part of its reserve army of labour when you aren't working" - J. Moufawad-Paul

SEX:

"A part of the bourgeoisie is desirous of redressing social grievances in order to secure the continued existence of bourgeois society. To this section belong economists, philanthropists, humanitarians, improvers of the condition of the working class, organisers of charity, members of societies for the prevention of cruelty to animals, temperance fanatics, hole-and-corner reformers of every imaginable kind. This form of socialism has, moreover, been worked out into complete systems" - Karl Marx

"Bakunin has become a monster, a huge mass of flesh and fat, and is barely capable of walking any more. To crown it all, he is sexually perverse and jealous of the seventeen year-old Polish girl who married him in Siberia because of his martyrdom. He is presently in Sweden, where he is hatching 'revolution' with the Finns" - Karl Marx

"I was told that questions of sex and marriage are the main subjects dealt with in the reading and discussion evenings of women comrades. They are the chief subject of interest, of political instruction and education. I could scarcely believe my ears when I heard it... But working women comrades discuss sexual problems and the question of forms of marriage in the past, present and future. They think it their most important duty to enlighten proletarian women on these subjects. The most widely read brochure is, I believe, the pamphlet of a young Viennese woman comrade on the sexual problem. What a waste!" - V.I. Lenin

"It seems to me that this superabundance of sex theories, which for the most part are mere hypotheses, and often quite arbitrary ones, stems from a personal need. It springs from the desire to justify one's own abnormal or excessive sex life before bourgeois morality and plead for tolerance towards oneself. This veiled respect for bourgeois morality is as repugnant to me as rooting about in all that bears on sex. No matter how rebellious and revolutionary it may be made to appear, it is in the final analysis thoroughly bourgeois. Intellectuals and others like them are particularly keen on this. There is no room for it in the Party, among the class-conscious, fighting proletariat" - V.I. Lenin

"I was also told that sex problems are a favorite subject in your youth organizations too, and that there are hardly enough lecturers on this subject. This nonsense is especially dangerous and damaging to the youth movement. It can easily lead to sexual excesses, to overstimulation of sex life and to wasted health and strength of young people. You must fight that too. There is no lack of contact between the youth movement and the women's movement. Our Communist women everywhere should cooperate methodically with young people. This will be a continuation of motherhood, will elevate it and extend it from the individual to the social sphere. Women's incipient social life and activities must be promoted, so that they can outgrow the narrowness of their Philistine, individualistic psychology centered on home and family. But this is incidental. In our country, too, considerable numbers of young people are busy 'revising bourgeois conceptions and morals' in the sex question. And let me add that this involves a considerable section of our best boys and girls, of our truly promising youth. It is as you have just said. In the atmosphere created by the aftermath of war and by the revolution which has begun, old ideological values, finding themselves in a society whose economic foundations are undergoing a radical change, perish, and lose their restraining force. New values crystallize slowly, in the struggle. With regard to relations between people, and between man and woman, feelings and thoughts are also becoming revolutionized. New boundaries are being drawn between the rights of the individual and those of the community, and hence also the duties of the individual" - V.I. Lenin

"The coercion of bourgeois marriage and bourgeois legislation on the family enhance the evil and aggravate the conflicts. It is the coercion of 'sacrosanct' property. It sanctifies venality, baseness, and dirt. The conventional hypocrisy of 'respectable' bourgeois society takes care of the rest. People revolt against the prevailing abominations and perversions. And at a time when mighty nations are being destroyed, when the former power relations are being disrupted, when a whole social world is beginning to decline, the sensations of the individual undergo a rapid change. A stimulating thirst for different forms of enjoyment easily acquires an irresistible force. Sexual and marriage reforms in the bourgeois sense will not do. In the sphere of sexual relations and marriage, a revolution is approaching in keeping with the proletarian revolution. Of course, women and young people are taking a deep interest in the complex tangle of problems which have arisen as a result of this. Both the former and the latter suffer greatly from the present messy state of sex relations. Young people rebel against them with the vehemence of their years. This is only natural. Nothing could be falser than to preach monastic self-denial and the sanctity of the filthy bourgeois morals to young people. However, it is hardly a good thing that sex, already strongly felt in the physical sense, should at such a time assume so much prominence in the psychology of young people. The consequences are nothing short of fatal. Ask Comrade Lilina about it. She ought to have had many experiences in her extensive work at educational institutions of various kinds and you know that she is a Communist through and through, and has no prejudices" - V.I. Lenin

"Youth's altered attitude to questions of sex is of course 'fundamental', and based on theory. Many people call it 'revolutionary' and 'Communist'. They sincerely believe that this is so. I am an old man, and I do not like it. I may be a morose ascetic, but quite often this so-called 'new sex life' of young people and frequently of the adults too seems to me purely bourgeois and simply an extension of the good old bourgeois brothel. All this has nothing in common with free love as we Communists understand it. No doubt you have heard about the famous theory that in Communist society satisfying sexual desire and the craving for love is as simple and trivial as 'drinking a glass of water'. A section of our youth has gone mad, absolutely mad, over this 'glass-of-water theory'. It has been fatal to many a young boy and girl. Its devotees assert that it is a Marxist theory. I want no part of the kind of Marxism which infers all phenomena and all changes in the ideological superstructure of society directly and blandly from its economic basis, for things are not as simple as all that. A certain Friedrich Engels has established this a long time ago with regard to historical materialism. I consider the famous 'glass-of-water' theory as completely un-Marxist and, moreover, as anti-social. It is not only what nature has given but also what has become culture, whether of a high or low level, that comes into play in sexual life. Engels pointed out in his Origin of the Family how significant it was that the common sexual relations had developed into individual sex love and thus became purer. The relations between the sexes are not simply the expression of a mutual influence between economics and a physical want deliberately singled out for physiological examination. It would be rationalism and not Marxism to attempt to refer the change in these relations directly to the economic basis of society in isolation from its connection with the ideology as a whole. To be sure, thirst has to be quenched. But would a normal person normally lie down in the gutter and drink from a puddle? Or even from a glass whose edge has been greased by many lips? But the social aspect is more important than anything else. The drinking of water is really an individual matter. But it takes two people to make love, and a third person, a new life, is likely to come into being. This deed has a social complexion and constitutes a duty to the community" - V.I. Lenin

"The revolution calls for concentration and rallying of every nerve by the masses and by the individual. It does not tolerate orgiastic conditions so common among d'Annunzio's decadent heroes and heroines. Promiscuity in sexual matters is bourgeois. It is a sign of degeneration. The proletariat is a rising class. It does not need an intoxicant to stupefy or stimulate it, neither the intoxicant of sexual laxity or of alcohol. It should and will not forget the vileness, the filth and the barbarity of capitalism. It derives its strongest inspiration to fight from its class position, from the Communist ideal. What it needs is clarity, clarity, and more clarity. Therefore, I repeat, there must be no weakening, no waste and no dissipation of energy Self-control and self-discipline are not slavery; not in matters of love either. But excuse me, Clara, I have strayed far from the point which we set out to discuss. Why have you not called me to order? Worry has set me talking. I take the future of our youth very close to heart. It is part and parcel of the revolution. Whenever harmful elements appear, which creep from bourgeois society to the world of the revolution and spread like the roots of prolific weeds, it is better to take action against them quickly. The questions we have dealt with are also part of the women's problems" - V.I. Lenin

RELIGION:

"Religion is the general theory of this world, its encyclopaedic compendium, its logic in popular form, its spiritual point d'honneur, its enthusiasm, its moral sanction, its solemn complement, and its universal basis of consolation and justification. It is the fantastic realisation of the human essence since the human essence has not acquired any true reality. The struggle against religion is, therefore, indirectly the struggle against that world whose spiritual aroma is religion. Religious suffering is, at one and the same time, the expression of real suffering and a protest against real suffering. Religion is the sigh of the oppressed creature, the heart of a heartless world, and the soul of soulless conditions. It is the opium of the people. The abolition of religion as the illusory happiness of the people is the demand for their real happiness. To call on them to give up their illusions about their condition is to call on them to give up a condition that requires illusions. The criticism of religion is, therefore, in embryo, the criticism of that vale of tears of which religion is the halo. Criticism has plucked the imaginary flowers on the chain not in order that man shall continue to bear that chain without fantasy or consolation, but so that he shall throw off the chain and pluck the living flower. The criticism of religion disillusions man, so that he will think, act, and fashion his reality like a man who has discarded his illusions and regained his senses, so that he will move around himself as his own true Sun" - Karl Marx

"It is the work of a man in deep sorrow who expresses his hope that the anger and hatred so generally evoked by suffering can be transformed into compassion and love; But what a strange logic, one that ties the very act of prediction of the mysteries of the dark ground, whereby 'x is y' really means, 'that which is x is that which is y.' Sheared of predicates of its own, the ground of unity ('that which is') is ensnared in darkness, where it is mysteriously joined to the heart. To speak (or sing) its truth is to lighten its burden through 'the generation of sound and meaning out of an interior so full that it can no longer remain in itself; What they all attempted to disclose was, mythically construed, the history of God's becoming. Forged in the painful contractions of primordial nature, god-Cronus, driven by alternating waves of fear and greed, devours his children. But when the gentle son steps forth, even old Cronus becomes gentle (and for the first time truly the Father), affirming the world in what we still celebrate as the act of creation; His purpose in illuminating the abyss of the pass was to uncover the origin of time itself; Caught between these poles is, of course, the world we now experience; In itself, the absolute future, like the absolute past, is hidden away in eternity; God in his wisdom hides in dark night not only the end of time to come from the beginningg of time past; Recognising it as such is the most difficult task facing humanity. Far from there being hame in the failure to complete the task, the failure itself is one of the secrets of divine wisdom: the compassionate heart is held open by the eternal return of the suffering it seeks to overcome; Imagining the contractions through which God was to give birth to himself was simply too much to bear: 'For man helps man; even God helps him. But nothing can assist the primal being, lost in its terrifying solitude. It has no choice but to fight through its chaotic condition alone and by itself; the image of a not-yet God himself undergoing hell, represents the only possible solution to the problem of why God would allow so much suffering in the world. To the degree that we are where God was, the affirmation of our need to suffer is a function of God's own self-affirmation; If Christianity has had to declare the very heart of Christianity heretical, it is presumably because its truth is too heavy to bear; Eighteen-eleven was the year of his solitude, when, still in mourning after the death of his Caroline; an exploration of his primordial past, the disclosure of the hell that God had to climb out of in order first to become God, a hell that those any less than divine still have to struggle with" - Karl Marx

"If we find that even in the country of complete political emancipation, religion not only exists, but displays a fresh and vigorous vitality, that is proof that the existence of religion is not in contradiction to the perfection of the state" - Karl Marx

"On the contrary, the perfect Christian state is the atheistic state, the democratic state, the state which relegates religion to a place among the other elements of civil society" - Karl Marx

"Everyone should be able to relieve religious and bodily nature without the police sticking their noses in" - Karl Marx

"Political democracy is Christian since in it man, not merely one man but everyman, ranks as sovereign, as the highest being" - Karl Marx

"That which is a creation of fantasy, a dream, a postulate of Christianity, i.e., the sovereignty of man - but man as an alien being different from the real man - becomes, in democracy, tangible reality, present existence, and secular principle" - Karl Marx

"Christianity attains, here, the practical expression of its universal-religious significance" - Karl Marx

"The consummation of the Christian state is the state which acknowledges itself as a state and disregards the religion of its members. The emancipation of the state from religion is not the emancipation of the real man from religion" - Karl Marx

"Political emancipation is, at the same time, the

dissolution of the old society on which the state alienated from the people, the sovereign power, is based. What was the character of the old society? It can be described in one word - feudalism" - Karl Marx

"Contempt for theory, art, history, and for man as an end in himself, is the real, conscious standpoint and the virtue of the man of money. The species-relation itself, the relation between man and woman, etc., becomes an object of trade!" - Karl Marx

"In America, which was the 'vanguard' of the age; the absolute separation of church and state had brought a religious renaissance in the great awakenings" - Karl Marx

"You can start a Communist revolution with the four gospels and revelation" - Friedrich Engels

"Three hundred years after its appearance Christianity was the recognised state religion in the Roman World Empire, and in barely sixty years socialism has won itself a position which makes its victory absolutely certain" - Friedrich Engels

"If [one] wonders [...] why, with the enormous concentration of landownership under the Roman emperors and the boundless sufferings of the working class of the time, which was composed almost exclusively of slaves, 'socialism did not follow the overthrow of the Roman Empire in the West,' it is because he cannot see that this 'socialism' did in fact, as far as it was possible at the time, exist and even became dominant - in Christianity" - Friedrich Engels

"We therefore see that the Christianity of that time, which was still unaware of itself, was as different as heaven from earth from the later dogmatically fixed universal religion of the Nicene Council; one cannot be recognised in the other. Here we have neither the dogma nor the morals of later Christianity but instead a feeling that one is struggling against the whole world and that the struggle will be a victorious one; an eagerness for the struggle and a certainty of victory which are totally lacking in Christians of today and which are to be found in our time only at the other pole of society, among the socialists. In fact, the struggle against a world that at the beginning was superior in force, and at the same time against the novators themselves, is common to the early Christians and the socialists. Neither of these two great movements were made by leaders or prophets – although there are prophets enough among both of them - they are mass movements. And mass movements are bound to be confused at the beginning; confused because the thinking of the masses at first moves among contradictions, lack of clarity and lack of cohesion, and also because of the role that prophets still play in them at the beginning. This confusion is to be seen in the formation of numerous sects which fight against one another with at least the same zeal as against the common external enemy. So it was with early Christianity, so it was in the beginning of the socialist movement, no matter how much that worried the well-meaning worthies who preached unity where no unity was possible" - Friedrich Engels

"The only service which one can still render to God is to declare atheism a compulsory article of faith" - Friedrich Engels

"If [a person] works honestly, takes part in our events, stands by our side in everything and expresses the wish to become a Communist - they must be admitted into the Party, whether they believe in Allah with his Muhammad or any other Totemic animal; this does us no harm" - J.V. Stalin

"The Soviet Government considers that the Sharia, as common law, is as fully authorised as that of any other of the peoples inhabiting Russia" - J.V. Stalin

"One should not close off people's worship. In any case, the people worship and pray. One should even open temples. But the books they read should be in Mongolian. And the monks should be in your hands" - J.V. Stalin

"The Soviet people, as Bolsheviks, have the following principle of building the leading organs of the state: if the Muslims prevail in the country, then the majority of government members should also be Muslim. You cannot violate people's religion. People will not understand, why the state is not led by the Muslims, while the majority of the country's population is Muslim. These are elementary things, but they did not understand that in Yugoslavia. It does not mean that only Muslims should be in the government. We should select capable people from among the national minorities in order to keep the unity of the people intact. Participation in the government of the representatives of ethnic and religious minorities will ensure the stability of the government" - (J.V. Stalin, speaking with Enver Hoxha)

"Regarding the three largest religious faiths of the world (Christianity, Islam and Buddhism), even up until now it exerts an enormous influence over the peoples of the world. Admittedly, our knowledge of these religions is small as currently our country does not have a proper research institution that uses a Marxist lens to analyse, research and study them, for example, right now there is not a single scholarly work that of which we can read and study this topic" - Mao Zedong

[In which moment did you become Communist?] "I became Communist because I was Catholic. I did not change religion, but I remained profoundly Catholic. I don't go to church but this doesn't matter; you don't ask people to go to church. I remained a Catholic, that is, an internationalist universalist" - Louis Althusser

[What role does Catholic culture have today?] "Oh… it has a giant role. In my view, today social revolution or a profound social change depends on the alliance between Catholics (I am not saying the church, though the church can also be part of it), the Catholics of the world, all religions of the world, and Communists" - Louis Althusser

"There were a large number of Christian churches in our country before the outbreak of the Fatherland Liberation War against the U.S. imperialists. These churches were destroyed by the planes of Americans who they themselves professed to be the so-called 'apostles of God.' The crucifixes, icons, Bibles, as well as their worshippers - all destroyed by U.S. bombs. And thus, it were the Americans who destroyed our churches and killed our religious. No god rescued us from this disaster. So after the war, our religious did not hurry to rebuild their churches and temples. Instead they focused their efforts on their survival, first rebuilding what they needed most: dwellings, homes, factories, schools" - Kim Il-sung

ASIATIC MODE OF PRODUCTION:

"There cannot, however, remain any doubt but that the misery inflicted by the British on Hindostan is of an essentially different and infinitely more intensive kind than all Hindostan had to suffer before. I do not allude to European despotism, planted upon Asiatic despotism, by the British East India Company, forming a more monstrous combination than any of the divine monsters startling us in the Temple of Salsette; All the civil wars, invasions, revolutions, conquests, famines, strangely complex, rapid, and destructive as the successive action in Hindostan may appear, did not go deeper than its surface. England has broken down the entire framework of Indian society, without any symptoms of reconstitution yet appearing. This loss of his old world, with no gain of a new one, imparts a particular kind of melancholy to the present misery of the Hindoo, and separates Hindostan, ruled by Britain, from all its ancient traditions, and from the whole of its past history; Now, the British in East India accepted from their predecessors the department of finance and of war, but they have neglected entirely that of public works. Hence the deterioration of an agriculture which is not capable of being conducted on the British principle of free competition, of laissez-faire and laissez-aller. But in Asiatic empires we are quite accustomed to see agriculture deteriorating under one government and reviving again under some other government. There the harvests correspond to good or bad government, as they change in Europe with good or bad seasons. Thus the oppression and neglect of agriculture, bad as it is, could not be looked upon as the final blow dealt to Indian society by the British intruder, had it not been attended by a circumstance of quite different importance, a novelty in the annals of the whole Asiatic world; It was the British intruder who broke up the Indian hand-loom and destroyed the spinning-wheel. England began with driving the Indian cottons from the European market; it then introduced twist into Hindostan, and in the end inundated the very mother country of cotton with cottons. From 1818 to 1836 the export of twist from Great Britain to India rose in the proportion of 1 to 5,200. In 1824 the export of British muslins to India hardly amounted to 1,000,000 yards, while in 1837 it surpassed 64,000,000 of yards. But at the same time the population of Dacca decreased from 150,000 inhabitants to 20,000. This decline of Indian towns celebrated for their fabrics was by no means the worst consequence. British steam and science uprooted, over the whole surface of Hindostan, the union between agriculture and manufacturing industry" - Karl Marx

"In short, the rural commune finds it in a state of crisis that will only end when the social system is eliminated through the return of modern societies to the 'archaic' type of communal property. In the words of an American writer, who supported in his work by the Washington government, is not at all to be suspected of revolutionary tendencies, ['the higher plane'] 'the new system' to which society is tending 'will be a revival, in a superior form, of an archaic social type.' We should not, then, be too frightened by the word 'archaic'" - Karl Marx

"On the ruins and remnants of a [Peruvian] socialist economy, they [the Spanish] established the bases of a feudal economy (- José Carlos Mariátegui); Artificially developed Communism of the Peruvians [Incas]" - Karl Marx

"Thus the absolute monarchy in Spain, bearing but a superficial resemblance to the absolute monarchies of Europe in general, is rather to he ranged in a class with

Asiatic forms of government. Spain, like Turkey remained an agglomeration of mismanaged republics with a nominal sovereign at their head... Despotism changed character in the different provinces with the arbitrary interpretation of the general laws by viceroys and governors; but despotic as was the government it did not prevent the provinces from subsisting with different laws and customs, different coins, military banners of different colours, and with their respective systems of taxation. The oriental despotism attacks municipal self-government only when opposed to its direct interests, but is very glad to allow those institutions to continue so long as they take off its shoulders the duty of doing something and spare it the trouble of regular administration" - Karl Marx

"This anticipation of coming stages of historic development, forced in itself, but a natural outcome of the life conditions of the plebeian grouop, is firsted noted in Germany, in the teachings of Thomas Muenzer and his party; Only in the teachings of Muenzer did these Communist notions find expression as the desires of a vital section of society. Through him they were formulated with a certain definiteness, and were afterwards found in every great convulsion of the people, until gradually, they merged with the modern proletarian movement" - Friedrich Engels

"Turks, particularly those of the Ottoman Empire in its heyday, are the most perfect nation on earth in every possible way. The Turkish language is the most perfect and melodious in the world... If a European is maltreated in Turkey, he has only himself to blame; your Turk hates neither the religion of the Frank, nor his character, but only his narrow trousers. Imitation of Turkish architecture, etiquette, etc. is strongly recommended. The author himself was several times kicked in the bottom by Turks, but subsequently realised that he alone was to blame... In short, only the Turk is a gentleman and freedom exists only in Turkey" - Friedrich Engels

"The most outstanding contribution of Ivan the Terrible

was that he was the first to introduce the government monopoly of external trade. Ivan the Terrible was the first and Lenin was the second" - J.V. Stalin

"The nomadic system of Mongolia and Central Asia has been directly linked with socialism" - Mao Zedong

"One of Caesar's first acts upon becoming consul was to have the proceedings of the Senate and Assembly publicly posted daily, making both bodies more accountable to the citizenry. During his first consulship in 59, he regularly disgarded auspices. He updated and streamlined the voter registration rolls. And he decisively terminated Cicero's political witch-hunts against popular leaders, supporting Clodius in driving Cicero into exile in 58 for what proved to be only a brief period. During his later consulships he divested the senatorial oligarchy of its unaccountable executive powers including its control over the treasury, and secured the powers of the people's tribunate to initiate legislation. Whether such moves are deemed despotic or democratic depends on the perspective from which they are viewed. He accumulated individual power in order to break the oligarchic stranglehold and thereby initiate popular reforms. Without too much overreaching, we might say his reign can be called a dictatorship of the proletarii, an instance of ruling autocratically against plutocracy on behalf of the citizenry's substantive interests" - (Michael Parenti, The Assassination of Julius Caesar: A People's History of Ancient Rome)

"The Mongols were responsible for the ability of the East Slavs to resume their expansion eastward. Such movement required a stronger centralised government, which arose under Muscovite leadership because the Mongols had weakened the petty Russian principalities and the power of the aristocracy (boiarstvo). The lower classes were thus unimpeded in supporting the creation of a powerful unified state which could protect Russia from the steppe; Nevskii's two feats were fighting off the Latin enemies and submitting in all humility to the Mongols, thus saving Russian national consciousness and Orthodoxy. The Mongols saved Russia from the Catholics by defeating Grand Prince Vitovt of Lithuania at the battle on the river Vorskla in 1399" - (George Vernadsky, Eurasianism, the Mongols and Russia)

"Urukagina claimed to have put an end to all this. He humbled the bureaucrats, he cut taxes and in some cases entirely abolished them; he restored the temple's property, but ensured that the priests no longer oppressed the lay public. He redressed the inequalities of power, the oppression of the poor by the wealthy: 'If the house of a rich man is next to the house of a poor man, and if the rich man says to the poor man, 'I want to buy it,' then if the poor man wishes to sell he may say 'pay me in silver as much as I think just, or reimburse me with an equivalent amount of barley'. But if the poor man does not wish to sell the house, the rich man may not force him.' He freed citizens who had fallen into irretrievable debt, or were falsely accused of theft or murder. 'He promised the god Ningirsu that he would not allow widows and orphans to be victimised by the powerful. He established freedom for the citizens of Lagash'" - (Paul Kriwaczek, Babylon, Mesopotamia and the birth of civilisation)

"Vipper's concept of popular monarchy may be described as 'divisive' rather than 'inclusive': a 'democratic monarchy' in which the ruler attempts to ally himself with the lower classes against the nobility" - Maureen Perrie

"A closer resemblance - as I have more than once taken occasion to notice - may be found between the Peruvian institutions and some of the despotic governments of Eastern Asia... Such were the Chinese, who the Peruvians resembled in their implicit obedience to authority, their mild yet somewhat stubborn temper, their solicitude for forms, their reverence for ancient usage, their skill in the minuter manufactures, their imitative rather than inventive cast of mind, and their invincible patience, which serves instead of an adventurous spirit for the execution of difficult undertakings. A still closer analogy may be found with the natives of Hindostan in their division into castes, their worship of the heavenly bodies and the elements of nature, and their acquaintance with the scientific principles of husbandry. To the ancient Egyptians, also, they bore considerable resemblance in the same particulars..." - (Historians)

"'If the sovereign was the patrimonial owner (votchinnik) of his tsardom, then it belonged to him as his property, with all the unconditionality of ownership rights [...]. If the power of the sovereign was based on the consciousness of the people (narodnaia massa), who saw the tsar and grand prince of all Rus' as the expression of national (narodnoe) unity and the symbol of national (natsional' naia) independence, then the democratic (demokraticheskii) character of this power is obvious [...] Thus power in Muscovy was both absolute and democratic'; But, while stressing the 'harmonic' nature of the Muscovite state system, which combined autocracy (samoderzhavie) with local self-government (samoupravlenie), Solonevich also argued that the lower classes, with their anti-boyar attitudes, played an important part in the creation of the Muscovite autocratic system; The monarchy was created and supported by the masses, including the peasants, and this imbued it with its democratic character. 'In place of an all-powerful despot wielding arbitrary power over cowering slaves, these studies have found a monarch ruling in council with this boyars and elites, constrained to rule according to custom, tradition, piety, and even law, enjoying a high degree of legitimacy in the eyes of his subjects'; But they do not exclude the possibility that peasants, if not serfs and slaves, might be included in the political community. Societal participation; that; describes the seventeenth-century state as a 'popular monarchy' (narodnaia monarhiia); Moscow sponsored and protected pretenders to the khanate of Kazan; in the eighteenth century, according to a recent estimate, fully one-third of Russian aristocratic families bore Turkic names; The Muscovite state showed tolerance to the Muslims in Russia, and in a very pronounced manner in the autonomous Khanate… until the end of the seventeenth century tens of thousands of Russian peasants were dependent on Muslim Tatars; 'Between the Russians and Tatars there is no noticeable mutual hatred and our people now are extraordinarily regretful about the departure of the latter'; 'The general opinion of those who know the Crimea is unanimously in favour of the Tatars. This people is quiet and submissive and does not have any sort of prejudice against the Russian government'; Toktu was young and inexperienced, and Nogai doubtless expected to find him a docile pupil. Within and without Kipchak, the great viceroy was treated as the real khan. The Russian chroniclers gave him the title of Tsar ('Tsar' was the common Russian title for the Khan: only later was it transferred to the native sovereign, the grand Duke of Muscovy)" - (Historians)

TERMINOLOGY:

"The bourgeoisie has disclosed how it came to pass that the brutal display of vigour in the Middle Ages, which reactionaries so much admire, found its fitting complement in the most slothful indolence. It has been the first to show what man's activity can bring about. It has accomplished wonders far surpassing Egyptian pyramids, Roman aqueducts, and Gothic cathedrals; it has conducted expeditions that put in the shade all former Exoduses of nations and crusades" - Karl Marx

"The lower middle class, the small manufacturer, the shopkeeper, the artisan, the peasant, all these fight against the bourgeoisie, to save from extinction their existence as fractions of the middle class. They are therefore not revolutionary, but conservative. Nay more, they are reactionary, for they try to roll back the wheel of history. If by chance, they are revolutionary, they are only so in view of their impending transfer into the proletariat; they thus defend not their present, but their future interests, they desert their own standpoint to place themselves at that of the proletariat" - Karl Marx

"[Reactionary] A political position that maintains a conservative response to change, including threats to social institutions and technological advances. Reaction is the reciprocal action to revolutionary movement. Reactionaries clamp down on differences of the emerging productive forces in society, and attempt to remove those differences, silence them, or segregate them in order to keep the stability of the established order" - (Encyclopedia of Marxism)

"Something is aufheben when it is superseded by

something else. 'Supersede' and 'transcend' do not carry the same connotation however as 'abolish,' in which the old is actually terminated and got rid of by that which supersedes it; 'sublation' carries the connotation of 'including' the old in the new, but is altogether too platonic and misses the sense of 'abolish.' Engels authorised the use of 'abolish' in the English translation of The Communist Manifesto where it talks of the aufheben of the family; this however gives leeway to those who would simply ban the institutions of religion, or dismiss the very existence of spiritual needs. The translators of the Introduction to the Critique of Hegel's Philosophy of Right variously used 'abolish' and 'supersede' according to context. Generally speaking, when reading English translations of Marx and Engels, the words 'abolish,' 'supersede' and 'sublate' are most likely translations of aufheben, and should be understood in that sense, as something being made obsolete by means of resolving the problems that gave rise to it in some new way" - (Encyclopedia of Marxism)

DOGMATISM:

"The Philosophers have only interpreted the world, in various ways. The point, however is to change it" - Karl Marx

"Volume One of Marx's Capital gives a detailed description of the condition of the British working class for about 1865, i.e. the time when Britain's industrial prosperity had reached its peak. I would therefore have had to repeat what Marx says. It will be hardly necessary to point out that the general theoretical standpoint of this book - philosophical, economical, political, - does not exactly coincide with my standpoint of today" - Friedrich Engels

"…They themselves do not for the most part understand the theory and treat it in doctrinaire and dogmatic fashion as something which, having once been learnt by rote, is sufficient as it stands for any and every need. To them it is a credo, not a guide to action. Besides which, they refuse to learn English on principle" - Friedrich Engels

"The masses must make themselves heard in order to propel the party ship forward. Then we will be able to face the future confidently" - Rosa Luxemburg

"We have made the start. When, at what date and time, and the proletariat of which nation will complete this process is not important. The important thing is that the ice has been broken; the road is open, the way has been shown" - V.I. Lenin

"Marxism is not a lifeless dogma, not a completed, ready-made, immutable doctrine, but a living guide to action" - V.I. Lenin

"One must not fear criticism, or gloss over

shortcomings; on the contrary, it is necessary to help to make them known and to see nothing discreditable in doing so. Only he can be discredited who conceals his shortcomings, who is unwilling to fight against evils, that is, precisely the man who ought to be discredited. It is necessary to be able to see the truth and to imbibe it from the masses and from all who are taking part in production. There is nothing worse than self-praise and self-satisfaction. It is possible to go forward only when, step by step, evils are sought out and overcome. At the same time, an end must be put to our established practice of humouring the masses – the workers. It should be remembered that in our country the workers, like ourselves, are not yet cultured, that often their group interests outweigh the interests of the working class as a whole; often they do not sufficiently realise that only their own useful labour, the productivity of their labour, can create the communist state, maintain their Soviet power. Every economic manager should wage a struggle to win prestige, to win the confidence of the working masses, but the struggle for this confidence should on no account employ the instrument of demagogy, of humouring the masses, satisfying them to the detriment and at the expense of the state, of the interests of the alliance with the peasants, of parochial requirements. The path of demagogy is perhaps the most harmful path, lulling the masses, deflecting them from the main tasks of the working class in production, diminishing the sacrifices the working class has made and, in the final analysis, one which is harmful for our industry..." - Felix E. Dzerzhinsky

"Oppose book worship; Seek truth from facts; No investigation, no right to speak" - Mao Zedong

"The Communist Party does not fear criticism because we are Marxists, the truth is on our side, and the basic masses, the workers and peasants, are on our side" - Mao Zedong

"Yet another form (of idealism) is to wave a 'red flag' to oppose the Red Flag; while peddling idealist apriorism and the idealist historical viewpoint. In the face of the class enemies constantly applying idealism to carry out anti-Party conspiratorial activities, a matter of major importance for the fate of the Party and the state, each and every revolutionary should rise up to voice his condemnation of idealism and must by no means think that it has nothing to do with him..." - Mao Zedong

"People may ask, since Marxism is accepted as the guiding ideology by the majority of the people in our country, can it be criticised? Certainly it can. Marxism is scientific truth and fears no criticism. If it did, and if it could be overthrown by criticism, it would be worthless. In fact, aren't the idealists criticising Marxism every day and in every way? And those who harbour bourgeois and petty-bourgeois ideas and do not wish to change - aren't they also criticising Marxism in every way? Marxists should not be afraid of criticism from any quarter. Quite the contrary, they need to temper and develop themselves and win new positions in the teeth of criticism and in the storm and stress of struggle. Fighting against wrong ideas is like being vaccinated - a man develops greater immunity from disease as a result of vaccination. Plants raised in hothouses are unlikely to be hardy. Carrying out the policy of letting a hundred flowers blossom and a hundred schools of thought contend will not weaken, but strengthen, the leading position of Marxism in the ideological field" - Mao Zedong

"All erroneous ideas, all poisonous weeds, all ghosts and monsters, must be subjected to criticism; in no circumstance should they be allowed to spread unchecked" - Mao Zedong

"If you don't study the negative stuff, you won't be able to refute it. Neither Marx nor Engels nor Lenin was like that. They made great efforts to learn and study all sorts of things, contemporary and past, and taught other people to do likewise" - Mao Zedong

"Our dogmatists are lazy-bones. They refuse to

undertake any painstaking study of concrete things, they regard general truths as emerging out of the void, they turn them into purely abstract unfathomable formulas, and thereby completely deny and reverse the normal sequence by which man comes to know truth... They understand nothing of the Marxist theory of knowledge" - Mao Zedong

"If we have shortcomings, we are not afraid to have them pointed out and criticised, because we serve the people. Anyone, no matter who, may point out our shortcomings. If he is right, we will correct them. If what he proposes will benefit the people, we will act upon it" - Mao Zedong

"When we say Marxism is correct, it is certainly not because Marx was a 'prophet' but because his theory has been proved correct in our practice and in our struggle. We need Marxism in our struggle. In our acceptance of his theory no such formalisation of mystical notions as that of 'prophecy' ever enters our minds. Many who have read Marxist books have become renegades from the revolution, whereas illiterate workers often grasp Marxism very well" - Mao Zedong

"When you are forced to read something, that probably is good for you. Some say that I have never committed any mistake. As a matter of fact, I believed in Confucius's feudalism when I was a little boy. Later, when I entered school, I believed in capitalism, taking [George] Washington and Napoleon as great heroes, and looking upon [Oliver] Cromwell, [Duke of] Wellington, and Admiral [Horatio] Nelson as wonderful human beings" - Mao Zedong

"You cannot carry out fundamental change without a certain amount of madness. In this case, it comes from nonconformity, the courage to turn your back on the old formulas, the courage to invent the future. It took the madmen of yesterday for us to be able to act with extreme clarity today. I want to be one of those madmen. We must dare to invent the future" - Thomas Sankara

"We cannot mechanically apply what Comrade Mao Zedong said about a particular question to another question, what he said in a particular place to another place, what he said at a particular time to another time, or what he said under particular circumstances to other circumstances" - Deng Xiaoping

"All sense of dialectics is lost when someone believes that today's economy is identical to the economy of 50 or 100 or 150 years ago, or that it is identical to the one in Lenin's day or to the time when Karl Marx lived" - Fidel Castro

BOURGEOIS IDEOLOGY:

"Throughout the civilised world the teachings of Marx evoke the utmost hostility and hatred of all bourgeois science (both official and liberal), which regards Marxism as a kind of 'pernicious sect'. And no other attitude is to be expected, for there can be no 'impartial' social science in a society based on class struggle. In one way or another, all official and liberal science defends wage-slavery, whereas Marxism has declared relentless war on that slavery. To expect science to be impartial in a wage-slave society is as foolishly naïve as to expect impartiality from manufacturers on the question of whether workers' wages ought not to be increased by decreasing the profits of capital" - V.I. Lenin

"Take our old Economists. They too howled that their opponents were conspirators, Jacobins (see the Rabocheye Dyelyo, especially No. 10, and Martynov's speech in the debate on the program at the Second Congress), that by plunging into politics they were divorcing themselves from the masses, that they were losing sight of the fundamentals of the working-class movement, ignoring the initiative of the workers, etc., etc. In reality these supporters of the 'initiative of the workers' were opportunist intellectuals who tried to foist on the workers their own narrow and philistine conception of the tasks of the proletariat. In reality the opponents of Economism, as everyone can see from the old Iskra, did not neglect or push into the background any of the aspects of Social-Democratic work, nor did they in the least forget the economic struggle; but they were able at the same time to present the urgent and immediate political tasks in their full scope and they opposed the transformation of the workers' party into an 'economic' appendage of the liberal bourgeoisie" - V.I. Lenin

"For the socialist of another country cannot expose the government and bourgeoisie of a country at war with 'his own' nation, and not only because he does not know that country's language, history, specific features, etc., but also because such exposure is part of imperialist intrigue, and not of internationalist duty" - V.I. Lenin

"They tell you that socialism would destroy your individuality. That would be miraculous - that would be a miracle! Because you have none. No man has any individuality who has got to beg for permission to live" - Eugene Debs

"Marxism is the sharpest weapon of the proletariat" - William Z. Foster

"A system cannot fail those it was never meant to protect" - W.E.B. Du Bois

"If you're not careful, the newspapers will have you hating the people who are being oppressed, and loving the people who are doing the oppressing" - Malcolm X

"[In order to rid society of bourgeois ideas], it is necessary at the same time to criticise and repudiate those representatives of the bourgeoisie who have sneaked into the party, the government and the army... [and] to clear them out or transfer some of them to other positions" - Mao Zedong

"That's all the media and the politicians are ever talking about - the things that separate us, things that make us different from one another. That's the way the ruling class operates in any society. They try to divide the rest of the people. They keep the lower and middle classes fighting with each other so that they, the rich, can run off with all the fucking money!" - George Carlin

"We're taught from an early age to be against Communists, yet most of us don't have the faintest idea what Communism is. Only a fool lets somebody else tell him who his enemy is" - Assata Shakur

HISTORY/ EDUCATION:

"Men make their own history, but they do not make it as they please; they do not make it under self-selected circumstances, but under circumstances existing" - Karl Marx

"The bourgeoisie turns everything into a commodity, even the writing of history. The best-paid historians are the ones best able to falsify history for the purposes of the bourgeoisie" - Friedrich Engels

"Sometimes, history needs a push; There are decades where nothing happens; and there are weeks where decades happen" - V.I. Lenin

"All over the world, wherever there are capitalists, freedom of the press means freedom to buy up newspapers, to buy writers, to bribe, buy and fake 'public opinion' for the benefit of the bourgeoisie" - V.I. Lenin

"We must not borrow the system of encumbering young people's minds with an immense acount of knowledge, nine-tenths of which was useless and one-tenth distorted. This, however, does not mean that we can restrict ourselves to Communist conclusions and learn only Communist slogans. You will not create communism that way. You can become a Communist only when you enrich your mind with a knowledge of all the treasures created by mankind" - V.I. Lenin

"Education is a weapon whose effects depend on who holds it in his hands and at who it is aimed" - J.V. Stalin

"The bourgeoisie, with its arbitrary, eclectic style of

history writing, has no idea of the process of past events, or how things arise in the present" - William Z. Foster

"In the United States, for over a hundred years, the ruling interests tirelessly propagated anticommunism among the populace, until it became more like a religious orthodoxy than a political analysis. During the Cold War, the anticommunist ideological framework could transform any data about existing Communist societies into hostile evidence. If the Soviets refused to negotiate a point, they were intransigent and belligerent; if they appeared willing to make concessions, this was but a skillful ploy to put us off our guard. By opposing arms limitations, they would have demonstrated their aggressive intent; but when in fact they supported most armament treaties, it was because they were mendacious and manipulative. If the churches in the U.S.S.R. were empty, this demonstrated that religion was suppressed; but if the churches were full, this meant the people were rejecting the regime's atheistic ideology. If the workers went on strike (as happened on infrequent occasions), this was evidence of their alienation from the collectivist system; if they didn't go on strike, this was because they were intimidated and lacked freedom. A scarcity of consumer goods demonstrated the failure of the economic system; an improvement in consumer supplies meant only that the leaders were attempting to placate a restive population and so maintain a firmer hold over them. If Communists in the United States played an important role struggling for the rights of workers, the poor, African-Americans, women, and others, this was only their guileful way of gathering support among disfranchised groups and gaining power for themselves. How one gained power by fighting for the rights of powerless groups was never explained. What we are dealing with is a nonfalsifiable orthodoxy, so assiduously marketed by the ruling interests that it affected people across the entire political spectrum" - Michael Parenti

"Real socialism, it is argued, would be controlled by the workers themselves through direct participation instead of being run by Leninists, Stalinists, Castroites, or other ill-willed, power-hungry, bureaucratic, cabals of evil men who betray revolutions. Unfortunately, this 'pure socialism' view is ahistorical and nonfalsifiable; it cannot be tested against the actualities of history. It compares an ideal against an imperfect reality, and the reality comes off a poor second. It imagines what socialism would be like in a world far better than this one, where no strong state structure of security force is required, where none of the value produced by the workers needs to be expropriated to rebuild society and defend it from invasion and internal sabotage. It is no suprise then that the pure socialists support every revolution except for the ones that succeed" - Michael Parenti

THE MASSES:

"First of all, the vanguard will divorce itself from the masses when it fails to perform its obligations as the vanguard of the people, when it fails to represent at all times and in all circumstances the maximum interests of the broadest possible sections of the people, when it fails to define correct tasks, policies and methods of work at the right time and when it fails to stick to the truth and correct its mistakes in good time. In other words, tailism and negligence willl lead to our estrangement from the masses; Secondly, the vanguard divroces itself from the masses when it fails to adopt a correct attitude and correct methods to lead them, when it fails to help them recognise in their own experience the correctness of the Partys slogans and act accordingly, when the slogans it adopts are too radical and the policies ultra-Left, or when the forms of struggle and organisation it advocated are impossible to carry out at the time or unacceptable to the masses. In other words, commandism, adventurism and closed-doorism will lead to isolation from the masses" - Liu Shaoqi

"As Stalin has said, leaders must maintain close ties with the masses, and the experience gained by both leaders and masses must be synthesised. Only thus can there be correct leadership" - Zhou Enlai

"The contradictions between ourselves and the enemy are antagonistic contradictions. Within the ranks of the people, the contradictions among the working people are non-antagonistic, while those between the exploited and the exploiting classes have a non-antagonistic as well as an antagonistic aspect. There have always been contradictions among the people, but they are different in content in each period of the revolution and in the period of building socialism. In the conditions prevailing in China today, the contradictions among the people comprise the contradictions within the working class, the contradictions within the peasantry, the contradictions within the intelligentsia, the contradictions between the working class and the peasantry, the contradictions between the workers and peasants on the one hand and the intellectuals on the other, the contradictions between the working class and other sections of the working people on the one hand and the national bourgeoisie on the other, the contradictions within the national bourgeoisie, and so on. Our People's Government is one that genuinely represents the people's interests, it is a government that serves the people. Nevertheless, there are still certain contradictions between this government and the people. These include the contradictions between the interests of the state and the interests of the collective on the one hand and the interests of the individual on the other, between democracy and centralism, between the leadership and the led, and the contradictions arising from the bureaucratic style of work of some of the state personnel in their relations with the masses. All these are also contradictions among the people. Generally speaking, the fundamental identity of the people's interests underlies the contradictions among the people" - Mao Zedong

"How should we judge whether a youth is a revolutionary? How can we tell? There can only be one criterion, namely, whether or not he is willing to integrate himself with the broad masses of workers and peasants and does so in practice. If he is willing to do so and actually does so, he is a revolutionary; otherwise he is a nonrevolutionary or a counter-revolutionary" - Mao Zedong

"As for people who are politically backward, Communists should not slight or despise them - but should befriend them - unite with them, and convince them and encourage them to go forward" - Mao Zedong

"The attitude of Communists towards any person who has made mistakes in his work should be one of persuasion in order to help him change and start afresh and not one of exclusion, unless he is incorrigible" - Mao Zedong

"To criticise the people's shortcomings is necessary… but in doing so we must truly take the stand of the people and speak out of whole-hearted eagerness to protect and educate them. To treat comrades like enemies is to go over to the stand of the enemy" - Mao Zedong

"The Chinese Communist Party is the only party in China, and in it's victory it will speak for the whole nation it cannot speak for the Russian people, or rule for the Third International, but only in the interests of the Chinese masses" - Mao Zedong

"If we tried to go on the offensive when the masses are not yet awakened, that would be adventurism. If we insisted on leading the masses to do anything against their will, we would certainly fail. If we did not advance when the masses demand advance, that would be Right opportunism" - Mao Zedong

"As revolutionaries we don't have the right to say that we are tired of explaining. We must never stop explaining. We know that when the people understand, they cannot help but follow us" - Thomas Sankara

"I just want to say something else do the do the one percent that top plutocracy which you know it's really not 1 percent you know that don't you, 1 percent would be 3 million people it's really more like a fraction about one-quarter of a tenth of 1% about 120,000 people who really compose the super-rich and have the wealth of America, and when people say whoa you know that the top 1% has as much wealth as the bottom 30 or 40% that's not true at all as the bottom 30-40 percent has nothing. I heard him [Robert Reich] say that the

140 richest billionaires have as much wealth as the poorest, oh what was it 75 million people. The poorest 75 million in America don't have a pot to spit in that most of them are in debt most of them are maxing out on their credit cards most of them are just barely getting by, how are you comparing these two. What what kind of a dazzling statistic is that supposed to be, but does that 1% believe their own mythologies? Yes of course people believe in their own virtue yes of course they believe in their own value to society of course. You think Mitt Romney doesn't think he's God's gift, well he's got a special problem with the Mormon stuff and all that but he thinks he's God's gift to to society for the most part. The class propaganda they put out elevates them, justifies their worth so why would they not believe it they find it very persuasive. We all find things very persuasive that are flattering to us rather things that are that are critical of us. You don't know what you're talking about what do you mean, that's what you say but when someone says something that's positive. You say oh you really think so hey, hmm they believed they believed you know it elevates them it justifies their wealth. So why would they not believe it, it's very persuasive because it serves their interests. They believe that the poor are the authors of their own poverty they believe their own wealth is earned and socially useful. It creates jobs it provides growth they believe the free market system is the most productive and beneficial in history they believe competing systems and reforms and government regulations are harmful and distract from the performance of the good things. They believe that government should not be a nanny state tending to the needs of the needy, let them learn self-reliance. Those people down there with their hands out at the same time they overlook the fact that their own class is not at all self-reliant no one is more reliant on government handouts than corporate America. They get tax breaks more than you and I get, they get about a hundred billion dollars a year out of every budget. Indirect subsidies, everything that they produce, almost everything, is, is subsidised by the

government. They get loan guarantees they get export subsidies they get equity grants and land giveaways, they get almost free leases on a lot of government land to do what, harvest the timber or mine the copper or drill for the oil. They get oil they get oil giveaways practically or leases or the land. I mean it'll be estimated that there's, that there's a fifteen billion dollars worth of oil on a certain reserve on government land and they'll issue the government release it to them for, for like half a million or a million peanuts or something so they can go ahead and take that. That's stealing from the public treasury, the airwaves, they get to lease the airwaves for a song for a song. Fox News gets to get these Airways the airwaves ladies and gentlemen brothers and sisters the airwaves are the property of the people of the United States, you'd never know it though. They're sent out and they're used to great profit by the media corporations and their advertisers and the like and they get bailouts they get billion-dollar bailouts, mom-and-pop doesn't get a bailout if things go down you go out of business you lose your grocery store you lose your little cafe whatever it is. Federal government does not give you a bailout and say hey you're too small to fail let's give you some more money to boost you up here a little bit. That doesn't happen in big corporate capitalism besides being hypocritical self-deluding and deluding us in an irrational system. Marx said it was a ruthlessly rational system that demystified and shattered the dark ages. You know there's that incredible paragraph in the Communist Manifesto where Marx and Engels talk about the dynamic productive energy of capitalism and how it broke loose from the shackles of a thousand years of the dark ages and if you read you know, and if you read the Enlightenment writers I had a book of an anthology of the enlightenment I started reading and I was so struck I mean I was just so struck by how naively enthusiastic they are" - Michael Parenti

CLASS:

"Once the aim of the proletarian movement - i.e., abolition of classes - is attained, the power of the state, which serves to keep the great majority of producers in bondage to a very small exploiter minority, disappears, and the functions of government become simple administrative functions. The Alliance draws an entirely different picture. It proclaims anarchy in proletarian ranks as the most infallible means of breaking the powerful concentration of social and political forces in the hands of the exploiters. Under this pretext, it asks the International, at a time when the Old World is seeking a way of crushing it, to replace its organisation with anarchy" - (Karl Marx, on the Juras Alliance)

"Wherever the class struggle is thrust aside as a distasteful, 'crude' manifestation, the only basis still left to socialism will be a 'true love of mankind' and empty phrases about 'justice'" - Karl Marx

"This class of petty-tradesmen, the great importance and influence of which we have already several times adverted to, may be considered as the leading class of the insurrection of May, 1849. There being, this time, none of the large towns of Germany among the center of the movement, the petty-trading class, which in middling and lesser towns always predominates, found the means of getting the direction of the movement into its hands. We have moreover, seen that, in this struggle for the Imperial Constitution, and for the rights of the German Parliament, there were the interests of this peculiar class at stake" - Karl Marx

"The great mass of so-called 'higher grade' workers

- such as state officials, military people, artists, doctors, priests, judges, lawyers, etc. - some of whom are not only not productive but in essence destructive, but who know how to appropriate to themselves a very great part of the 'material' wealth partly through the sale of their 'immaterial' commodities and partly by forcibly imposing the latter on other people - found it not at all pleasant to be relegated economically to the same class as clowns and menial servants and to appear merely as people partaking in the consumption, parasites on the actual producers (or rather agents of production). This was a peculiar profanation precisely of those functions which had hitherto been surrounded with a halo and had enjoyed superstitious veneration. Political economy in its classical period, like the bourgeoisie itself in its parvenu period, adopted a severely critical attitude to the machinery of the State, etc. At a later stage it realised and - as was shown too in practice - learnt from experience that the necessity for the inherited social combination of all these classes, which in part were totally unproductive, arose from its own organisation" - Karl Marx

"Some work better with their hands, others with their heads, one as a manager, engineer, technologist, etc., the other as overseer, the third as manual labourer or even drudge. An ever-increasing number of types of labour are included in the immediate concept of productive labour, and those who perform it are classed as productive workers, workers directly exploited by capital and subordinated to its process of production and expansion" - Karl Marx

"The same singer, when engaged by an entrepreneur who has her sing in order to make money, is a productive worker, for she directly produces capital" - Karl Marx

"The division of labour, which we already saw above as one of the chief forces of history up till now, manifests itself also in the ruling class as a division of mental and material labour, so that inside this class one part appears as the thinkers of the class (its active, conceptive ideologists, who make the perfecting of the illusion of the class about itself their chief source of livelihood), while the others' attitude to these ideas and illusions is more passive and receptive, because they are in reality the active members of this class and have less time to make up illusions and ideas about themselves. Within this class this cleavage can even develop into a certain opposition and hostility between the two parts, which, however, in the case of a practical collision, in which the class itself is endangered, automatically comes to nothing, in which case there also vanishes the semblance that the ruling ideas were not the ideas of the ruling class and had a power distinct from the power of this class. The existence of revolutionary ideas in a particular period presupposes the existence of a revolutionary class; about the premises for the latter sufficient has already been said above" - Karl Marx

"The distinction between skilled and unskilled labour rests in part on pure illusion, or, to say the least, on distinctions that have long since ceased to be real, and that survive only by virtue of a traditional convention; in part on the helpless condition of some groups of the working-class, a condition that prevents them from exacting equally with the rest the value of their labour-power. Accidental cirumstances here play so great a part, that these two forms of labour sometimes change places" - Karl Marx

"The petty-bourgeois democratic party in Germany is very powerful. It not only embraces the great majority of the urban middle class, the small industrial merchants and master craftsmen; it also includes among its followers the peasants and rural proletariat in so far as the latter has not yet found support among the independent proletariat of the towns. The relationship of the revolutionary worker's party to the petty-bourgeois democrats is this: it cooperates with them against the party which they aim to overthrow; it opposes them wherever they wish to secure their own position" - Karl Marx

"A certain strata of the working class who have been bribed [with] imperialist superprofits and converted to watchdogs of capitalism and corruptors of the labour movement" - V.I. Lenin

"As a matter of fact, the exposures merely dealt with the relations between the workers in a given trade and their employers, and all they achieved was that the sellers of labour power learned to sell their 'commodity' on better terms and to fight the purchasers over a purely commercial deal; Social Democracy [Workers movement] represents the working class, not in its relation to a given group of employers alone, but in its relation to all classes of modern society and to the state as an organised political force. Hence, it follows that not only must Social-Democrats not confine themselves exclusively to the economic struggle, but that they must not allow the organisation of economic exposures to become the predominant part of their activities. We must take up actively the political education of the working class and the development of its political consciousness" - V.I. Lenin

"The so-called 'working' peasant is in fact a small proprietor, or a petty-bourgeois, who nearly always either hires himself out to work for somebody else or hires workers himself. Being a small proprietor, the 'working' peasant also vacillates in politics between the masters and the workers, between the bourgeoisie and the proletariat" - V.I. Lenin

"The question arises: what elements predominate? Clearly in a small-peasant country, the petty-bourgeois element predominates and it must predominate, for the great majority of those working the land are small commodity producers" - V.I. Lenin

"It is also clear that, in general, the arrest of the Kadets and quasi-Kadets was the necessary and correct measure to take... What a tragedy, you're thinking! What an injustice! Intellectuals in prison for several days or even weeks just to prevent the massacre of tens of thousands of workers and peasants... The forces of the workers and peasants are growing and getting stronger in their fight to overthrow the bourgeoisie and their acomplices, the educated classes, the lackeys of capital, who consider themselves the brains of the nation. In fact they are not its brains but its shit" - V.I. Lenin

"We have a similar situation as regards the problem of the abolition of the antithesis between mental and physical labour. This too is a well-known problem which was discussed by Marx and Engels long ago. The economic basis of the antithesis between mental and physical labour is the exploitation of the physical workers by the mental workers. Everyone is familiar with the gulf under which capitalism divided the physical workers of enterprises from the managerial personnel. We know that this gulf gave rise to a hostile attitude on the part of the workers towards managers, foremen, engineers and other members of the technical staff, whom the workers regarded as their enemies" - J.V. Stalin

"Engels has created a lot of confusion here. There was a time when we used to boast that the technical staff and the engineers would receive not more than what the qualified workers get. Engels did not understand a thing about production and he confounded us too. It is as ridiculous as the other opinion that the higher administrative staff must be changed every so often. If we had gone along with this everything would have been lost" - J.V. Stalin

"The landlord class and the comprador class. [A comprador, in the original sense of the word, was the Chinese manager or the senior Chinese employee in a foreign commercial establishment. The compradors served foreign economic interests and had close connection with imperialism and foreign capital]. In economically backward and semi-colonial China the landlord class and the comprador class are wholly appendages of the international bourgeoisie, depending upon imperialism for their survival and growth.

These classes represent the most backward and most reactionary relations of production in China and hinder the development of her productive forces. Their existence is utterly incompatible with the aims of the Chinese revolution. The big landlord and big comprador classes in particular always side with imperialism and constitute an extreme counterrevolutionary group. Their political representatives are the Étatistes and the right-wing of the Kuomintang" - Mao Zedong

"Marx pointed out that ordinary engineers and technicians join in the creation of surplus value. That is to say, they, too, are exploited by the capitalists" - Deng Xiaoping

"Unlike the dominant tendency within contemporary stratification theory, Marxian class analysis is less interested in the prestige, status, rank, or honorific order of individuals, their style of life, family background, and social connections, than in their economic function and power to change the mode of production and distribution and to alter the course of future history" - Donald C. Hodges

"Class gets its significance from the process of surplus extraction. The relationship between worker and owner is essentially and exploitative one, involving the constant transfer of wealth from those who labour (but do not own) to those who own (but do not labour). This is how some people get richer and richer without working, or with doing only a fraction of the work that enriches them, while others toil hard for an entire lifetime only to end up with little or nothing. Both orthodox social scientists and 'Left' ABC [Anything But Class] theorists treat the diverse social factions within the non-capitalist class as classes unto themselves; so they speak of a 'blue-collar class,' a 'professional class,' and the like. In doing so, they claim to be moving beyond a 'reductionist' Marxist dualistic model of classes. But what is more reductionist than to ignore the underlying dynamics of economic power and the conflict between capital and labour? What is more misleading than to treat occupational groups as autonomous classes, giving attention to every social group in capitalist society except the capitalist class itself, to every social conflict except class conflict? Both conventional and 'Left' ABC theorists have difficulty understanding that the creation of a managerial or technocratic social formation constitutes no basic change in the property relations of capitalism, no creation of new classes. Professionals and managers are not an autonomous class as such. Rather they are mental workers who live much better than most other employees but who still serve the accumulation process on behalf of corporate owners" - Michael Parenti

PEASANTS:

"The soil (and this, economically speaking, includes water) in the virgin state in which it supplies man with necessaries or the means of subsistence ready to hand, exists independently of him, and is the universal subject of human labour. All those things which labour merely separates from immediate connexion with their environment, are subjects of labour spontaneously provided by Nature. Such are fish which we catch and take from their element, water, timber which we fell in the virgin forest, and ores which we extract from their veins. If, on the other hand, the subject of labour has, so to say, been filtered through previous labour, we call it raw material; such is ore already extracted and ready for washing. All raw material is the subject of labour, but not every subject of labour is raw material: it can only become so, after it has undergone some alteration by means of labour" - Karl Marx

"The Communist peasant community no less than the feudal corvée farm and similar institutions maintain their economic organisation by subjecting the labour power, and the most important means of production, the land, to the rule of law and custom" - Rosa Luxemburg

"Can a class-conscious worker forget the democratic struggle for the sake of the socialist struggle, or forget the latter for the sake of the former? No, a class-conscious worker calls himself a Social-Democrat for the reason that he understands the relation between the two struggles. He knows that there is no other road to socialism save the road through democracy, through political liberty. He therefore strives to achieve democratism completely and consistently in order to attain the ultimate goal - socialism. Why are the conditions for the democratic struggle not the same as those for the socialist struggle? Because the workers will certainly have different allies in each of those two struggles. The democratic struggle is waged by the workers together with a section of the bourgeoisie, especially the petty-bourgeoisie. On the other hand, the socialist struggle is waged by the workers against the whole of the bourgeoisie. The struggle against the bureaucrat and the landlord can and must be waged together with all the peasants, even the well-to-do and the middle peasants. On the other hand, it is only together with the rural proletariat that the struggle against the bourgeoisie, and therefore against the well-to-do peasants too, can be properly waged" - V.I. Lenin

"Capitalism would not be capitalism if the 'pure' proletariat were not surrounded by a large number of exceedingly motley types intermediate between the proletarian and the semi-proletarian (who earns his livelihood in part by the sale of his labour power), between the semi-proletarian and the small peasant (and petty-artisan, handicraft worker and small master in general), between the small peasant and the middle peasant, and so on, and if the proletariat itself were not divided into more developed and less developed strata, if it were not divided according to territorial origin, trade, sometimes according to religion, and so on. And from all this follow the necessity, the absolute necessity, for the vanguard of the proletariat, for its class-conscious section, for the Communist Party, to resort to manoeuvres, agreements and compromises with the various groups of proletarians, with the various parties of the workers and small masters" - V.I. Lenin

"Particular attention should be paid to Marx's extremely profound remark that the destruction of the bureaucratic-military state machine is 'the precondition for every real people's revolution'. This idea of a people's revolution seems strange coming from Marx, so that the Russian Plekhanovites and Mensheviks, those followers of Struve who wish to be regarded as Marxists, might possibly declare such an expression to be a 'slip of the pen' on Marx's part. They have reduced Marxism to such a state of wretchedly liberal distortion that nothing exists for them beyond the antithesis between bourgeois revolution and proletarian revolution, and even this antithesis they interpret in an utterly lifeless way. If we take the revolutions of the 20th century as examples we shall, of course, have to admit that the Portuguese and the Turkish revolutions are both bourgeois revolutions. Neither of them, however, is a 'people's' revolution, since in neither does the mass of the people, their vast majority, come out actively, independently, with their own economic and political demands to any noticeable degree. By contrast, although the Russian bourgeois revolution of 1905-07 displayed no such 'brilliant' successes as at time fell to the Portuguese and Turkish revolutions, it was undoubtedly a 'real people's' revolution, since the mass of the people, their majority, the very lowest social groups, crushed by oppression and exploitation, rose independently and stamped on the entire course of the revolution the imprint of their own demands, their attempt to build in their own way a new society in place of the old society that was being destroyed. In Europe, in 1871, the proletariat did not constitute the majority of the people in any country on the Continent. A 'people's' revolution, one actually sweeping the majority into its stream, could be such only if it embraced both the proletariat and the peasants. These two classes then constituted the 'people'. These two classes are united by the fact that the 'bureaucratic-military state machine' oppresses, crushes, exploits them. To smash this machine, to break it up, is truly in the interest of the 'people', of their majority, of the workers and most of the peasants, is 'the precondition' for a free alliance of the poor peasant and the proletarians, whereas without such an alliance democracy is unstable and socialist transformation is impossible. As is well known, the Paris Commune was actually working its way toward such an alliance, although it did not reach its goal owing to a number of circumstances, internal and external. Consequently, in speaking of a 'real people's revolution', Marx, without in the least discounting the special features of the petty-bourgeois (he spoke a great deal about them and often), took strict account of the actual balance of class forces in most of the continental countries of Europe in 1871. On the other hand, he stated that the 'smashing' of the state machine was required by the interests of both the workers and the peasants, that it united them, that it placed before them the common task of removing the 'parasite' and of replacing it by something new" - V.I. Lenin

"Can the majority of the peasants in Russia demand and carry out the nationalisation of the land? Certainly it can. Would this be a socialist revolution? It would not. It would still be a bourgeois revolution, for the nationalisation of the land is a measure that is not incompatible with the existence of capitalism. It is, however, a blow to private ownership of the most important means of production. Such a blow would strengthen the proletarians and semi-proletarians far more than was the case during the revolutions of the seventeenth, eighteenth and nineteenth centuries" - V.I. Lenin

"Indeed, is it not clear that as far as the proletariat is concerned the struggle for the republic is inconceivable without an alliance with the petty-bourgeois masses? Is it not clear that without the revolutionary dictatorship of the proletariat and the peasantry there is not a shadow of hope for the success of this struggle?; Whatever the form, whatever the origin, whatever the conditions, one thing at any rate is clear - that the provisional revolutionary government must have the support of definite classes. One has only to remember this simple truth to realise that the provisional revolutionary government can be nothing else but the revolutionary dictatorship of the proletariat and the peasantry" - V.I. lenin

"Here I stand on the frontier between the old, capitalist

world and the new, socialist world. Here on this frontier I unite the efforts of the proletarians of the West and of the peasantry of the East in order to shatter the old world. May the god of history be my aid" - J.V. Stalin

"It is the peasants who are the source of China's industrial workers. In the future, additional tens of millions of peasants will go to the cities and enter factories. If China is to build up powerful national industries and many large modern cities, there will have to be a long process of transformation of rural into urban inhabitants. It is the peasants who constitute the main market for China's industry. Only they can supply foodstuffs and raw materials in great abundance and absorb manufactured goods in great quantities. It is the peasants who are the source of the Chinese army. The soldiers are peasants in military uniform, the mortal enemies of the Japanese aggressors. It is the peasants who are the main political force for democracy in China at the present stage. Chinese democrats will achieve nothing unless they rely on the support of the 360 million peasants. It is the peasants who are the chief concern of China's cultural movement at the present stage. If the 360 million peasants are left out, do not the 'elimination of illiteracy', 'popularisation of education', 'literature and art for the masses' and 'public health' become largely empty talk? In saying this, I am of course not ignoring the political, economomic and cultural importance of the rest of the people numbering about 90 million, and in particular am not ignoring the working class, which is politically the most conscious and therefore qualified to lead the whole revolutionary movement. Let there be no misunderstanding. It is absolutely necessary not only for Communists but for every democrat in China to grasp these points" - Mao Zedong

"There are two lines. Either stubbornly oppose the Chinese peasants' endeavour to settle the problem of democracy and the people's livelihood, and become corrupt, ineffectual and utterly incapable of fighting Japan; or firmly support the Chinese peasants in their endeavour, and gain the great of allies, constituting 80 percent of the population, thereby forging tremendous fighting strength. The former is the line of the Kuomintang government, the latter is the line of China's Liberated Areas. The line of the opportunists is to vacillate between the two, to profess support for the peasants and yet lack to resolve to reduce rent and interest, arm the peasants or establish democratic political power in the rural areas" - Mao Zedong

"It is the peasants who made the idols, and when the time comes they will cast the idols aside with their own hands; there is no need for anyone else to do it for them prematurely. The Communist Party's propaganda policy in such matters should be, 'Draw the bow without shooting, just indicate the motions.' It is for the peasants themselves to cast aside the idols, pull down the temples to the martyred virgins and the arches to the chaste and faithful widows; it is wrong for anybody else to do it for them" - Mao Zedong

TRANSITIONAL NATURE OF COMMUNISM:

"No social order is ever destroyed before all the productive forces for which it is sufficient have been developed, and new superior relations of production never replace older ones before the material conditions for their existence have matured within the framework of the old society..." - Karl Marx

""What we have to deal with here is a Communist society, not as it has developed on its own foundations, but, on the contrary, just as it emerges from capitalist society; which is thus in every respect, economically, morally, and intellectually, still stamped with the birthmarks of the old society from whose womb it emerges. Accordingly, the individual producer receives back from society - after the deductions have been made - exactly what he gives to it... These defects are inevitable in the first phase of Communist society as it is when it has just emerged after prolonged birth pangs from capitalist society. Right can never be higher than the economic structure of society and its cultural development conditioned thereby. In a higher phase of Communist society, after the enslaving subordination of the individual to the division of labour, and therewith also the antithesis between mental and physical labour, has vanished; after labour has become not only a means of life but life's prime want; after the productive forces have also increased and with the all-around development of the individual, and all the springs of co-operative wealth flow more abundantly - only then can the narrow horizon of bourgeois right be crossed in its entirety and society inscribe on its banners; From each according to his ability, to each according to his needs!" - Karl Marx

"The idea held by some socialists that we need capital but not the capitalists is altogether wrong. It is posited within the concept of capital that the objective conditions of labour - and these are its own product - take on a personality towards it, or, what is the same, that they are posited as the property of a personality alien to the worker. The concept of capital contains the capitalist" - Karl Marx

"The Communists therefore, are on the one hand, practically, the most advanced and resolute section of the working-class parties of every country, that section which pushes forward all others; on the other hand, theoretically, they have over the great mass of the proletariat the advantage of clearly understanding the line of march, the conditions, and the ultimate general results of the proletarian movement. The immediete aim of the Communists is the same as that of all other proletarian parties: formation of the proletariat into a class, overthrow of the bourgeois supremacy, conquest of political power by the proletariat" - Karl Marx

"The working class did not expect miracles from the Commune. They have no ready-made utopias to introduce par décret du peuple. They know that in order to work out their own emancipation, and along with it that higher form to which present society is irresistably tending by its own economical agencies, they will have to pass through long struggles, through a series of historic processes, transforming circumstances and men. They have no ideals to realise, but to set free the elements of the new society with which old collapsing bourgeois society itself is pregnant. In the full consciousness of their historic mission, and with the heroic resolve to act up to it, the working class can afford to smile at the coarse invective of the gentlemen's gentlemen with pen and inkhorn, and at the didactic patronage of well-wishing bourgeois-doctrinaires, pouring forth their ignorant platitudes and sectarian crotchets in the oracular tone of scientific infallibility" - Karl Marx

"Development of productive forces (which itself implies the actual empirical existence of men in their world-historical, instead of local, being) is an absolutely necessary practical premise because without it want is merely made general, and with destitution the struggle for necessities and all the old filthy business would necessarily be reproduced" - Karl Marx

"Every change in the social order, every revolution in property relations, is the necessary consequence of the creation of new forces of production which no longer fit into the old property relations... no more than existing forces of production can at one stroke be multiplied to the extent necessary for the creation of a communal society. In all probability, the proletarian revolution will transform existing society gradually and will be able to abolish private property only when the means of production are available in sufficient quantity" - Friedrich Engels

"'Will it be possible for private property to be abolished at one stroke?' - No, no more than existing forces of production can at one stroke be multiplied to the extent necessary for the creation of a communal society. In all probability, the proletarian revolution will transform existing society gradually and will be able to abolish private property only when the means of production are available in sufficient quantity" - Friedrich Engels

"From that time forward Socialism was no longer an accidental discovery of this or that ingenious brain, but the necessary outcome of the struggle between two historically developed classes - the proletariat and the bourgeoisie. Its task was no longer to manufacture a system of society as perfect as possible, but to examine the historico-economic succession of events from which these classes and their antagonism had of necessity sprung, and to discover in the economic conditions thus created the means of ending the conflict" - Friedrich Engels

"Though social production remains, the determination of value still prevails in the sense that the regulation of labour-time and the distribution of social labour among various production groups becomes more essential than ever, as well as the keeping of accounts on this" - Friedrich Engels

"The proletariat seizes from state power and turns the means of production into state property to begin with. But thereby it abolishes itself as the proletariat, abolishes all class distinctions and class antagonisms, and abolishes also the state as state. Society thus far, operating amid class antagonisms, needed the state, that is, an organisation of the particular exploiting class, for the maintenance of its external conditions of production, and, therefore, especially, for the purpose of forcibly keeping the exploited class in the conditions of oppression determined by the given mode of production (slavery, serfdom or bondage, wage-labour). The state was the official representative of society as a whole, its concentration in a visible corporation. But it was this only insofar as it was the state of that class which itself represented, for its own time, society as a whole: in ancient times, the state of slave-owning citizens; in the Middle Ages, of the feudal nobility; in our own time, of the bourgeoisie. When at last it becomes the real representative of the whole of society, it renders itself unnecessary. As soon as there is no longer any social class to be held in subjection, as soon as class rule, and the individual struggle for existence based upon the present anarchy in production, with the collisions and excesses arising from this struggle, are removed, nothing more remains to be held in subjection - nothing necessitating a special coercive force, a state. The first act by which the state really comes forward as the representative of the whole of society - the taking possession of the means of production in the name of society - is also its last independent act as a state. State interference in social relations becomes, in one domain after another, superfluous, and then dies down of itself. The government of persons is replaced by the administration of things, and by the conduct of processes of production. The state is not 'abolished'. It withers away. This gives the measure of the value of the phrase 'a free people's state', both as to its justifiable use for a long time from an agitational point of view, and as to its ultimate scientific insufficiency; and also of the so-called anarchists' demand that the state be abolished overnight" - Friedrich Engels

"In all probability, the proletarian revolution will transform existing society gradually and will be able abolish private property only when the means of production are in sufficient quantity" - Friedrich Engels

"So long as it is not possible to produce so much that there is enough for all all. With more left over for expanding social capital and extending the forces of production... there must always be a ruling class directing the use of society's productive forces, and a poor oppressed class" - Friedrich Engels

"Socialised production upon a predetermined plan becomes henceforth possible. The development of production makes the existence of different classes of society thenceforth an anachronism. In proportion as anarchy in social production vanishes, the political authority of the State dies out. Man, at last the master of his own form of social organisation, becomes at the same time the lord over Nature, his own master - free" - Friedrich Engels

[Do you intend to replace the existing social order by community of property at one stroke?] "We have no such intention. The development of the masses cannot be ordered by decree. It is determined by the development of the conditions in which these masses live, and therefore proceeds gradually" - Friedrich Engels

[How do you think the transition from the present situation to community of property is to be effected?] "The first, fundamental condition for the introduction of community of property is the political liberation of the proletariat through a democratic constitution" - Friedrich Engels

"In any socialist revolution. After the proletariat seizes power and basically finishes the task of depriving exploiters and supressing their revolt. It is bound to give priority to the fundamental task of creating a social structure higher than that of the capitalists and improving labour productivity" - V.I. Lenin

"No one, I think, in studying the question of the economic system of Russia, had denied its transitional character. Nor, I think, has any Communist denied that the term Socialist Soviet Republic implies the determination of Soviet power to achieve the transition to socialism, and not that the new economic system is recognised as a socialist order" - V.I. Lenin

"Socialism is inconceivable without large-scale capitalist engineering based on the latest discoveries of modern science. It is inconceivable without planned state organisation which keeps tens of millions of people to the strictest observance of a unified standard in production and distribution. We Marxists have always spoken of this, and it is not worth while wasting two seconds talking to people who do not understand even this (anarchists and a good half of the Left Socialist-Revolutionaries)" - V.I. Lenin

"You will find that, given a really revolutionary-democratic state, state - monopoly capitalism inevitably and unavoidably implies a step, and more than one step, towards socialism! For if a huge capitalist undertaking becomes a monopoly, it means that it serves the whole nation. If it has become a state monopoly, it means that the state (i.e., the armed organisation of the population, the workers and peasants above all, provided there is revolutionary democracy) directs the whole undertaking. In whose interest? Either in the interest of the landowners and capitalists, in which case we have not a revolutionary-democratic, but a reactionary-bureaucratic state, an imperialist republic. Or in the interest of revolutionary democracy - and then it is a step towards socialism. For socialism is merely the next step forward from state-capitalist monopoly. Or, in other words, socialism is merely state-capitalist monopoly which is made to serve the interests of the whole people and has to that extent ceased to be capitalist monopoly" - V.I. Lenin

"State capitalism would be a step forward as compared with the present state of affairs in our Soviet Republic... I can imagine with what noble indignation some people will recoil from these words. What! The transition to state capitalism in the Soviet Socialist Republic would be a step forward? Isn't this the betrayal of socialism? We must deal with this point in detail. Our state capitalism differs essentially from the state capitalism in countries that have bourgeois governments in that the state with us is represented not by the bourgeoisie, but by the proletariat, who has succeeded in winning the full confidence of the peasantry. On the contrary. The development of capitalism. Controlled and regulated by the proletarian state (i.e... 'state' capitalism in this sense of the term). is advantageous and necessary in an extremely devastated and backward small-peasant country..." - V.I. Lenin

"Socialism is not a ready-made system that will be mankind's benefactor. Socialism is the class struggle of the present-day proletariat as it advances from one objective today to another objective tomorrow for the sake of its basic objective, to which it is coming nearer every day" - V.I. Lenin

"In order to renovate our state apparatus we must at all costs set out, first, to learn, secondly to learn, and thirdly to learn, to learn, and then see to it that learning shall not remain a dead letter, or a fashionable catch-phrase, that learning shall really become part of our very being, that it shall actually and fully become a constituent element of our social life" - V.I. Lenin

"It means that, to a certain extent, we are re-creating capitalism. We are doing this quite openly. It is state capitalism. But state capitalism in a society where power belongs to capital, and state capitalism in a proletarian state, are two different concepts. In a capitalist state, capitalism means that it is recognised by the state and controlled by it for the benefit ofthe bourgeoisie, and to the detriment the proletariat. In the proletarian state, the same thing is done for the benefit of the working class, for the purpose withstanding the as yet strong bourgeoisie, and offighting it. It goes without saying that we must grant concessions to the foreign bourgeoisie, to foreign capital. Without the slightest denationalisation, we shall lease mines, forests and oilfields to foreign capitalists, and receive exchange manufactured goods, machinery etc., and thus restore our own industry" - V.I. Lenin

"The concessionaire is a capitalist. He conducts his business on capitalist lines, for profit, and is willing to enter into an agreement with the proletarian government in order to obtain superprofits or raw materials which he cannot otherwise obtain, or can obtain only with great difficulty" - V.I. Lenin

"There was only one such country at the close of the last century, when Anti-Duhring was published - Britain. There the development of capitalism and the concentration of production both in industry and in agriculture had reached such a point that it would have been possible, in the event of the assumption of power by the proletariat, to convert all the country's means of production into public property and to put an end to commodity production" - J.V. Stalin

"What then do we propose? We propose the establishment, after the thorough defeat of the Japanese aggressors, of a state system which we call New Democracy, namely, a united-front democratic alliance based on the overwhelming majority of the people, under the leadership of the working class. It is this kind of state system that truly meets the demands of the overwhelming majority of the Chinese population, because it can win and indeed has been winning the approval, first, of millions of industrial workers and tens of milions of handicraftsmen and farm labourers, second, of the peasantry, which constitutes 80 percent of China's population, i.e., 360 million out of a population of 450 million, and third, of the large numbers of the urban petty-bourgeoisie as well as the national bourgeoisie, the englightened gentry and other patriots. Of course, there are still contradictions among those classes, notably the contradiction between labour and capital, and consequently each has its own particular demands. It would be hypocritical and wrong to deny the existence of these contradictions and differing demands. But throughout the stage of New Democracy, these contradictions, these differing demands, will not grow and transcend the demands which we all have in common and should not be allowed to do so; they can be adjusted. Given such adjustment, these classes can together accomplish the political, economic and cultural tasks of the new-democratic state" - Mao Zedong

"No matter to what degree we open up to the outside world and admit foreign capital. It's relative magnitude will be small and it can't affect our system of socialist public ownership of the means of production. Absorbing foreign capital and technology and even allowing foreigners to construct plants in China can only play a complementary role to our efforts to develop the productive forces in a socialist society. Of course, this will bring some decadent capitalist influences into China. We are aware of this possibility: it's nothing to be afraid of" - Deng Xiaoping

"Our reform is an experiment not only for China but also for the rest of the world. We believe the experiment will succeed. If it does, our experience may be useful to the cause of world socialism and to other developing countries. If we assume that by mid-21st century our population will have reached 1.5 billion and that we shall a per capita GNP of $4,000, then our total annual GNP will be $6 trillion, and we will place China in the front ranks of nations. When we reach that goal, we shall not only have blazed a new path for the peoples of the Third World, who represent quarters of the world's population, but also - and this is even more important - shall have demonstrated to manking that socialism is the only path and that it is superior to capitalism" - Deng Xiaoping

"At present, we are still a relatively poor nation. It is impossible for us to undertake many international proletarian obligations, so our contributions remain small. However, once we have accomplished the four modernisations and the national economy has expanded, our contributions to mankind, and especially to the Third World, will be greater. As a socialist country, China shall always belong to the Third World and shall never seek hegemony. This idea is understandable because China is still quite poor, and is therefore a Third World country in the real sense of the term. The question is whether or not China will practise hegemony when it becomes more developed in the future. My friends, you are younger than I, so you will be able to see for yourselves what happens at that time. If it remains a socialist country, China will not practise hegemony and it will still belong to the Third World. Should China become arrogant, however, act like an overlord and give orders to the world, it would no longer be considered a Third World country. Indeed, it would cease to be a socialist country. I first addressed these points in a speech delivered at the Special Session of the United Nations General Assembly in 1974. The current foreign policy, which was formulated by Chairman Mao Zedong and Premier Zhou Enlai, will be passed on to our descendants" - Deng Xiaoping

"We want to do business. Quite right, business will be done. We are against no one except the domestic and foreign reactionaries who hinder us from doing business. Everybody should know that it is none other than the imperialists and their running dogs, the Chiang Kai-shek reactionaries, who hinder us from doing business and also from establishing diplomatic relations with foreign countries. When we have beaten the internal and external reactionaries by uniting all domestic and international forces, we shall be able to do business and establish diplomatic relations with all foreign countries on the basis of equality, mutual benefit and mutual respect for territorial integrity and sovereignty" - Mao Zedong

"Western economics' knowledge about finance, prices, currency, markets, competition, trade, exchange rates, industries, enterprises, growth, management, etc., reflects the general laws of socialised mass production and market economy, and should be used for reference. At the same time, with regard to foreign countries, especially Western economics, we must insist on removing the rough and the essence, removing the falsehood and keeping the truth, insisting on focusing on me and using it for me. For the content that reflects the attributes and values of the capitalist system, and for the content that has the color of Western ideology, Can't copy it. In our economics teaching, we must talk about Marxist political economy. We must talk about the political economy of socialism in contemporary China, and we must not be marginalised" - Xi Jinping

"Socialist politics with Chinese characteristics does not

exclude political participation by private enterprise owners as long as they follow the basic principles of the leadership of the CPC, people as masters of the country, and rule of law. Therefore, the ruling Party should allow the private enterprise owners to participate in politics within the framework of the system with Chinese characteristics and grant them full expression of their economic needs and political will. Of course, their political participation should be conducive, rather than detrimental, to safeguard the purity and vanguard nature of the ruling Party and the healthy development of socialist modernisation with Chinese characteristics" - Jin Huiming

Different Types of Socialism:

"In order to arouse sympathy the aristocracy was obliged to lose sight, apparently, of its own interests, and to formulate their indictment against the bourgeoisie in the interest of the exploited working class alone. Thus the aristocracy took their revenge by singing lampoons on their new masters and whispering in his ears sinister prophesies of the coming catastrophe. In this way arose feudal Socialism: half lamentation, half lampoon; half an echo of the past, half menace of the future; at times, by its bitter, witty and incisive criticism, striking the bourgeoisie to the very heart's core; but always ludicrous in its effect, through total incapacity to comprehend the march of modern history. The aristocracy, in order to rally the people to them, waved the proletarian alms-bag in front for a banner. But the people, so often as it joined them, saw on their hindquarters the old feudal coats of arms, and deserted with loud and irreverent laughter" - Karl Marx

"[How do Communists differ from socialists?] The so-called socialists are divided into three categories. [Reactionary Socialists:] The first category consists of adherents of a feudal and patriarchal society which has already been destroyed, and is still daily being destroyed, by big industry and world trade and their creation, bourgeois society. This category concludes, from the evils of existing society, that feudal and patriarchal society must be restored because it was free of such evils. In one way or another, all their proposals are directed to this end. This category of reactionary socialists, for all their seeming partisanship and their scalding tears for the misery of the proletariat, is nevertheless energetically opposed by the Communists for the following reasons: (i) It strives for something which is entirely impossible. (ii) It seeks to establish the rule of the aristocracy, the guildmasters, the small producers, and their retinue of absolute or feudal monarchs, officials, soldiers, and priests - a society which was, to be sure, free of the evils of present-day society but which brought it at least as many evils without even offering to the oppressed workers the prospect of liberation through a Communist revolution. (iii) As soon as the proletariat becomes revolutionary and Communist, these reactionary socialists show their true colors by immediately making common cause with the bourgeoisie against the proletarians. [Bourgeois Socialists:] The second category consists of adherents of present-day society who have been frightened for its future by the evils to which it necessarily gives rise. What they want, therefore, is to maintain this society while getting rid of the evils which are an inherent part of it. To this end, some propose mere welfare measures - while others come forward with grandiose systems of reform which, under the pretense of re-organising society, are in fact intended to preserve the foundations, and hence the life, of existing society. Communists must unremittingly struggle against these bourgeois socialists because they work for the enemies of Communists and protect the society which Communists aim to overthrow. [Democratic Socialists:] Finally, the third category consists of democratic socialists who favor some of the same measures the Communists advocate, as described in Question 18, not as part of the transition to Communism, however, but as measures which they believe will be sufficient to abolish the misery and evils of present-day society. These democratic socialists are either proletarians who are not yet sufficiently clear about the conditions of the liberation of their class, or they are representatives of the petty-bourgeoisie, a class which, prior to the achievement of democracy and the socialist measures to which it gives rise, has many interests in common with the proletariat. It follows that, in moments of action, the Communists will have to come to an understanding with these democratic socialists, and in general to follow as far as possible a common policy with them - provided that these socialists do not enter into the service of the ruling bourgeoisie and attack the Communists. It is clear that this form of co-operation in action does not exclude the discussion of differences" - Friedrich Engels

We Live In Socialism:

"Aside from the stock-company business, which represents the abolition of the capitalist private industry on the basis of the capitalist system itself and destroys private industry as it expands and invades new spheres of production" - Karl Marx

"The co-operative factories of the labourers themselves represent within the old form the first sprouts of the new, although they naturally reproduce, and must reproduce, everywhere in their actual organisation all the shortcomings of the prevailing system. But the antithesis between capital and labour is overcome within them, if at first only by way of making the associated labourers into their own capitalist, i.e., by enabling them to use the means of production for the employment of their own labour. They show how a new mode of production naturally grows out of an old one, when the development of the material forces of production and of the corresponding forms of social production have reached a particular stage. Without the factory system arising out of the capitalist mode of production there could have been no co-operative factories. Nor could these have been developed without the credit system arising out of the same mode of production. The credit system is not only the principal basis for the gradual transformation of capitalist private enterprises into capitalist stock companies, but equally offers the means for the gradual extension of co-operative enterprises on a more or less national scale. The capitalist stock companies, as much as the co-operative factories, should be considered as transitional forms from the capitalist mode of production to the associated one, with the only distinction that the antagonism is resolved negatively in the one and positively in the other" - Karl Marx

"It reproduces a new financial aristocracy, a new variety of parasites in the shape of promoters, speculators and simply nominal directors a whole system of swindling and cheating by means of corporation promotion, stock issuance, and stock speculation. It is private production without the control of private property... Success and failure both lead here to a centralisation of capital, and thus to expropriation on the most enormous scale. Expropriation extends here from the direct producers to the smaller and the medium-sized capitalists themselves. It is the point of departure for the capitalist mode of production; its accomplishment is the goal of this production. In the last instance, it aims at the expropriation of the means of production from all individuals" - Karl Marx

"This result of the ultimate development of capitalist production is a necessary transitional phase towards the reconversion of capital into the property of producers, although no longer as the private property of the individual producers, but rather as the property of associated producers, as outright social property. On the other hand, the stock company is a transition toward the conversion of all functions in the reproduction process which still remain linked with capitalist property, into mere functions of associated producers, into social functions; It is the abolition of capital as private property within the framework of capitalist production itself" - Karl Marx

"The ideas of the ruling class are in every epoch the ruling ideas, i.e. the class which is the ruling material force of society, is at the same time its ruling intellectual force. The class which has the means of material production at its disposal, has control at the same time over the means of mental production, so that thereby, generally speaking, the ideas of those who lack the means of mental production are subject to it. The ruling ideas are nothing more than the ideal expression of the dominant material relationships, the dominant material relationships grasped as ideas; hence of the relationships which make the one class the ruling one, therefore, the ideas of its dominance. The individuals composing the ruling class possess among other things consciousness, and therefore think. Insofar, therefore, as they rule as a class and determine the extent and compass of an epoch, it is self-evident that they do this in its whole range, hence among other things rule also as thinkers, as producers of ideas, and regulate the production and distribution of the ideas of their age: thus their ideas are the ruling ideas of the epoch. For instance, in an age and in a country where royal power, aristocracy, and bourgeoisie are contending for mastery and where, therefore, mastery is shared, the doctrine of the separation of powers proves to be the dominant idea and is expressed as an 'eternal law'" - Karl Marx

"According to the materialist conception of history, the ultimately determining element in history is the production and reproduction of real life. Other than this neither Marx nor I have ever asserted. Hence if somebody twists this into saying that the economic element is the only determining one, he transforms that proposition into a meaningless, abstract, senseless phrase. The economic situation is the basis, but the various elements of the superstructure - political forms of the class struggle and its results, to wit: constitutions established by the victorious class after a successful battle, etc., juridical forms, and even the reflexes of all these actual struggles in the brains of the participants, political, juristic, philosophical theories, religious views and their further development into systems of dogmas - also exercise their influence upon the course of the historical struggles and in many cases preponderate in determining their form. There is an interaction of all these elements in which, amid all the endless host of accidents (that is, of things and events whose inner interconnection is so remote or so impossible of proof that we can regard it as non-existent, as negligible), the economic movement finally asserts itself as necessary. Otherwise the application of the theory to any period of history would be easier than the solution of a simple equation of the first degree" - Friedrich Engels

"Oppression by force was replaced by corruption; the sword, as the first social lever, by gold" - Friedrich Engels

"The materialist conception of history starts from the proposition that the production of the means to support human life and, next to production, the exchange of things produced, is the basis of all social structure; that in every society that has appeared in history, the manner in which wealth is distributed and society divided into classes or orders is dependent upon what is produced, how it is produced, and how the products are exchanged. From this point of view, the final causes of all social changes and political revolutions are to be sought, not in men's brains, not in men's better insights into eternal truth and justice, but in changes in the modes of production and exchange. They are to be sought, not in the philosophy, but in the economics of each particular epoch. The growing perception that existing social institutions are unreasonable and unjust, that reason has become unreason, and right wrong, is only proof that in the modes of production and exchange changes have silently taken place with which the social order, adapted to earlier economic conditions, is no longer in keeping" - Friedrich Engels

"The present situation of society - this is now pretty generally conceded - is the creation of the ruling class of today, of the bourgeoisie. The mode of production peculiar to the bourgeoisie, known, since Marx, as the capitalist mode of production, was incompatible with the feudal system, with the privileges it conferred upon individuals, entire social ranks and local corporations, as well as with the hereditary ties of subordination which constituted the framework of its social organisation. The bourgeoisie broke up the feudal system and built upon its ruins the capitalist order of society, the kingdom of free competition, of personal liberty, of the equality, before the law, of all commodity owners, of all the rest of the capitalist blessings. Thenceforward, the capitalist mode of production could develop in freedom. Since steam, machinery, and the making of machines by machinery transformed the older manufacture into modern industry, the productive forces, evolved under the guidance of the bourgeoisie, developed with a rapidity and in a degree unheard of before. But just as the older manufacture, in its time, and handicraft, becoming more developed under its influence, had come into collision with the feudal trammels of the guilds, so now modern industry, in its complete development, comes into collision with the bounds within which the capitalist mode of production holds it confined. The new productive forces have already outgrown the capitalistic mode of using them. And this conflict between productive forces and modes of production is not a conflict engendered in the mind of man, like that between original sin and divine justice. It exists, in fact, objectively, outside us, independently of the will and actions even of the men that have brought it on. Modern Socialism is nothing but the reflex, in thought, of this conflict in fact; its ideal reflection in the minds, first, of the class directly suffering under it, the working class" - Friedrich Engels

"In the trusts, freedom of competition changes into its

very opposite - into monopoly; and the production without any definite plan of capitalistic society capitulates to the production upon a definite plan of the invading socialistic society. Certainly, this is so far still to the benefit and advantage of the capitalists. But, in this case, the exploitation is so palpable, that it must break down. No nation will put up with production conducted by trusts, with so barefaced an exploitation of the community by a small band of dividend-mongers" - Friedrich Engels

"The growing perception that existing social institutions are unreasonable and unjust, that reason has become unreason, and right wrong, is only proof that in the modes of production and exchange changes have silently taken place with which the social order, adapted to earlier economic conditions, is no longer in keeping. From this it also follows that the means of getting rid of the incongruities that have been brought to light must also be present, in a more or less developed condition, within the changed modes of production themselves" - Friedrich Engels

"[O]nly people who shut their eyes so as not to see, and stuff their ears so as not to hear, can fail to notice that all over the world the birth pangs of the old, capitalist society, which is pregnant with socialism, have begun" - V.I. Lenin

"Capitalist property is impersonal. Finance has taken it upon itself to tear the last veils that masked this impersonality; In capitalist collectivism, the shareholders and obligors, between whom there is no relationship of kinship or nationality, and who do not know each other, collectively own the company (railway, spinning mill, foundry, mine, etc.). It is necessarily undivided, although its owners are scattered throughout every corner; these do not have - nor could they have - the use of their property, but collect the fruit individually, without providing any work" - Paul La Farge

In Defence of Chinese Socialism:

"Nor will we explain to them that it is only possible to achieve real liberation in the real world and by employing real means, that slavery cannot be abolished without the steam-engine and the mule and spinning-jenny, serfdom cannot be abolished without improved agriculture, and that, in general, people cannot be liberated as long as they are unable to obtain food and drink, housing and clothing in adequate quality and quantity" - Karl Marx

"The so-called 'socialist society' is not anything immutable. Like all other social formations, it should be conceived in a state of constant flux and change. Its crucial difference from the present order consists naturally in production organised on the basis of common ownership by the nature of all means of production" - Friedrich Engels

"Get down to business, all of you! You will have capitalists beside you, including foreign capitalists, concessionaires and leaseholders. They will squeeze profits out of you amounting to hundreds per cent; they will enrich themselves, operating alongside of you. Let them. Meanwhile you will learn from them the business of running the economy, and only when you do that will you be able to build a Communist republic. Since we must necessarily learn quickly, any slackness in this respect is a serious crime. And we must undergo this training, because we have no other way out. You must remember that our land is impoverished after man years of trial and suffering, and has no socialist France or socialist England as neighbours which could help us with their highly developed technology and their highly developed industry. Bear that in mind! We must remember that at present all their highly developed technology and highly developed industry belong to the capitalists, who are fighting us" - V.I. Lenin

"'Firmly establish the new-democratic social order.' That's a harmful formulation. In the transition period changes are taking place all the time and socialist factors are emerging every day. How can this 'new-democratic social order' be 'firmly established'? It would be very difficult indeed to 'establish' it 'firmly'! For instance, private industry and commerce are being transformed, and if an order is 'established' in the second half of the year, it will no longer hold 'firm' next year. And changes are taking place in mutual aid and co-operation in agriculture from year to year too. The period of transition is full of contradictions and struggles. Our present revolutionary struggle is even more profound than the revolutionary armed struggle of the past. It is a revolution that will bury the capitalist system and all other systems of exploitation once and for all. The idea, 'Firmly establish the new-democratic social order', goes against the realities of our struggle and hinders the progress of the socialist cause" - Mao Zedong

"'Don't you want to abolish state power?' Yes, we do, but not right now. We cannot do it yet. Why? Because imperialism still exists, because domestic reaction still exists, because classes still exist in our country; Our present task is to strengthen the people's state apparatus - mainly the people's army, the people's police and the people's courts - in order to consolidate national defence and protect the people's interests; The foreign reactionaries who accuse us of practicing 'dictatorship' or 'totalitarianism' are the very persons who practice it. They practice the dictatorship or totalitarianism of one class, the bourgeoisie, over the proletariat and the rest of the people. They are the very persons Sun Yat-sen spoke of as the bourgeoisie of modern states who oppress the common people; The state apparatus, including the army, the police and the courts, is the instrument by which one class oppresses another. It is an instrument for the oppression of antagonistic classes, it is violence and not 'benevolence.' We definitely do not apply a policy of benevolence to the reactionaries and towards the reactionary activities of the reactionary classes" - Mao Zedong

"The socialist society could probably be divided into

two phases. The first one is undeveloped socialism and the second one is relatively developed socialism. The latter may need much longer time to be achieved than the former" - Mao Zedong

"In a country such as China completing socialist construction is a tough task. Hence it's still early to say we've completed our socialist construction" - Mao Zedong

"Understanding China's realities is the fundamental basis for understanding all the problems of the revolution" - Mao Zedong

"The behaviour of the police in China was a revelation to me. They are there to protect and help the people, not to oppress them. Their courtesy was genuine; no division or suspicion exists between them and the citizens. This impressed me so much that when I returned to the United States and was met by the Tactical Squad at San Francisco airport (they had been called out because nearly a thousand people came to the airport to welcome us back), it was brought home to me all over again that the police in our country are an occupying, repressive force. I pointed this out to a customs officer in San Francisco, a Black man, who was armed, explaining to him that I felt intimidated seeing all the guns around. I had just left a country, I told him, where the army and police are not in opposition to the people but are their servants" - Huey P. Newton

"We shall not forget that the idea [of socialism] is not dead, but rather in a few countries the socialist society actually exists. Here, I am thinking of the People's Republic of China, which especially in current days has reinforced its determination to continue the successful development of socialism. After all, this is a country of 1.2 billion people. As you know, I've been to China [in 1986], and I can say with deep conviction that the ideas of Marx, Engels, Lenin, and Mao Zedong will keep getting realised with success. We have the valiant Vietnam, which fares the socialist path, and refused to be brought to its knees by the U.S. imperialists. And we have the beacon in Latin America: the brave Cuba under Fidel Castro. So socialism as such still actually exists; however the idea of course is in existence since Marx and Engels, founded on the basis of science, and it cannot be shaken by temporary setbacks" - Erich Honecker

"Deng Xiaoping Tried to save the G.D.R.:

'Comrade Egon Krenz

Today I held extensive talks with comrade Lin Hanxiong, minister of urban planning (who first visited the G.D.R. in 1982 to revitalise relations). Comrade Lin Hanxiong stated that the fate of socialism in the G.D.R. is of utmost strategic importance for world socialism and for the victory of socialism in the P.R.C. The CPC leadership is ready to do whatever is necessary to support the survival of socialism in the G.D.R. In light of complicated labour shortages in the G.D.R., the P.R.C. is willing to offer any required amount of skilled labour in any necessary qualification. The P.R.C. does not expect any payment in foreign exchange, because they consider it political assistance. Balance settlement could be done by goods. Comrade Lin Hanxiong announced his willingness to travel to Berlin on short notice to engage in direct talks with the responsible state organs. The P.R.C. is ready for very short term decisions. Comrade Lin Hanxiong stressed that ideally a reply by the G.D.R. should arrive before the 5th congress of the CC CPC at the beginning of November. Request answer.

- Berthold 27.10. 14.00'

<![if !supportLists]>· <![endif]>Peking" -1 -2

"The course of China's successful revolution and national construction is inextricably linked to Mao Zedong Thought. Mao Zedong, throughout the course of his life, sacrificed greatly and has made profound contributions and achievements that would, fundamentally, remain eternal for the hearts of the Chinese people. But, Mao Zedong just like any other human being, had his weaknesses and has made mistakes. When we analyse and explore Mao Zedong's mistakes, it is obvious that we should recognise who and which individual is responsible, but at the same time we should always recognise the sheer complexity of historical background and the conditions of which these very mistakes were made. It is only through this that we can objectively, scientifically, and which is ultimately the correct Marxist method of handling history, approach important historical figures like Chairman Mao; The traits, character and essence of Mao Zedong's errors and the issues of Lin Biao and the 'Gang of Four' are not the same. Chairman Mao throughout the majority of his life has done innumerable great things. He has, in multiple occasions, lead, guided and ultimately saved our party and our country during dire conditions and times of crises. Without Chairman Mao, to the very least, we, the Chinese people, would be still left astray in a far darker state of chaos for a far more longer time. Chairman Mao's greatest contribution is his efforts to blend, link and unite Marxist theory with the conditions of China, which ultimately led to the successful path of China's revolution; The Communist Party of China's 'left' errors can be traced back to the late 1950s. But these errors are not solely Chairman Mao's responsibility or fault" - Deng Xiaoping

"It's true that [Mao] made mistakes in a certain period, but he was after all a principal founder of the Chinese Communist Party and the People's Republic of China. In evaluating his merits and mistakes, we hold that his mistakes were only secondary. What he did for the Chinese people can never be erased. In our hearts, we Chinese people will always cherish him as a founder of our Party and our state" - Deng Xiaoping

"The aim of Socialism is to make all our people

prosperous, not create polarisation. If our policies lead to polarisation, it would mean that we had failed; if a new bourgeoisie emerged, it would mean we had strayed from the right path" - Deng Xiaoping

"At present some people, especially young people, are sceptical about the socialist system, alleging that socialism is not as good as capitalism. Such ideas must be firmly corrected. The socialist system is one thing, and the specific way of building socialism is another. Counting from the October Revolution of 1917, the Soviet Union has been engaging in building socialism for 63 years, but it is still in no position to boast about how we do it. It is true that we don't have enough experience either, and perhaps it is only now that we have begun in earnest to search for a better road. Nevertheless, the superiority of the socialist system has already been proved, even though it still needs to be displayed in more convincing ways, but first and foremost it must be revealed in the rate of economic growth and in economic efficiency. Otherwise, there will be no point in our trying to blow our own horn. And to achieve a high rate of economic growth and high efficiency, it is essential to carry out our political line consistently and unfalteringly" - Deng Xiaoping

"So, to build socialism it is necessary to develop the productive forces. Poverty is not socialism. To uphold socialism, a socialism that is to be superior to capitalism, it is imperative first and foremost to eliminate poverty. True, we are building socialism, but that doesn't mean that what we have achieved so far is up to the socialist standard. Not until the middle of the next century, when we have reached the level of the moderately developed countries, shall we be able to say that we have really built socialism and to declare convincingly that it is superior to capitalism. We are advancing towards that goal" - Deng Xiaoping

"The socialist system has been basically established in China, the principal contradiction within the country was no longer the contradiction between the proletariat and the bourgeoisie but the one resulted from the need of the people for rapid economic development" - Deng Xiaoping

"The masses are the source of our strength and the mass viewpoint and the mass line are our cherished traditions. The Party's organisations, its rank and file members and cadres must be one with the masses and never stand against them. Any party organisation that deplorably loses tough with the masses and does not mend its ways is forfeiting the source of its strength and will invariably fail and be rejected by the people" - Deng Xiaoping

"It is their direction to continuously self-improve and develop socialism. It means that China is constantly changing and as it changes, they need to constantly reform the system in order to improve" - Deng Xiaoping

"The essence of Marxism is seeking truth from facts. That's what we should advocate, not book worship. The reform and open policy have been successful not because we relied on books, but because we relied on practice and sought truth from facts" - Deng Xiaoping

"I haven't read too many books, but there is one thing I believe in: Chairman Mao's principle of seeking truth from facts. That is the principle we relied on when we were fighting wars and we continue to rely on it in construction and reform" - Deng Xiaoping

"Whether it promotes the growth of the productive forces in a socialist society, increases the overall strength of the socialist state, and raises living standards" - Deng Xiaoping

"'Those who suffer from it dare not say a word or take a step that isn't mentioned in books, documents or the speeches of leaders: everything has to be copied.' And a little over a decade later, he returned to this thought. 'The world changes every day and modern science and technology in particular develop rapidly. A year today is the equivalent of several decades, a century or even a longer period of in ancient times. Anyone who fails to carry Marxism forward with new thinking and a new viewpoint is not a true Marxist; When everything has to be done by the book, when thinking turns rigid and blind faith is the fashion, it is impossible for a party or a nation to progress. Its life will cease and that party or nation will perish.' He encouraged, 'We should be bolder than before in conducting reform and opening up to the outside and have the courage to experiment'" - Deng Xiaoping

"'Reform and Opening up' comes from. The experimentation and reform can then be tied directly to Mao's own work 'Oppose Book Worship!'" - Deng Xiaoping

"The course of China's successful revolution and national construction is inextricably linked to Mao Zedong Thought. Mao Zedong, throughout the course of his life, sacrificed greatly and has made profound contributions and achievements that would, fundamentally, remain eternal for the hearts of the Chinese people. But, Mao Zedong just like any other human being, had his weaknesses and has made mistakes. When we analyse and explore Mao Zedong's mistakes, it is obvious that we should recognise who and which individual is responsible, but at the same time we should always recognise the sheer complexity of historical background and the conditions of which these very mistakes were made. It is only through this that we can objectively, scientifically, and which is ultimately the correct Marxist method of handling history, approach important historical figures like Chairman Mao; The traits, character and essence of Mao Zedong's errors and the issues of Lin Biao and the 'Gang of Four' are not the same. Chairman Mao throughout the majority of his life has done innumerable great things. He has, in multiple occasions, lead, guided and ultimately saved our party and our country during dire conditions and times of crises. Without Chairman Mao, to the very least, we, the Chinese people, would be still left astray in a far darker state of chaos for a far more longer time. Chairman Mao's greatest contribution is his efforts to blend, link and unite Marxist theory with the conditions of China, which ultimately led to the successful path of China's revolution; The Communist Party of China's 'left' errors can be traced back to the late 1950s. But these errors are not solely Chairman Mao's responsibility or fault" - Deng Xiaoping

"The aim of Socialism is to make all our people prosperous, not create polarisation. If our policies lead to polarisation, it would mean that we had failed; if a new bourgeoisie emerged, it would mean we had strayed from the right path" - Deng Xiaoping

"China is not a superpower, nor will she ever seek to be one. If one day China should change her colour and turn into a superpower, if she too should play the tyrant in the world, and everywhere subject others to her bullying, aggression and exploitation, the people of the world should identify her as social-imperialism, expose it, oppose it and work together with the Chinese people to overthrow it" - Deng Xiaoping

"Ours is an economically backwards country with a population of one billion. If we took the capitalist road, a small number of people in certain areas would quickly grow rich, while the overwhelming majority of the people would remain in poverty, scarcely able to feed and clothe themselves. Only the socialist system can eradicate poverty" - Deng Xiaoping

"Observe calmly; secure our position; cope with affairs calmly; hide our capacities and bide our time; be good at maintaining a low profile; and never claim leadership" - Deng Xiaoping

"Absorbing foreign capital and technology and even allowing foreigners to construct plants in China can only play a complementary role to our effort to develop the productive forces in a socialist society. Of course, this will bring some decadent capitalist influences into China. We are aware of this possibility; it's nothing to be afraid of" - Deng Xiaoping

"We mustn't fear to adopt the advanced management methods applied in capitalist countries. The very essence of socialism is the liberation and development of the productive systems. Socialism and market economy are not incompatible. We should be concerned about right-wing deviations, but most of all, we must be concerned about left-wing deviations" - Deng Xiaoping

"No matter to what degree China opens up to the outside world and admits foreign capital, its relative magnitude will be small and it can't affect our system of socialist public ownership of the means of production" - Deng Xiaoping

"We cannot say that everything developed in capitalist countries is of a capitalist nature. For instance, technology, science - even advanced production management is also a sort of science - will be useful in any society or country" - Deng Xiaoping

"Nevertheless, the superiority of the socialist system has already been proved, even though it still needs to be displayed in more convincing ways, but first and foremost it must be revealed in the rate of economic growth and in economic efficiency. Otherwise, there will be no point in our trying to blow our own horn. And to achieve a high rate of economic growth and high efficiency, it is essential to carry out our political line consistently and unfalteringly" - Deng Xiaoping

"I am convinced that more and more people will come to believe in Marxism, because it is a science. Using historical materialism, it has uncovered the laws governing the development of human society… So don't panic, don't think that Marxism has disappeared, that it's not useful anymore and that it has been defeated. Nothing of the sort!" - Deng Xiaoping

"Poverty is not socialism… socialism means eliminating poverty. Unless you are developing the productive forces and raising people's living standards, you cannot. To be rich is glorious" - Deng Xiaoping

"At the higher stage of Communism, when the productive forces will be greatly developed and the principle 'from each according to his ability, to each according to his needs' will be practised, personal interests will be acknowledged still more and more personal needs will be satisfied" - Deng Xiaoping

"China is no longer the China of the feudal lords, nor the constant victim of the aggressions of colonial and imperial powers. Henceforth, no one will be able to scorn and humiliate China. This is the new China that emerges with the victorious national liberation struggles and the socialist revolution. Everything was forged through feats of heroism and long marches, which were exploits unsurpassable in human history. Everything was carried out under the immortal ideas of Marxism-Leninism and their wise application [words indistinct] of China. Eternal glory to the Communist Party, to its founders and leaders, and to the heroic population capable of such a feat. Glory and honor, too, and most rightfully so, to the great revolutionary strategist, Mao Zedong. The path China has had to travel following liberation has been long, difficult, and risky in a world where imperialism exercised and still exercises power and hegemonic influence. The Chinese Communists, as they themselves admit, also had to struggle against their own mistakes. It is up to them, not us, to judge that. What is an unquestionable and certain fact is that the Chinese people are indissolubly united around their revolutionary vanguard today. Colossal successes have been attained. The era of disasters and famines has been left behind. Only socialism could have been capable of the miracle of feeding; clothing; providing with footwear, jobs, education, and healthcare; raising life expectancy to 70; and providing decorous shelter for more than 1 billion human beings in a minute portion of the planet's arable land. Thanks to such a feat at this difficult and critical time for the world's peoples, in China over one-fifth of humanity remains under the banner of socialism" - Fidel Castro

"Xi Jinping is one of the strongest and most capable revolutionary leaders I have met in my life" - Fidel Castro

"The People's Republic of China originates from the biggest anti-colonial revolution of our history, and an anti-colonial revolution can only be said to truly succeed if it can add a successful economic independence to its political independence. In this respect, there is a continuity between Mao Zedong and Deng Xiaoping. The latter introduced his new plan on the basis of two main considerations. Firstly, he believed that a call to the revolutionary spirit of sacrifice can only succeed in moments of particular political enthusiasm; in the long term it is impossible to develop the productive forces (and so combat misery) without economic incentives, and therefore without competition and without markets. On top of this, during times of crises and following the collapse of the U.S.S.R., the west held the monopoly over high technology, and as such it was impossible for China to access this high technology without opening itself up to international markets. Thanks also to the achievements orchestrated by the Maoist era (with its massive promotion of education, eradication of infectious diseases, etc.), the new plan, despite its blatant contradictions can boast an incredible success: 600 million people or 660 million people (according to other estimates) liberated from misery, infrastructures worthy of a first world economy, growth in the process of industrialisation from its coast areas to its inland areas, rapid incrementation of salaries for several years and a growing concern for environmental issues. By focusing on the key role of the achievement in the safekeeping of independence and of national sovereignty, and by encouraging the old colonies to pursue their own economic independence, China can today be seen as the centre of the anti-colonial revolution - which began in the 20th Century and is still in process under its different guises to this day. And by reminding ourselves of the pivotal role the public sphere should play in any economy, China constitutes an alternative in opposition to the economic liberalism and to the consensus dictated by Washington" - Domenico Losurdo

"The founding of the CPC and creation of the new China were major events in human history. Since then, China, a great nation representing progressive and left revolutionary forces, has made important theoretical and practical contributions to Marxism-Leninism by holding high the banner of socialism. Comrade Mao Zedong, one of the founding delegates, as party leader made major contributions to revolutionary struggle and the national liberation of China, which was large and impoverished. Today after more than four decades of reform and opening up, China is recognised throughout the world with a strong economic base, which is supported by a huge domestic market and experience gained in exploration of socialism with Chinese characteristics. We see in China a united, industrious people, with a historic memory, millennial culture, and highly trained capable and committed cadres. Above all, we see a party that has firmly and wisely addressed the greatest adversities and has been able to place integrated development, institutions, rule of law, and the people at the center of its work. The CPC's effective battle against Covid-19 and the visible results in eradicating poverty are recent and admirable examples of its response to the people's demands" - Miguel Díaz-Canel

"The present world is open... Reviewing our history, we have concluded that one of the most important reasons for China's long years of stagnation and backwardness was its policy of closing the country to outside contact. Our experiences show that China cannot rebuild itself behind closed doors and that it cannot develop in isolation from the rest of the world" - Xi Jinping

"To build China into a modern socialist country that is prosperous, strong, democratic, culturally advanced, and harmonious and achieve the great rejuvenation of the Chinese nation by the middle of the century" - Xi Jinping

"We should promote open, innovative and inclusive development that benefits all. The 2008 global financial crisis has taught us that allowing capital to blindly pursue profit will result in chaos, and that global prosperity cannot be built on the shaky foundations of a market without moral constraints. The growing gap between rich and poor is both unfair and unsustainable. It is important for us to use both the invisible hand and the visible hands to form synergy between market forces and government functions and strive to achieve both efficiency and fairness" - Xi Jinping

"Men make their own history, but they do not make it as they please; they do not make it under self-selected circumstances, but under circumstances existing already, given and transmitted from the past" - Xi Jinping

"There are some bored foreigners, with full stomachs, who have nothing better to do that point fingers at us… First, China doesn't export Revolution; second, China doesn't export hunger and poverty; third, China doesn't come and cause you headaches, what more is there to be said?" - Xi Jinping

"China pursues an independent foreign policy of peace, and is ready to enhance friendship and cooperation with all other countries on the basis of the Five Principles of Peaceful Coexistence. China is the first country to make partnership-building a principle guiding its relations with other countries. It has formed partnerships of various forms with over 90 countries and regional organisations, and will expand its circle of friends around the world" - Xi Jinping

"Socialism is the primary stage of Communism and Communism is our highest ideal. What we are doing now belongs to the primary stage of socialism, but we must stay true to why we started out and stay true to our loftiest goal. We cannot be evasive and vague with our words on this issue" - Xi Jinping

"Developed Western countries have long-term economic, technological and military advantages over China, and the Communist Party of China (CPC) must understand that some of the leaders and the Western countries behind them will use their own strengths to criticise socialism. [China should] Fully appreciate the objective reality of the long-term advantage that Western developed countries have in the economic, scientific and military fields, and conscientiously prepare for all aspects of long-term cooperation and (at the same time) the struggle between the two social systems. [The CPC also had to] face the reality that some people compare the good qualities of the developed countries of the West with the shortcomings of the socialist development of our country and criticise it. [Although the CPC at one time made] big mistakes, [such as the cultural revolution], [the history of the party is] on the whole, great. Those who criticise the revolution that brought the Communist Party to power in 1949 are simply trying to provoke its overthrow. [China, needs to adhere to the important economic reforms begun in 1978, without which the ruling party] could have perished. [The CPC] may even have faced a serious crisis, such as the threat of the death of the party and the death of the country that the Soviet Union and the countries of Eastern Europe have already suffered. But China, has proven that skeptics are wrong" - Xi Jinping

"First, we will take Eastern Europe, then the masses of Asia, then we will encircle the United States, which will be the last bastion of capitalism. We will not have to attack. It will fall like an overripe fruit into our hands" - Xi Jinping

"To study and research Marxism, one should not adopt a simple and superficial attitude. Some people have not read classics of Marxism, and they express their opinions when they know little about them. This is an irresponsible attitude and goes against the spirit of science" - Xi Jinping

"Both history and reality tell us that only socialism can save China. Only socialism with Chinese characteristics can develop China. This is a conclusion of the history and the choice of the people" - Xi Jinping

"All party organs and members should be frugal and make determined efforts to oppose ostentation and reject hedonism" - Xi Jinping

"The capitalist road was tried and found wanting; reformism, liberalism, social Darwinism, anarchism, pragmatism, populism, syndicalism - they were all given their moment on the stage. They all failed to solve the problems of China's future destiny. It is Marxism-Leninism and Mao Zedong Thought that guided the Chinese people out of the darkness of that long night and established a New China" - Xi Jinping

"No theory in history can match Marxism in terms of rationale, truth, and spread, and no theory has exerted such a huge influence on the world as Marxism. This proves the truth and vigor in Marxism and its irreplaceable role in understanding, reshaping and advancing the world" - Xi Jinping

"Although there is a vast ocean between China and Latin America, we are connected heart and soul. We are bound together not only be profound traditional friendship and close interests, but also by our common pursuit of beautiful dreams" - Xi Jinping

"I believe that, for real Communists, Stalin weighs no less than Lenin, and in a percentage of right decisions, he doesn't even have an equal in world history" - Xi Jinping

"In America you can change the party but not the policy, in China you can't change the party but the policy can change" - Eric Li

"If we do not take into consideration the objective dialectical law of the new superseding the old but look for a "pure" socialism free from both vestiges of the old and rudiments of the new, we are likely to fall victim to a metaphysical point of view" - Xue Muqiao

"Zhou said he hoped that a coalition government would come into being if Chiang admitted the CPC as an equal partner. 'The United States will find us more cooperative than the Guomindang. China must industrialise. This can only be done by free enterprise and with the aid of foreign capital. Chinese and American interests are correlated. The two countries fit well together.' Mao went further, hinting that, although dedicated to socialism, the CPC would delay drastic social reforms for 'twenty years or more... should American help be forthcoming.' He and Zhou envisaged for China something akin to the Marshall Plan that later put Western Europe back on its feet. 'The U.S.S.R has suffered greatly from the war... It will be far too busy with its own reconstruction. We are quite willing to make concessions.' 'Revolution is a very gradual process, and we shall have to go through a comparatively long new-democratic stage,' asserted Zhou Enlai. This long-term policy, advocating a mixed economy, would be the one that Zhou would endeavor to pursue through the following decades. And even though at times contrary winds blew, and schemes utterly different took hold for a while, the 'opening of China,' attributed to Deng Xiaoping in the 1980s, goes right back to those concepts forged by Zhou Enlai and Mao in 1944 in Yenan" - (Biography of Zhou Enlai)

Post-Stalin U.S.S.R.:

"The proletarian state will gradually turn, as socialist construction succeeds, capitalist relations are eradicated and the capitalists disappear, into a state of the whole people" - (Mikhail Kalinin, What the Soviet government is doing to achieve democracy, 1926)

"Unlike bourgeois constitutions, the draft of the new Constitution of the U.S.S.R. proceeds from the fact that there are no longer any antagonistic classes in society; that society consists of two friendly classes, of workers and peasants; that it is these classes, the labouring classes, that are in power; that the guidance of society by the state (the dictatorship) is in the hands of the working class, the most advanced class in society, that a constitution is needed for the purpose of consolidating a social order desired by, and beneficial to, the working people" - J.V. Stalin

"I started working as soon as I learned how to walk. Until the age of fifteen, I worked as a shepherd. I tended, as the foreigners say when they use the Russian language, 'the little cows,' I was a sheepherder, I herded cows for a capitalist, and that was before I was fifteen. After that, I worked at a factory for a German, and I worked in a French-owned mine, I worked at a Belgian-owned chemical factory, and [now] I'm the Prime Minister of the great Soviet state. And I am in no way ashamed of my past because all work is worthy of respect. Work as such cannot be dirty, it is only conscience that can be" - N.S. Khrushchev

"The power of our society and state in connection with the transformation of the dictatorship of the proletariat into a national state is not only not weakening, but, on the contrary, is increasing many times, because new sources of our power are being added to the former sources of our strength. Along with the constant increase in economic potential, the social base of our state has strengthened and expanded, the society has become unified and monolithic as never before. And this is the main source of the state's strength. Every worker, every peasant, every intellectual can say: the state is we, his policy is our policy, the task is to develop and strengthen him, to protect him from all encroachments - this is our common task. (Prolonged applause). And why, in fact, is the state itself preserved, although the main thing that gave rise to it, class antagonism, has disappeared? This is explained by the fact that the tasks that society can solve only with the help of the state have not yet been exhausted. These tasks and functions of the socialist state are clearly defined in the draft Program of our party. - N.S. Khrushchev

"Our State, which arose as a state of the dictatorship of the proletariat, developed at a new, modern stage into a state of the whole people, an organ of expression of the interests and will of the whole people. Insofar as the working class is the most advanced, organised force of the Soviet society, it exercises its leading role even during the period of extensive Communist construction. The working class will complete its role as leader of society with the construction of Communism when the classes disappear" - N.S. Khrushchev

"The dictatorship of the proletariat born of the socialist revolution played a world-historic role in securing the victory of socialism in the U.S.S.R. At the same time, in the process of building socialism she herself has undergone changes. In connection with the liquidation of the exploiting classes, the function of suppressing their resistance has died out" - N.S. Khrushchev

"Naturally, when socialism won in our country completely and finally, and we entered the period of the expanded the building of Communism, the conditions that caused the need for a dictatorship of the proletariat, its internal tasks were done" - N.S. Khrushchev

"I would like to focus on some of the fundamental issues of modern international development that determine not only the course of current events, but also future prospects. These are questions about the peaceful coexistence of the two systems, about the possibility of preventing wars in the modern era and about the forms of transition of various countries to socialism" - N.S. Khrushchev

"When we talk about the fact that in the competition of

two systems - capitalist and socialist - will win the socialist system, this does not at all mean that victory will be achieved through the armed intervention of the socialist countries in internal affairs of the capitalist countries" - N.S. Khrushchev

"The stated provisions of the Marxist-Leninist theory are they also overturn the notorious formulation of the question of "ex-port of the revolution ". It is Marxism, in contrast to all bourgeois ideological concepts, proved that revolutions occur do not occur by order, not because of the desires of individuals, but due to the natural course of the historical process. "Of course," Lenin pointed out, "there are people who think that a revolution can be born in a foreign country by order, by co-announcement. These people are either madmen or provocateurs... We know that they cannot be made either by order or by agreement that they grow when tens of millions of people come to the conclusion that it is impossible to live like this any longer" - N.S. Khrushchev

"In this fight against the skeptics and capitulators, the Trotskyites, Zinovievites, Bukharinites and Kamenevites, there was definitely welded together, after Lenin's death, that leading core of the Party... that upheld the great banner of Lenin, rallied the Party behind Lenin's behests, and brought the Soviet people onto the broad paths of industrialising the country and collectivising the rural economy. The leader of this core and the guiding force of the Party and the state was Comrade Stalin" - N.S. Khrushchev

"Three weeks later (After the Secret Speech), before eight hundred guests at a Chinese Embassy reception, he declared that being a Communist was 'inseparable from being a Stalinist,' so that even though 'mistakes' had been made in the struggle against the enemies of Marxism-Leninism, 'may God grant that every Communist will be able to fight for the interests of the working class as Stalin fought.' Communism's enemies had tried to exploit his criticism of Stalin's shortcomings to undermine the Soviet regime. But 'nothing will come of this, gentlemen, any more than you will be able to see your ears without a mirror'"

"'In the Romanian capital of Bucharest, at the International Meeting of Communist and Workers Parties (November 1960), Mao and Khrushchev respectively attacked the Soviet and the Chinese interpretations of Marxism-Leninism as the wrong road to world socialism in the U.S.S.R. and in China. Mao said that Khrushchev's emphases on consumer goods and material plenty would make the Soviets ideologically soft and un-revolutionary, to which Khrushchev replied: 'If we could promise the people nothing, except revolution, they would scratch their heads and say: 'Isn't it better to have good goulash?"

'In the context of the tri-polar Cold War, Khrushchev doubted Mao's mental sanity, because his unrealistic policies of geopolitical confrontation might provoke nuclear war between the capitalist and the Communist blocs. To thwart Mao's warmongering, Khrushchev cancelled foreign-aid agreements and the delivery of Soviet atomic bombs to the P.R.C.'"

"Our enemies like to depict us Leninists as advocates of violence always and everywhere. True, we recognise the need recognise the need for the revolutionary transformation of capitalist society into socialist society. It is this that distinguishes the revolutionary Marxists from the reformists, the opportunists. There is no doubt that in a number of capitalist countries the violent overthrow of the dictatorship of the bourgeoisie and the sharp aggravation of class struggle connected with this are inevitable. But the forms of social revolution vary. It is not true that we regard violence and civil war as the only way to remake society. It will be recalled that in the conditions that arose in April 1917 Lenin granted the possibility that the Russian Revolution might develop peacefully" - N.S. Khrushchev

"Liberation wars will continue to exist as long as imperialism exists, as long as colonialism exists. These are revolutionary wars. Such wars are not only admissible but inevitable since the colonialists do not grant independence voluntarily... We recognise such wars, we help and will help the people striving for their independence... These uprisings must not be identified with wars among states, with local wars, since in these uprisings the people are fighting for implementation of their right for self-determination, for independence social and national development" - N.S. Khrushchev

"The stated provisions of the Marxist-Leninist theory are they also overturn the notorious formulation of the question of 'ex-port of the revolution'. It is Marxism, in contrast to all bourgeois ideological concepts, proved that revolutions occur do not occur by order, not because of the desires of individuals, but due to the natural course of the historical process. 'Of course,' Lenin pointed out, 'there are people who think that a revolution can be born in a foreign country by order, by co-announcement. These people are either madmen or provocateurs... We know that they cannot be made either by order or by agreement that they grow when tens of millions of people come to the conclusion that it is impossible to live like this any longer" - N.S. Khrushchev

"To strengthen the cause of peace in the entire world it would be of great importance to establish strong friendly relations between the two major powers of the world, the Soviet Union and the United States of America. We believe that if the basis of relations between the U.S.S.R. and the U.S.A. was based on the known five principles of peaceful coexistence, it would be truly a remarkable value for all of humanity and it would certainly be healthy to the people of America, no less than the peoples of the Soviet Union and all other nations. The principles are mutual respect for territorial integrity and sovereignty, non-aggression, non-interference in each other's internal affairs, equality and mutual benefit, peaceful coexistence and economic cooperation are now shared and supported by two dozen states" - N.S. Khrushchev

"In advocating peaceful coexistence, we of course have no intention of saying that there are no contradictions between socialism and capitalism, that complete 'harmony' can be established between them, or that it is possible to reconcile the Communist and bourgeois ideologies. Such a viewpoint would be tantamount to retreating from Marxism-Leninism. The ideological differences are irreconcilable and will continue so" - N.S. Khrushchev

"Berlin is the testicles of the West… Every time I want to make the West scream, I squeeze on Berlin" - N.S. Khrushchev

"The system under which some states sell arms to others is not for our invention. France, Britain and the United States have long since been supplying arms to very many countries, and particularly to the countries whose governments take the most hostile attitude towards the Soviet Union. Therefore we have nothing else to do but to act in the same way. We sell arms to countries which ask us to do so and want to be friendly with us. Apparently they buy arms because they fear the countries which you supply with arms. Thus we are doing only the same thing which you have been doing for a long time. If the Western powers want to come to agreement on this score, we are willing to do so. We said this as far back as 1955 in London and made a statement to this effect. The Soviet Union is prepared to reach agreement that no country should sell its arms to any other country" - N.S. Khrushchev

"Our enemies like to depict us Leninists as advocates of violence always and everywhere. True, we recognise the need recognise the need for the revolutionary transformation of capitalist society into socialist society. It is this that distinguishes the revolutionary Marxists from the reformists, the opportunists. There is no doubt that in a number of capitalist countries the violent overthrow of the dictatorship of the bourgeoisie and the sharp aggravation of class struggle connected with this are inevitable. But the forms of social revolution vary. It is not true that we regard violence and civil war as the only way to remake society. It will be recalled that in the conditions that arose in April 1917 Lenin granted the possibility that the Russian Revolution might develop peacefully... Leninism teaches us that the ruling class will not surrender their power voluntarily. And the greater or lesser degree of intensity which the struggle may assume, the use or the non-use of violence in the transition to socialism, depends on the resistance of the exploiters, on whether the exploiting class itself resorts to violence, rather than the proletariat. In this connection the question arises of whether it is possible to go over to socialism by using parliamentary means. No such course was open to the Russian bolsheviks... Since then, however, the historical situation has undergone radical changes which make possible a new approach to the question. The forces of socialism and democracy have grown immeasurably throughout the world, and capitalism has become much weaker... In these circumstances the working class, by rallying around itself the working peasantry, the intelligentsia, all patriotic forces, and resolutely repulsing the opportunist elements who are incapable of giving up the policy of compromise with the capitalists and landlords, is in a position to defeat the reactionary forces opposed to the interests of the people, to capture a stable majority in parliament, and transform the latter from an organ of bourgeois democracy into a genuine instrument of the people's will... In the countries where capitalism is still strong and has a huge military and police apparatus at its disposal, the reactionary forces will, of course, inevitably offer serious resistance. There the transition to socialism will be attended by a sharp class, revolutionary struggle. Whatever the form of transition to socialism, the decisive and indispensable factor is the political leadership of the working class headed by its vanguard. Without this there can be no transition to socialism" - N.S. Khrushchev

"I once said, 'We will bury you,' and I got into trouble with it. Of course we will not bury you with a shovel. Your own [American] working class will bury you" - N.S. Khrushchev

"Even now we feel that Stalin was devoted to Communism, he was a Marxist, this cannot and should not be denied" - N.S. Khrushchev

"When it is a question of fighting against imperialism we can state with conviction that we are all Stalinists. We can take pride that we have taken part in the fight for the advance of our great cause against our enemies. From that point of view I am proud that we are Stalinists" - N.S. Khrushchev

"Do you think when two representatives holding diametrically opposing views get together and shake hands, the contradictions between our systems will simply melt away? What kind of a daydream is that?" - N.S. Khrushchev

"The Soviet people and Government helped us both morally and materially in the years of our struggle for independence, and. they continue to help us in every way: with credits, industrial plants and specialists" - (President Henri Boumedienne of Algeria, in New Times, June 9, 1965)

"We Communists have got to string along with the capitalists for a while. We need their agriculture and their technology. But we are going to continue massive military programs... (soon) we will be in a position to return to a much more aggressive foreign policy designed to gain the upper-hand..." - L.I. Brezhnev

"We stand for the dismantling of foreign military bases. We stand for a reduction of armed forces and armaments in areas where military confrontation is especially dangerous, above all in central Europe" - L.I. Brezhnev

"We are entirely for the idea that Europe shall be free

from nuclear weapons, from medium-range weapons as well as tactical weapons. That would be a real zero option" - L.I. Brezhnev

"It stands to the Party's credit that millions upon millions of Soviet men of every nation and nationality have adopted internationalism - once the ideal of a handful of Communists - as their deep conviction and standard of behaviour. This was a true revolution in social thinking, and one which it is hard to overestimate" - L.I. Brezhnev

"When external and internal forces hostile to the development of socialism try to turn the development of a given socialist country in the direction of the restoration of the capitalist system, when a threat arises to the cause of socialism in that country... this is no longer merely a problem for that country's people, but a common problem, the concern of all socialist countries" - L.I. Brezhnev

"Our Party supports and will continue to support peoples fighting for their freedom. In so doing, the Soviet Union does not look for advantages, does not hunt for concessions, does not seek political domination and is not after military bases. We act as we are bid by our revolutionary conscience, our Communist convictions" - L.I. Brezhnev

"Our militant union with peoples which still have to carry on an armed struggle against the colonialists constitutes an important element of our line in international affairs" - L.I. Brezhnev

"Of late, attempts have been made in the U.S.A. - at a high level and in a rather cynical form - to play the 'Chinese card' against the U.S.S.R. This is a shortsighted and dangerous policy" - L.I. Brezhnev

"We must fight actively and persistently for peace and detente... [with] a calm and clear confirmation of our course towards detente and towards the development of good, mutually beneficial relations with the United States" - L.I.

Brezhnev

"Some bourgeois leaders raise a howl over the solidarity of Soviet Communists, the Soviet people, with the struggle of other peoples for freedom and progress. This is either naivete or a deliberate befuddling of minds. Detente and peaceful coexistence have to do with interstate relations. This means above all that conflicts between countries are not to be settled by war, by the use or threat of force. Detente cannot abolish or alter the laws of class struggle. No one should expect that detente will cause Communists to reconcile themselves with capitalist exploitation or that monopolists will become revolutionists. On the other hand, strict observance of the principle of non-interference in the affairs of other states and respect for their independence and sovereignty is one of the essential conditions of detente. We make no secret of the fact that we see detente as the way to create more favorable conditions for peaceful socialist and Communist construction. This only confirms that socialism and peace are indissoluble. As for the ultra-leftist assertion that peaceful coexistence is the next thing to 'helping capitalism' and 'freezing the socio-political status quo', our reply is this: every revolution is above all a natural result of the given society's internal development. Life itself has refuted the inventions about 'freezing of the status quo'. Suffice it to recall the far-reaching revolutionary changes in the world in recent years - L.I. Brezhnev

"Socialist emulation spells out innovation by the people. Underlying it are the people's high level of consciousness and initiative. It is this initiative that helps to reveal and tap the potentialities of production, and enhance efficiency and quality. But in practice - there's no hiding it - socialist commitments are sometimes not worked out from below but handed down from above, from higher bodies. This is prejudicial to the very spirit of labour emulation. In it the emphasis should be on upwardly revised plans and other similar initiatives going from below to the top: worker-team-factory-industry. Only then should these initiatives be dovetailed with the state plan. This accords with the nature of socialist emulation and with the planned character of our economy" - L.I. Brezhnev

"In the present epoch, when the international class struggle has grown extremely acute, the danger of Right and 'Left' deviations and of nationalism in the Communist movement has grown more tangible than ever before. The struggle against Right- and 'Left'-wing opportunism and nationalism cannot therefore be conducted as a campaign calculated for only some definite span of time. The denunciation of opportunism of all kinds was and remains an immutable law for all Marxist-Leninist Parties" - L.I. Brezhnev

"The most important thing in my life, its leitmotif, has been the constant and close contacts with working people, with workers and peasants" - L.I. Brezhnev

"The substance of socialist democracy lies in efficient socialist organisation of all society for the sake of every individual, and in the socialist discipline of every individual for the sake of all society" - L.I. Brezhnev

"Communists have always viewed the national question through the prism of the class struggle, believing that its solution has to be subordinated to the interests of the Revolution, to the interests of socialism. That is why Communists and all fighters for socialism believe that the main aspect of the national question is unification of the working people, regardless of their national origin, in the common struggle against every type of oppression, and for a new social system which rules out exploitation of the working people" - L.I. Brezhnev

"The defeat of Nazi Germany signified the victory of progress over reaction, humanity over barbarism and the victory of socialism over imperialist obscurantism. This victory opened the road for advancing the revolutionary struggle of the working class, a national liberation movement on an unprecedented scale and the destruction of the shameful colonial system" - L.I. Brezhnev

"We want the world socialist system to be a well-knit family of nations, building and defending the new society together, and mutually enriching each other with experience and knowledge, a family, strong and united, which the people of the world would regard as the prototype of the future world community of free nations" - L.I. Brezhnev

"The progress of the African peoples is unthinkable without the fraternal and sincere assistance of the Soviet Union" - (President Sekou Toure of Guinea, October 2, 1965)

"What fool (durak) invented this word perestroika? Why rebuild the house? Is there anything wrong in the Soviet Union? We are fine! What is there to rebuild? It is necessary to improve, reorganise, but why, if the house is not falling apart, why does it need to be rebuilt?" - Volodymyr Shcherbytsky

"There never was and never will be an anti-Soviet Communism" - Janos Kadar

"Without the existence of the Soviet Union the socialist revolution in Cuba could not have been possible" - (Fidel Castro, speech in the Red Square, April 28, 1963)

"How could the Soviet Union be classified as imperialist? Where are its monopolist enterprises? What is its participation in multinational companies? What industries, what mines, what petroleum deposits does it own in the undeveloped world? What worker is exploited in any country of Asia, Africa or Latin America by Soviet capital? The economic cooperation which the Soviet Union is offering Cuba and many other countries did not come from the sweat and the sacrifice of exploited workers of other peoples, but from the sweat and effort of Soviet workers" - Fidel Castro

"Reconversion to the production of consumer goods would be at best a painful process, and could be disastrous, for no one knew whether the American economy could maintain full employment in peacetime. The Soviet Union needed heavy industrial equipment, partly to rebuild its war-devastated economy and partly to satisfy its people's long denied desire for more consumer goods. Moscow could solve its reconstruction problems, it appeared, by placing massive orders for industrial equipment with American firms. Filling these orders would help the United States deal with its own post war reconversion problems and, in the process would begin to integrate the Soviet Union into the multilateral system of world trade to which Washington attached such great importance. Both countries, it seemed, had a strong interest in promoting this most promising of economic partnerships" - (John Gaddis Smith, The United States and the origins of the Cold War)

"Then the economy. After all, why have they already moved to the NEP? Because even the prodrazverstka didn't work, couldn't. It was impossible to provide large cities with food. Therefore, they moved to the market economy, to the NEP, then quickly turned it down. You know, what I'm saying now is my personal conclusions, my personal analysis. Planned economy has certain advantages, it makes it possible to concentrate national resources on the implementation of the most important tasks. This was how the health care issues were resolved, which was an absolute merit of the Communist Party of that time. So the issues of education were resolved- an absolute merit of the Communist Party of that time. Thus, the issues of industrialisation in the defense sector were resolved. I think that if it were not for the concentration of national resources, the Soviet Union would not have been able to prepare for war with Nazi Germany. And there would be a great chance of defeat with disastrous consequences for our statehood, for the Russian people and other peoples of the Soviet Union. Therefore, these are all absolute advantages. But in the end, insensitivity to changes, insensitivity to technological revolutions, to new technological structures led to the collapse of the economy" - V.V. Putin

"What can I say? We have been doing this for a long time: we have been saying the whole time that the working class is the leading political force in our country. It was a Soviet stamp, but in fact it is. It's just that the essence of working professions is changing. You probably know this not worse, but even better than I do" - V.V. Putin

"I liked Communist and socialist ideas very much and I like them still. [Putin insisted he was never just a] functionary [when it came to party matters and said that the Moral Code of the Builder of Communism - a set of rules to be followed by all party members -] resembles the Bible a lot" - V.V. Putin

"Many people now fear the United States, but neither I (nor the Russian people) subscribe to this fear. My view is that the ridiculous little U.S. lapdogs make lots of noise, but they lack the ability to back it up. When U.S. leaders with no dignity or virtue are elected into office, the U.S. is sullied as a nation. This debilitating internal process weakens the U.S. on the external international stage. The U.S. would do well to study the virtuous thinking of Mao Zedong, as he gave China her dignity back. In fact, under the expert leadership of Mao Zedong, the Chinese people were able to 'stand-up'! It is through the work of Mao Zedong that I learned to counter U.S. hegemony in the world. Just as Mao Zedong stood-up to the tyrannical West, I too have stood up to the tyrannical West. Just as Mao Zedong is vilified by the tyrannical West, I too am vilified by the tyrannical West. That is why I can state with absolute certainty that Mao Zedong is my hero and role model" - V.V. Putin

Revisionism:

"It is the business of the International Working Men's Association to combine and generalise the spontaneous movements of the working classes, but not to dictate or impose any doctrinary system whatever. The Congress should, therefore, proclaim no special system of co-operation, but limit itself to the enunciation of a few general principles. (a.) We acknowledge the co-operative movement as one of the transforming forces of the present society based upon class antagonism. Its great merit is to practically show, that the present pauperising, and despotic system of the subordination of labour to capital can be superseded by the republican and beneficent system of the association of free and equal producers. (b.) Restricted, however, to the dwarfish forms into which individual wages slaves can elaborate it by their private efforts, the co-operative system will never transform capitalist society. to convert social production into one large and harmonious system of free and co-operative labour, general social changes are wanted, changes of the general conditions of society, never to be realised save by the transfer of the organised forces of society, viz., the state power, from capitalists and landlords to the producers themselves. (c.) We recommend to the working men to embark in co-operative production rather than in co-operative stores. The latter touch but the surface of the present economical system, the former attacks its groundwork. (d.) We recommend to all co-operative societies to convert one part of their joint income into a fund for propagating their principles by example as well as by precept, in other words, by promoting the establishment by teaching and preaching. (e.) In order to prevent co-operative societies from degenerating into ordinary middle-class joint stock companies (societes par actions), all workmen employed, whether shareholders or not, ought to share alike. As a mere temporary expedient, we are willing to allow shareholders a low rate of interest" - Karl Marx

"It seems that every worker's party in a great country can grow only through internal strife, this is based on the general law of dialectical development. The German Party became what it is in the struggle between the Eisenachers and the Lassalleans" - Friedrich Engels

"To confine Marxism to the theory of class struggle means curtailing Marxism, distorting it, reducing it to something acceptable to the bourgeoisie. Only he is a Marxist who extends the recognition of the class struggle and the recognition of the dictatorship of the proletariat" - V.I. Lenin

"The party which entered into a compromise with the German imperialists by signing the Treaty of Brest-Litovsk had been evolving its internationalism in practice ever since the end of 1914. It was not afraid to call for the defeat of the tsarist monarchy and to condemn 'defence of country' in a war between two imperialist robbers. The parliamentary representatives of this party preferred exile in Siberia to taking a road leading to ministerial portfolios in a bourgeois government. The revolution that overthrew tsarism and established a democratic republic put this party to a new and tremendous test - it did not enter into any agreements with its 'own' imperialists, but prepared and brought about their overthrow. When it had assumed political power, this party did not leave a vestige of either landed or capitalist ownership. After making public and repudiating the imperialists' secret treaties, this party proposed peace to all nations, and yielded to the violence of the Brest-Litovsk robbers only after the Anglo-French imperialists had torpedoed the conclusion of a peace, and after the Bolsheviks had done everything humanly possible to hasten the revolution in Germany and other countries. The absolute correctness of this compromise, entered into by such a party in such a situation, is becoming ever clearer and more obvious with every day. The Mensheviks and the Socialist-Revolutionaries in Russia (like all the leaders of the Second International throughout the world, in 1914–20) began with treachery - by directly or indirectly justifying 'defence of country', i.e., the defence of their own predatory bourgeoisie. They continued their treachery by entering into a coalition with the bourgeoisie of their own country, and fighting, together with their own bourgeoisie, against the revolutionary proletariat of their own country. Their bloc, first with Kerensky and the Cadets, and then with Kolchak and Denikin in Russia - like the bloc of their confrères abroad with the bourgeoisie of their respective countries - was in fact desertion to the side of the bourgeoisie, against the proletariat. From beginning to end, their compromise with the bandits of imperialism meant their becoming accomplices in imperialist banditry" - V.I. Lenin

"It is necessary that our cadres have a thorough knowledge of Marxist economic theory. The first, old generation of Bolsheviks were very solid theoretically. We learnt Capital by heart, made conspectuses, held discussions and tested each others' understanding. This was our strength and it helped us a lot. The second generation was less prepared. They were busy with practical matters and construction. They studied Marxism from booklets. The third generation is being brought up on satirical and newspaper articles. They do not have any deep understanding . They need to be provided with food that is easily digestible. The majority has been brought up not by studying Marx and Lenin but on quotations. If matters continue further in this way people would soon degenerate. In America people argue: We need dollars, why do we need theory? Why do we need science? With us people may think similarly: 'when we are building socialism why do we need Capital?' This is a threat for us - it is degradation, it is death. In order not to have such a situation even partially we have to improve the level of economic understanding" - J.V. Stalin

"The Party becomes strong by purging itself of opportunist elements. The source of factionalism in the Party is its opportunists elements. The proletariat is not an isolated class. It is consistently replenished by the influx of peasants, petty-bourgeois and intellectuals proletarianised by the development of capitalism. At the same time the upper stratum of the proletariat, principally trade union leaders and members of parliament who are fed by the bourgeoisie out of the super-profits extracted from the colonies, is undergoing a process of decay. 'This stratum of bourgeoisified workers, or the 'labour aristocracy,' says Lenin, 'who are quite philistine in their mode of life, in the size of their earnings and in their entire outlook, is the principal prop of the Second International, and, in our days, the principal social (not military) prop of the bourgeoisie. For they are real agents of the bourgeoisie in the working-class movement, the labour lieutenants of the capitalist class..., real channels of reformism and chauvinism'" - J.V. Stalin

"The Communist bureacrat is the most dangerous type of bureaucrat. Why? Because he masks his bureaucracy with the title of Party member" - J.V. Stalin

"Social-chauvinism and opportunism are the same in their political essence; class collaborationism, repudiation of the proletarian dictatorship, rejection of revolutionary action, obeisance to bourgeois legality, non-confidence in the proletariat, and confidence in the bourgeoisie. The political ideas are identical, and so is the political content of their tactics. Social-chauvinism is the direct continuation and consummation of Millerandism, Bernsteinism, and British liberal-labour policies, their sum, their total, their highest achievement" - Thomas Sankara

Ultra-Leftism:

"The Executive Committee of the Third International must, in my opinion, positively condemn, and call upon the next congress of the Communist International to condemn both the policy of refusing to work in reactionary trade unions in general (explaining in detail why such refusal is unwise, and what extreme harm it does to the cause of the proletarian revolution)" - V.I. Lenin

"He who does not work shall not eat" - V.I. Lenin

"Owing to the present circumstances the whole world is

developing faster than we are. While developing, the capitalist world is directing all its forces against us. That is how the matter stands! That is why we must devote special attention to this struggle" - V.I. Lenin

"Some people believe that Marxism and Anarchism are based on the same principles and that the disagreements between them concern only tactics, so that, in the opinion of these people, no distinction whatsoever can be drawn between these two trends. This is a great mistake. We believe that the Anarchists are real enemies of Marxism. Accordingly, we also hold that a real struggle must be waged against real enemies" - J.V. Stalin

"The People's Communes were to represent a shortcut to Communism. Three years of toil would lead to ten thousand years of happiness. Poetry was displacing Marxism as a guide to economics" - R. Palme Dutt

"If your not an Anarchist by the time your twenty you have no heart, if your not a Marxist-Leninist by thirty you have no brain" - Erich Honecker

"Thus the very premise of petty-bourgeois radicalism is that it is impossible to win the working class in the struggle against capitalism. From this it follows that mass concepts of struggle are not possible, necessary or realistic. This leads to actions based on small elite groups - or to individual action. Because this concept is not concerned with winning over masses, it promotes and condones actions that alienate masses. There is an inner logic to this path. Specific actions are taken because there is a lack of confidence in mass -in class - actions. These ill-considered actions result in widening the gap between the petty-bourgeois radical movements and the masses. This widening gap then becomes 'proof' that you cannot win masses and therefore the line of conduct of these movements is justified. Each step leads to a further isolation. This is the inner logic of petty-bourgeois radicalism" - Gus Hall

"Lucanamarca. Neither they nor we have forgotten it, to be sure, because they got an answer that they didn't imagine possible. More than 80 were annihilated, that is the truth. And we say openly that there were excesses, as was analysed in 1983. But everything in life has two aspects. Our task was to deal a devastating blow in order to put them in check, to make them understand that it was not going to be so easy. On some occasions, like that one, it was the Central Leadership itself that planned the action and gave instructions. That's how it was. In that case, the principal thing is that we dealt them a devastating blow, and we checked them and they understood that they were dealing with a different kind of people's fighters, that we weren't the same as those they had fought before. This is what they understood. The excesses are the negative aspect... If we were to give the masses a lot of restrictions, requirements and prohibitions, it would mean that deep down we didn't want the waters to overflow. And what we needed was for the waters to overflow, to let the flood rage, because we know that when a river floods its banks it causes devastation, but then it returns to its riverbed... [T]he main point was to make them understand that we were a hard nut to crack, and that we were ready for anything, anything" - Abimael 'Gonzalo' Guzmán

"They (Maoists) were in the forefront along with the Trotskyites and the anarchists, and the social democrats marching together in one orchestra. Don't forget the Zionists, throw them in there. And they all wanted one head, and that was comrade Stalin's head. So it shows you that's the reason they were all after him. It was only under comrade Stalin's rule that the Communist movement was united. Think about that. We were the most powerful force on this planet; Marxism-Leninism on the other hand, is like being balanced on a tightrope. If you sway right you fall for right-revisionism, and if you sway left you fall for left-revisionism (ultra-leftism/dogmatism/book-worship), we as Marxist-Leninists must maintain balance and hold the golden centre of Stalin" - Angelo D'Angelo

"Real socialism, it is argued, would be controlled by the workers themselves through direct participation instead of being run by Leninists, Stalinists, Castroites, or other ill-willed, power-hungry, bureaucratic, cabals of evil men who betray revolutions. Unfortunately, this 'pure socialism' view is ahistorical and nonfalsifiable; it cannot be tested against the actualities of history. It compares an ideal against an imperfect reality, and the reality comes off a poor second. It imagines what socialism would be like in a world far better than this one, where no strong state structure of security force is required, where none of the value produced by the workers needs to be expropriated to rebuild society and defend it from invasion and internal sabotage. It is no suprise then that the pure socialists support every revolution except for the ones that succeed" - Michael Parenti

"Western Marxism is basically a kind of Marxism which has, as a key characteristic, never exercised political power. It is a Marxism that has, more and more frequently, concerned itself with philosophical and aesthetic issues. It has pulled back, for example, from criticism of political economy and the problem of the conquest of political power. More and more it has taken a historical distance from the concrete experiences of socialist transition in the Soviet Union, China, Viet Nam, Cuba and so forth. This Western Marxism considers itself to be superior to eastern Marxism because it hasn't tarnished Marxism by transforming it into an ideology of the State like, for example, Soviet Marxism, and it has never been authoritarian, totalitarian or violent. This Marxism preserves the purity of theory to the detriment of the fact that it has never produced a revolution anywhere on the face of the Earth - this is a very important point. Wherever a victorious socialist revolution has taken place in the West, like Cuba, it is much more closely associated with the so-called eastern Marxism than with this western Marxism produced in Western Europe, the United States, Canada and parts of South America" - Michael Parenti

"I hadn't met Western 'revolutionaries' before... What astonished us the most about this group was that they were opposed to nationalism, a doctrine we hold dearly as a colonised and dissipated people" - Leila Khaled

Elections:

"Even where there is no prospect of achieving their election the workers must put up their own candidates to preserve their independence, to gauge their own strength and to bring their revolutionary position and party standpoint to public attention" - Karl Marx

"If, by the way, either of the two parties into which the educated section of the English people is split deserves any preference, it is the Tories. In the social circumstances of England the Whig is himself too much of an interested party to be able to judge; industry, that focal point of English society, is in his hands and makes him rich; he can find no fault in it and considers its expansion the only purpose of all legislation, for it has given him his wealth and his power. The Tory on the other hand, whose power and unchallenged dominance have been broken by industry and whose principles have been shaken by it, hates it and sees in it at best a necessary evil. This is the reason for the formation of that group of philanthropic Tories whose chief leaders are Lord Ashley, Ferrand, Walter, Oastler, etc., and who have made it their duty to take the part of the factory workers against the manufacturers. Thomas Carlyle too was originally a Tory and still stands closer to that party than to the Whigs. This much is certain: a Whig would never have been able to write a book that was half so humane as Past and Present" - Friedrich Engels

"There is no place yet in America for a third party, I believe. The divergence of interests even in the same class group is so great in that tremendous area that wholly different groups and interests are represented in each of the two big parties, depending on the locality, and almost each particular section of the possessing class has its representatives in each of the two parties to a very large degree, though today big industry forms the core of the Republicans on the whole, just as the big landowners of the South form that of the Democrats. The apparent haphazardness of this jumbling together is what provides the splendid soil for the corruption and the plundering of the government that flourish there so beautifully. Only when the land - the public lands - is completely in the hands of the speculators, and settlement on the land thus becomes more and more difficult or falls prey to gouging - only then, I think, will the time come, with peaceful development, for a third party. Land is the basis of speculation, and the American speculative mania and speculative opportunity are the chief levers that hold the native-born worker in bondage to the bourgeoisie. Only when there is a generation of native-born workers that cannot expect anything from speculation any more will we have a solid foothold in America. But, of course, who can count on peaceful development in America! There are economic jumps over there, like the political ones in France - to be sure, they produce the same momentary retrogressions. The small farmer and the petty-bourgeois will hardly ever succeed in forming a strong party; they consist of elements that change too rapidly - the farmer is often a migratory farmer, farming two, three, and four farms in succession in different states and territories, immigration and bankruptcy promote the change in personnel, and economic dependence upon the creditor also hampers independence - but to make up for it they are a splendid element for politicians, who speculate on their discontent in order to sell them out to one of the big parties afterward. The tenacity of the Yankees, who are even rehashing the Greenback humbug, is a result of their theoretical backwardness and their Anglo-Saxon contempt for all theory. They are punished for this by a superstitious belief in every philosophical and economic absurdity, by religious sectarianism, and by idiotic economic experiments, out of which, however, certain bourgeois cliques profit" - Friedrich Engels

"This so-called bipartisan system prevailing in America and Britain has been one of the most powerful means in preventing the rise of an independent working class, i.e., genuinely socialist, party" - V.I. Lenin

"The Nazi party is the party of big business, on the same principle, if not in the exact form, that the Democratic and Republican parties are the parties of big business in the U.S.A." - William Z. Foster

"I like rightists. People say you are rightists, that the Republican Party is to the right, that Prime Minister Heath is also to the right; I am comparatively happy when these people on the right come into power" - (Mao Zedong, speaking to Richard Nixon)

"If the people are awakened only for voting but enter a dormant period soon after, if they are given a song and dance during campaigning but have no say after the election, or if they are favored during canvassing but are left out in the cold after the election, such a democracy is not a true democracy" - Xi Jinping

Populism:

"In short, the Communists everywhere support every revolutionary movement against the existing social and political order of things. In all these movements, they bring to the front, as the leading question in each, the property question, no matter what its degree of development at the time" - Friedrich Engels

"…[Engels] is proved by his preface to the second edition of The Condition of the Working Class in England, 1892. Here he speaks of an 'aristocracy among the working class', of a 'privelaged minority of the workers', in contradistinction to the 'great mass of working people'. 'A small, privelaged, protected minority' of the working class alone was 'permanently benefitted' by the privelaged position of England in 1848-1868, whereas 'the great bulk of them experienced at best but a temporary improvement'; In the nineteenth century the 'mass organisations' of the English trade unions were on the side of the bourgeois labour party. Marx and Engels did not reconcile themselves to it on this ground; they exposed it. They did not forget, firstly, that the trade union organisations directly embraced a minority of the proletariat. In England then, as in Germany now, not more than one-fifth of the proletariat was organised. No one can seriously think it possible to organise the majority of the proletariat under capitalism; Neither we nor anyone else can calculate precisely what portion of the proletariat is following and will follow the social-chauvinists and opportunists. This will be revealed only by the struggle, it will be definitely decided only by the socialist revolution. But we know for certain that the 'defenders of the fatherland' in the imperialist war represent only a minority. And it is therefore our duty, if we wish to remain socialists to go down lower and deeper, to the real masses; this is the whole meaning and the whole purport of the struggle against opportunism. By exposing the fact that the opportunists and social-chauvinists are in reality betraying and selling the interests of the masses, that they are defending the temporary privelages of a minority of the workers, that they are the vehicles of bourgeois ideas and influences, that they are really allies and agents of the bourgeoisie, we teach the masses to appreciate their true political interests, to fight for socialism and for the revolution through all the long and painful vicissitudes of imperialist wars and imperialist armistices" - V.I. Lenin

"[...] Bishop Nikon, quoting a letter from a peasant, does write: 'The land, bread and other important questions of our

Russian life and of the region do not appear to reach either the hands or the hearts of the authorities or the Duma. These questions and such solution of them as is possible are regarded as 'utopian', 'hazardous', untimely. Why do you keep silent, what are you waiting for? For moods and revolts for which those same 'undernourished', hungry, unfortunate peasants will be shot down? We are afraid of 'big' issues and reforms, we limit ourselves to trivialities and trifles, good though they may be.' That is what Bishop Nikon writes. And that is what very many Black-hundred peasants think. It is quite understandable why Bishop Nikon had to be removed from Damn affairs and Duma speeches for such statements. Bishop Nikon expresses his Black-Hundred democracy in arguments that are, in essence, very far from correct. The land, bread and all other important questions do reach the hands and hearts (and pockets) of the 'authorities' and the Duma; Under such circumstances, the cries about the Black-Hundred danger are the result either of absolute ignorance or of hypocrisy. And it is those who conceal their real aims and act behind the scenes that must play the hypocrite. The Mensheviks are raising an outcry about the Black-Hundred danger in order to divert the workers' attention from the game they, the Mensheviks, are playing, or did play recently, by joining the petty-bourgeois bloc and bar gaining with the Cadets" - V.I. Lenin

"It would be hard to imagine any greater ineptitude or greater harm to the revolution than that caused by the 'Left' revolutionaries! Why, if we in Russia today, after two and a half years of unprecedented victories over the bourgeoisie of Russa and the Entente, were to make 'recognition of the dictatorship' a condition of trade union membership, we would be doing a very foolish thing, damaging our influence among the masses, and helping the Mensheviks. The task devolving on Communists is to convince the backward elements, to work among them, and not to fence themselves off from them with artificial and childishly 'Left' slogans" - V.I. Lenin

"The struggle for immediate and direct improvement of conditions, is alone capable of rousing the most backward strata of the exploited masses, gives them a real education and transforms them - during a revolutionary period - into an army of political fighters within the space of a few months" - V.I. Lenin

"The trade unions have never embraced more than one-fifth of the wage-workers in capitalist society, even under the most favourable circumstances, even in the most advanced countries, after decades and sometimes even centuries of development of bourgeois-democratic civilisation and culture. Only a small upper section were members, and of them only a very few were lured over and bribed by the capitalists to take their place in capitalist society as workers' leaders. The American socialists called these people 'labour lieutenants of the capitalist class'. In that country of the freest bourgeois culture, in that most democratic of bourgeois republics, they saw most clearly the roled played by this tiny upper section of the proletariat who had virtually entered the service of the bourgeoisie as its deputies, who were bribed and bought by it, and who came to form those groups of social-patriots and defence advocates of which Ebert and Scheidemann will always remain the perfect heroes" - V.I. Lenin

Distorters of Marxism:

"These gentlemen think that when they have changed the names of things they have changed the things themselves. This is how these profound thinkers mock at the whole world" - Friedrich Engels

"It is impossible fully to grasp Marx's Capital, and especially its first chapter, if you have not studied through and understood the whole of Hegel's logic. Consequently, none of the Marxists for the past half century have understood Marx!" - V.I. Lenin

"What is now happening to Marx's theory has, in

the course of history, happened repeatedly to the theories of revolutionary thinkers and leaders of oppressed classes fighting for emancipation. During the lifetime of great revolutionaries, the oppressing classes constantly hounded them, received their theories with the most savage malice, the most furious hatred and the most unscrupulous campaigns of lies and slander. After their death, attempts are made to convert them into harmless icons, to canonise them, so to say, and to hallow their names to a certain extent for the 'consolation' of the oppressed classes and with the object of duping the latter, while at the same time robbing the revolutionary theory of its substance, blunting its revolutionary edge and vulgarising it. Today, the bourgeoisie and the opportunists within the labour movement concur in this doctoring of Marxism. They omit, obscure, or distort the revolutionary side of this theory, its revolutionary soul. They push to the foreground and extol what is or seems acceptable to the bourgeoisie. All the social-chauvinists are now 'Marxists' (don't laugh!). And more and more frequently German bourgeois scholars, only yesterday specialists in the annihilation of Marxism, are speaking of the 'national-German' Marx, who, they claim, educated the labour unions which are so splendidly organised for the purpose of waging a predatory war!" - V.I. Lenin

"However, the Bernsteinian and 'critical' trend, to which the majority of the legal Marxists turned, deprived the socialists of this opportunity and demoralised the socialist consciousness by vulgarising Marxism, by advocating the theory of the blunting of social contradictions, by declaring the idea of the social revolution and of the dictatorship of the proletariat to be absurd, by reducing the working-class movement and the class struggle to narrow trade-unionism and to a 'realistic' struggle for petty, gradual reforms. This was synonymous with bourgeois democracy's denial of socialism's right to independence and, consequently, of its right to existence; in practice it meant a striving to convert the nascent working-class movement into an appendage of the liberals" - V.I. Lenin

"But what the workers' cause needs is the unity of Marxists, not unity between Marxists, and opponents and distorters of Marxism" - V.I. Lenin

"Why should we bother to reply to Kautsky? He would reply to us, and we would have to reply to his reply. There's no end to that. It would be quite enough for us to announce that Kautsky is a traitor to the working class, and everyone will understand everything" - V.I. Lenin

Rights:

"The right of man to liberty is based not on the association of man with man, but on the separation of man from man. It is the right of this separation, the right of the restricted individual, withdrawn into himself. The practical application of man's right to liberty is man's right to private property" - Karl Marx

Imperialism:

"The money powers prey upon the nation in times of peace and conspire against it in times of adversity. It is more despotic than a monarchy. More insolent than autocracy. And more selfish than bureaucracy. It denounces as public enemies. All who question its methods or throw light upon its crimes" - Abraham Lincoln

"The British fleet is a knife held permanently at the throat of Europe; should any nation evince an ability to emerge from the position of a mere customer for British products, and become a successful competitor of Britain in the markets of the world, that knife is set in operation to cut that throat" - James Connolly

"If you remove the English army tomorrow and hoist the green flag over Dublin Castle, unless you set about the organisation of the Socialist Republic your efforts would be in vain. England would still rule you. She would rule you through her capitalists, through her landlords, through her financiers, through the whole array of commercial and individualist institutions she has planted in this country and watered with the tears of our mothers and the blood of our martyrs. England would still rule you to your ruin, even while your lips offered hypocritical homage at the shrine of that Freedom whose cause you had betrayed. Nationalism without Socialism - without a reorganisation of society on the basis of a broader and more developed form of that common property which underlay the social structure of Ancient Erin - is only national recreancy" - James Connolly

"Imperialism is as much our mortal enemy as is capitalism. That is so. No Marxist will forget, however, that capitalism is progressive compared with feudalism and that imperialism is progressive compared with pre-monopoly capitalism. Hence, it is not our duty to support every struggle against imperialism. We will not support the struggle of the reactionary classes against imperialism: We will not support an uprising of the reactionary classes against imperialism and capitalism" - V.I. Lenin

"On the one hand, there is the tendency of the bourgeoisie and the opportunists to convert a handful of very rich and privileged nations into 'eternal' parasites on the body of the rest of mankind, to 'rest on the laurels' of the exploitation of Negroes, Indians, etc., keeping them in subjection with the aid of the excellent weapons of extermination provided by modern militarism. On the other hand, there is the tendency of the masses, who are more oppressed than before and who bear the whole brunt of imperialist wars, to cast off this yoke and to overthrow the bourgeoisie. The fact that is that 'bourgeois labour parties,' as a political phenomenon, have already been formed in all the foremost capitalist countries, and that unless determined and relentless struggle is waged all along the line against these parties - or groups, trends, etc., it is all the same - there can be no question of a struggle against imperialism, or of Marxism, or of a socialist labour movement" - V.I. Lenin

"Capitalism in its imperialist phase is a system which considers war to be a legitimate instrument for settling international disputes, a legal method in fact, if not in law" - J.V. Stalin

"The same must be said of the revolutionary character of national movements in general. The unquestionably revolutionary character of the vast majority of national movements is as relative and peculiar as is the possible revolutionary character of certain particular national movements. The revolutionary character of a national movement under the conditions of imperialist oppression does not necessarily presuppose the existence of proletarian elements in the movement, the existence of a revolutionary or a republican programme of the movement, the existence of a democratic basis of the movement. The struggle that the Emir of Afghanistan is waging for the independence of Afghanistan is objectively a revolutionary struggle, despite the monarchist views of the Emir and his associates, for it weakens, disintegrates and undermines imperialism; whereas the struggle waged by such 'desperate' democrats and 'Socialists,' 'revolutionaries' and republicans as, for example, Kerensky and Tsereteli, Renaudel and Scheidemann, Chernov and Dan, Henderson and Clynes, during the imperialist war was a reactionary struggle, for its results was the embellishment, the strengthening, the victory, of imperialism. For the same reasons, the struggle that the Egyptians merchants and bourgeois intellectuals are waging for the independence of Egypt is objectively a revolutionary struggle, despite the bourgeois origin and bourgeois title of the leaders of Egyptian national movement, despite the fact that they are opposed to socialism; whereas the struggle that the British 'Labour'

Government is waging to preserve Egypt's dependent position is for the same reason a reactionary struggle, despite the proletarian origin and the proletarian title of the members of the government, despite the fact that they are 'for' socialism. There is no need to mention the national movement in other, larger, colonial and dependent countries, such as India and China, every step of which along the road to liberation, even if it runs counter to the demands of formal democracy, is a steam-hammer blow at imperialism, i.e., is undoubtedly a revolutionary step" - J.V. Stalin

"We cannot be indifferent to what happens anywhere in the world, because a victory by any country over imperialism is our victory, just as any country's defeat is a defeat for all of us" - Ernesto 'Che' Guevara

"The United States has set up hundreds of military bases in many countries all over the world. China's territory of Taiwan, Lebanon and all military bases of the United States on foreign soil are so many nooses around the neck of U.S. imperialism. The nooses have been fashioned by the Americans themselves and by nobody else, it is they themselves who have put these nooses round their own necks, handing the ends of the ropes to the Chinese people, the peoples of the Arab countries and all the peoples of the world who love peace and oppose aggression. The longer the U.S. aggressors remain in those places, the tighter the nooses around their necks will become" - Mao Zedong

"No matter what classes, parties or individuals in an oppressed nation join the revolution, and no matter whether they themselves are conscious of the point or understand it, so long as they oppose imperialism, their revolution becomes part of the proletarian-socialist world revolution and they become its allies" - Mao Zedong

"The basic cause of development in a thing is not external, but internal, and lies in internal contradictions.

Everything has its internal contradictions, hence motion and development. Contradictions within a thing are the basic cause of its development, while its relationship with other things, their interconnection and interaction, is a secondary cause; There are many contradictions in the process of development of a complex thing, and one of them is necessarily the principal contradiction whose existence and development determine or influence the existence and development of the other contradictions. For instance, in capitalist society the two forces in contradiction, the proletariat and the bourgeoisie, form the principal contradiction. The other contradictions, such as those between the remnant feudal class and the bourgeoisie, between the peasant petty-bourgeoisie and the bourgeoisie, between the proletariat and the peasant petty-bourgeoisie, between the non-monopoly capitalists and the monopoly capitalists, between bourgeois democracy and bourgeois fascism, among the capitalist countries and between imperialism and the colonies, are all determined or influenced by this principal contradiction. In a semi-colonial country such as China, the relationship between the principal contradiction and the non-principal contradictions presents a complicated picture. When imperialism launches a war of aggression against such a country, all its various classes, except for some traitors, can temporarily unite in a national war against imperialism. At such a time, the contradiction between imperialism and the country concerned becomes the principal contradiction, while all the contradictions among the various classes within the country (including what was the principal contradiction, between the feudal system and the great masses of the people) are temporarily relegated to a secondary and subordinate position. So it was in China in the Opium War of 1840, the Sino-Japanese War of 1894 and the Yi Ho Tuan War of 1900, and so it is now in the present Sino-Japanese War. But in another situation, the contradictions change position. When imperialism carries on its oppression not by war, but by milder means - political, economic and cultural - the ruling classes in semi-colonial countries capitulate to imperialism, and the two form an alliance for the joint oppression of the masses of the people" - Mao Zedong

"Our policy toward the national bourgeoisie has been to redeem their property; on the contrary, in that period our policy should still have been to protect the national bourgeoisie and win it over so as to enable us to concentrate our efforts on fighting the chief enemies" - Mao Zedong

"In our country, the contradiction between the working class and the national bourgeoisie comes under the category of contradictions among the people. By and large, the class struggle between the two is a class struggle within the ranks of the people, because the Chinese national bourgeoisie has a dual character. In the period of the bourgeois-democratic revolution, it had both a revolutionary and a conciliationist side to its character. In the period of the socialist revolution, exploitation of the working class for profit constitutes one side of the character of the national bourgeoisie, while its support of the Constitution and its willingness to accept socialist transformation constitute the other. The national bourgeoisie differs from the imperialists, the landlords and the bureaucrat-capitalists. The contradiction between the national bourgeoisie and the working class is one between exploiter and exploited, and is by nature antagonistic. But in the concrete conditions of China, this antagonistic contradiction between the two classes, if properly handled, can be transformed into a non-antagonistic one and be resolved by peaceful methods. However, the contradiction between the working class and the national bourgeoisie will change into a contradiction between ourselves and the enemy if we do not handle it properly and do not follow the policy of uniting with, criticising and educating the national bourgeoisie, or if the national bourgeoisie does not accept this policy of ours" - Mao Zedong

"People of the world, unite and defeat the U.S. aggressors and all their running dogs! People of the world, be courageous, and dare to fight, defy difficulties and advance wave upon wave. Then the whole world will belong to the people. Monsters of all kinds shall be destroyed!" - Mao Zedong

"If the imperialists insist on launching WW3, it is certain that several hundred million more will turn to socialism, and then there will not be much room left on earth for the imperialists; it's also likely that the whole structure of imperialism will utterly collapse" - Mao Zedong

"A new upsurge in the struggle against U.S. imperialism is now emerging throughout the world. Ever since the Second World War, U.S. imperialism and its followers have been continuously launching wars of aggression and the people in various countries have been continuously waging revolutionary wars to defeat the aggressors. The danger of a new world war still exists, and the people of all countries must get prepared. But revolution is the main trend in the world today" - Mao Zedong

"Why does NATO keep expanding towards Russia? They have the same goals as Napolean and Hitler. Which is to obtain Russia's oil, gas, coal and steel. This is clear as daylight" - Muammar Gaddafi

"Obama wants to kill me, to take away the freedom of our country, to take away our free housing, our free medicine, our free education, our free food and replace it with American style thievery called 'capitalism,' but all of us in the Third World know what that means, it means corporations run the countries, run the world and the people suffer" - Muammar Gaddafi

"'If you take food, fuel and housing out of the equation, inflation has been quite moderate' To be sure, and if you remove a few other major items, it disappears altogether. A key reason why the United States is becoming increasingly like the Third World is because corporate America is going Third World, literally, not only downgrading jobs and downsizing, but moving whole industries to Asia, Latin America, and Africa. The aim of modern imperialism is not to accumulate colonies nor even just to provide outlets for capitalist investment and access to natural resources. The economist Paul Sweezy noted that the overall purpose is to turn Third World nations into economic appendages the industrialised countries, encouraging the growth of those kinds of economic activities, that complement the advanced capitalist economies and thwarting those kinds that might compete with them; Perhaps Sweezy relies too much on the nation-state as the unit of analysis. The truth is, the investor class also tries to reduce its own population to a client-state status. The aim of imperialism is not a national one but an international class goal, to exploit and concentrate power not only over Guatamalans, Indonesians, and Saudis, but Americans, Canadians, and everyone else" - Michael Parenti

Nationalism:

"One after another, these 'nations' used the freshly granted freedom to ally themselves with German imperialism against the Russian Revolution as its mortal enemy, and, under German protection, to carry the banner of counter-revolution into Russia itself. The little game with the Ukraine at Brest, which caused a decisive turn of affairs in those negotiations and brought about the entire inner and outer political situation at present prevailing for the Bolsheviks, is a perfect case in point. The conduct of Finland, Poland, Lithuania, the Baltic lands, the nations of the Caucasus, shows most convincingly that we are dealing here not with an exceptional case, but with a typical phenomenon. To be sure, in all these cases, it was really not the 'people' who engaged in these reactionary policies, but only the bourgeois and petty-bourgeois classes, who - in sharpest opposition to their own proletarian masses - perverted the 'national right of self-determination' into an instrument of their counter-revolutionary class policies. But - and here we come to the very heart of the question - it is in this that the utopian, petty-bourgeois character of this nationalistic slogan resides: that in the midst of the crude realities of class society, especially when class antagonisms are sharpened to the uttermost, it is simply converted into a means of bourgeois class rule; Or take the Ukraine. At the beginning of the century, before the tomfoolery of 'Ukrainian nationalism' with its silver rubles and its 'Universals' and Lenin's hobby of an 'independent Ukraine' had been invented, the Ukraine was the stronghold of the Russian revolutionary movement. From there, from Rostov, from Odessa, from the Donetz region, flowed out the first lava streams of the revolution (as early is 1902-1904), which kindled all South Russia into a sea of flame, thereby preparing the uprising of 1905. The same thing was repeated in the present revolution, in which thc South Russian proletariat supplies the elite troops of the proletarian phalanx. Poland and the Baltic lands have been, since 1905, the mightiest and most dependable hearths of revolution, and in them the socialist proletariat has played an outstanding role. How does it happen then, that in all these lands the counter-revolution suddenly triumphs? The nationalist movement, just because it tore the proletariat loose from Russia, crippled it thereby, and delivered it into the hands of the bourgeoisie of the border countries; To be sure, without the help of German imperialism, without 'the German rifle butts in German fists,' as Kautsky's 'Neue Zeit' put it, the Lubinskys and other little scoundrels of the Ukraine, the Erichs and Mannerheims of Finland, and the Baltic barons would never have gotten the better of the socialist masses of the workers in their respective lands. But national separatism was the Trojan horse inside which the German 'comrades,' bayonets in hand, made their entrance into all those lands. The real class antagonisms and relations of military force brought about German intervention; Ukrainian nationalism in Russia was something quite different from, let us say, Czechish, Polish or Finnish nationalism in that the former was a mere whim, a folly of a few dozen petty-bourgeois intellectuals without the slightest roots in the economic, political or psychological relationships of the country; it was without any historical tradition, since the Ukraine never formed a nation or government, was without any national culture, except for the reactionary-romantic poems of Shevschenko. It is exactly as if, one fine day, the people living in the Wasserkante should want to found a new Low-German (Plattdeutsche) nation and government! And this ridiculous pose of a few university professors and students was inflated into a political force by Lenin and his comrades through their doctrinaire agitation concerning the 'right of self-determination including etc.' To what was at first a mere farce they lent such importance that the farce became a matter of the most deadly seriousness - not as a serious national movement for which, afterward as before, there are no roots at all, but as a shingle and rallying flag of counter-revolution! At Brest, out of this addled egg crept thc German bayonets" - Rosa Luxemburg

"The demand for a 'yes' or 'no' reply to the question of secession in the case of every nation may seem a very 'practical' one. In reality it is absurd; it is metaphysical in theory, while in practice it leads to subordinating the proletariat to the bourgeoisie's policy. The bourgeoisie always places its national demands in the forefront, and does so in categorical fashion. With the proletariat, however, these demands are subordinated to the interests of the class struggle. Theoretically, you cannot say in advance whether the bourgeois-democratic revolution will end in a given nation seceding from another nation, or in its equality with the latter; in either case, the important thing for the proletariat is the ensure the development of its class. For the bourgeoisie it is important to hamper this development by pushing the aims of its 'own' nation before those of the proletariat. That is why the proletariat confines itself, so to speak, to the negative demand for recognition of the right to self-determination, without giving guarantees to any nation, and without undertaking to give anything at the expense of another nation" - V.I. Lenin

"As a matter of fact, 'cultural-national autonomy', i.e., the absolutely pure and consistent segregating of education according to nationality, was invented not by the capitalists (for the time being they resort to cruder methods to divide the workers) but by the opportunist, philistine intelligentsia of Austria. There is not a trace of this brilliantly philistine and brilliantly nationalist idea in any of the democratic West-European countries with mixed populations. This idea of the despairing petty-bourgeois could arise only in Eastern Europe, in backward, feudal, clerical, bureaucratic Austria, where all public and political life is hampered by wretched, petty squabbling (worse still: cursing and brawling) over the question of languages. Since cat and dog can't agree, let us at least segregate all the nations once and for all absolutely clearly and consistently in 'national curias' for educational purposes! - such is the psychology that engendered this foolish idea of 'cultural-national autonomy'. The proletariat, which is conscious of and cherishes its internationalism, will never accept this nonsense of refined nationalism" - V.I. Lenin

"The British are as cunning as the fox and as changeable as the weather and they are not ashamed of themselves... Britain seeks friendship only with those which can render her services, and when her friends are too weak to be of any use to her, they must be sacrificed in her interests. Britain's tender regard for her friends is like the delicate care usually shown by farmers in the rearing of silkworks; after all the silk has been drawn from the cocoons, they are destroyed by fire or used as food for the fish. The present friends of Britain are no more than silkworms; When England befriends another country, the purpose is not to maintain a cordial relationship for the sake of friendship but to utilise that country as a tool to fight a third country. When an enemy has been shorn of his power, he is turned into a friend, and the friend who has become strong, into an enemy. England always remains in a commanding position; she makes other countries fight her wars and she herself reaps the fruits of victory; The key policy of England is to attack the strongest enemy with the help of the weaker countries and join the weakened enemy in checking the growth of a third country. The British foreign policy has remained basically unchanged for two centuries" - Sun Yat-sen

"Sometimes the emergence of independent states means the strengthening of imperialism" - (N. Bukharin, The Politics and Economics of the Transition Period)

"This does not mean, of course, that the proletariat must support every national movement, everywhere and always, in every individual concrete case. It means that support must be given to such national movements as tend to weaken, to overthrow imperialism, and not to strengthen and preserve it. Cases occur when the national movements in certain oppressed countries came into conflict with the interests of the development of the proletarian movement. In such cases support is, of course, entirely out of the question" - J.V. Stalin

"National autonomy is contrary to the whole course of development of nations. It calls for the organisation of nations; but can they be artificially welded together if life, if economic development tears whole groups from them and disperses these groups over various regions? There is no doubt that in the early stages of capitalism nations become welded together. But there is also no doubt that in the higher stages of capitalism a process of dispersion of nations sets in, a process whereby a whole number of groups separate off from the nations, going off in search of a livelihood and subsequently settling permanently in other regions of the state; in the course of this these settlers lose their old connections and acquire new ones in their new domicile, and from generation to generation acquire new habits and new tastes, and possibly a new language. The question arises: is it possible to unite into a single national union groups that have grown so distinct? Where are the magic links to unite what cannot be united? Is it conceivable that, for instance, the Germans of the Baltic Provinces and the Germans of Transcaucasia can be 'united into a single nation'? But if it is not conceivable and not possible, wherein does national autonomy differ from the utopia of the old nationalists, who endeavoured to turn back the wheel of history?" - J.V. Stalin

"Leninism is Lenin's formulation in his report of the Commission on the National and Colonial Question to the Second Congress of the Communist International: 'It is unquestionable that the proletariat of the advanced countries can and should give help to the working masses of the backward countries, and that the backward countries can emerge from their present stage of the development when the victorious proletariat of the Soviet Republics extends a helping hand to these masses and is in a position to give them support'" - J.V. Stalin

Fascism:

"In all capitalist countries. The capitalists, faced with the task of drastically slashing the living standards of the workers and poor peasants and, where the political crisis is acute, the job of trying to save the capitalist system itself, no longer find adequate their bourgeois 'democracy,' of which the Social Democracy is a part, to hold the rebellious masses in check. Consequently, with the aid of the Social Democrats, or Social Fascists, they are transforming the masked 'democratic' capitalist dictatorship into open Fascist dictatorship, with its extreme demagogy and use of violence against the workers and poor peasants" - William Z. Foster

"No less unsatisfactory are the attempted anti-fascist interpretations of fascism in terms of ideology or abstract political conceptions. The conventional anti-fascist ideological interpretations of fascism see in fascism only the principle of 'dictatorship' or 'violence.' This approach, which is the hallmark of the liberal and social democratic schools of thought in relation to fascism, see fascism as the parallel extreme to Communism, both being counterposed to bourgeois 'democracy.' Fascism is defined as 'Dictatorship from the Right' in contrast to Communism as 'Dictatorship from the Left'; The specific character of fascism cannot be defined in terms of abstract ideology or political first principles. The specific character of Fascism can only be defined by laying bare its class-basis, the system of class-relations within which it develops and functions, and the class-role which it performs. Only so can fascism be seen in its concrete reality, corresponding to a given historical stage of capitalist development and decay; In the first place, all the abstract general conceptions which are paraded as the peculiar outlook of fascism have no distinctive character whatever, but are common to a thousand schools of bourgeois political philosophy, which are not yet fascist and in particular to all national-conservative schools; In the second place, it is in fact incorrect to look for an explanation of fascism in terms of a political theory, in ideological terms. Fascism, as its leaders are frequently fond of insisting, developed as a movement in practice without a theory" - R. Palme Dutt

"Overpopulation (like the simultaneous 'overproduction') is only relative to the capitalist conditions of production. [This] reactionary and vicious propaganda [conceals], under [the] cover of obsolete clerical superstitions, the true social causes of poverty and misery" - R. Palme Dutt

Production:

"What kept production in true, or more or less true, proportions? It was demand that dominated supply, that preceded it. Production followed close on the heels of consumption. Large-scale industry, forced by the very instruments at its disposal to produce on an ever-increasing scale, can no longer wait for demand. Production precedes consumption, supply compels demands" - Karl Marx

"Not as with the instrument, which the worker animates and makes into his organ with his skill and strength, and whose handling therefore depends on his virtuosity. Rather, it is the machine which possesses skill and strength in place of the worker, is itself the virtuoso, with a soul of its own in the mechanical laws acting through it; and it consumes coal, oil etc., just as the worker consumes food, to keep up its perpetual motion. The worker's activity, reduced to a mere abstraction of activity, is determined and regulated on all sides by the movement of the machinery, and not the opposite. The science which compels the inanimate limbs of the machinery, by their construction, to act purposefully, as an automaton, does not exist in the worker's consciousness, but rather acts upon him through themachine as an alien power, as the power of the machine itself" - Karl Marx

"If the whole working day were to shrink to the length of its necessary component, surplus labour would vanish, something which is impossible under the regime of capital. Only the abolition of the capitalist form of production would permit the reduction of the working day to the necessary labour-time. But even in that case the latter would expand to take up more of the day, and for two reasons: first, because the worker's conditions of life would improve, and his aspirations become greater, and second, because a part of what is now surplus labour would then count as necessary labour, namely the labour which is necessary for the formation of a social fund for reserve and accumulation" - Karl Marx

"The possessor of money or commodities actually turns into a capitalist in such cases only where the minimum sum advanced for production greatly exceeds the maximum of the Middle Ages" - Karl Marx

"Let us take, first of all, the words 'proceeds of labour' in the sense of the product of labour; then the co-operative proceeds of labour are the total social product. From this must now be deducted: First cover for replacement of the means of production used up. Second additional portion for expansion of production. Third, reserve or insurance funds to provide against accidents dislocations caused by natural calamities, etc. Before this is divided among the individuals, there has to be deducted again, from it: First the general costs of administration not belonging to production. This part will, from the outset, be very considerably restricted in comparison with present-day society, and it diminishes in proportion as the new society develops. Second, that which is intended for the common satisfaction of needs, such as schools, health services, etc. From the outset, this part grows considerably in comparison with present-day society, and it grows in proportion as the new society develops. Third, funds for those unable to work, etc., in short, for what is included under so-called poor relief today. The 'undiminished' proceeds of labour have already unnoticeably become converted into the 'diminished' proceeds, although what the producer is deprived of in his capacity as a private individual benefits him directly or indirectly in his capacity as a member of society" - Karl Marx

"To begin with, a commodity, in the language of the English economists, is 'any thing necessary, useful or pleasant in life', an object of human wants, a means of existence in the widest sense of the term. Use-value as an aspect of the commodity coincides with the physical palpable existence of the commodity. Wheat, for example, is a distinct use-value differing from the use-values of cotton, glass, paper, etc. A use-value has value only in use, and is realised only in the process of consumption. One and the same use-value can be used in various ways. But the extent of its possible application is limited by its existence as an object with distinct properties. It is, moreover, determined not only qualitatively but also quantitatively. Different use-values have different measures appropriate to their physical characteristics; for example, a bushel of what, a quire of paper, a yard of linen" - Karl Marx

"A commodity is, in the first place, an object outside us, a thing that by its properties satisfies human wants of some sort or another. The nature of such wants, whether, for instance, they spring from the stomach or from fancy, makes no difference. Neither are we here concerned to know how the object satisfies these wants, whether directly as means of subsistence, or indirectly as means of production" - Karl Marx

"Thus, the products now produced socially were not appropriated by those who had actually set in motion the means of production and actually produced the commodities, but by the capitalists. The means of production, and production itself had become in essence socialised. But they were subjected to a form of appropriation which presupposes the private production of individuals, under which, therefore, everyone owns his own product and brings it to market. The mode of production is subjected to this form of appropriation, although it abolishes the conditions upon which the latter rests. This contradiction, which gives to the new mode of production its capitalistic character, contains the germ of the whole of the social antagonisms of today. The greater the mastery obtained by the new mode of production over all decisive fields of production and in all economically decisive countries, the more it reduced individual production to an insignificant residium, the more clearly was brought out the incompatibility of socialised production with capitalistic appropriation; The first capitalists found, as we have said, wage-labour ready-made for them. But it was exceptional, complementary, accessory, transitory wage-labour. The agricultural labourer, though, upon occasion, he hired himself out by the day, had a few acres of his own land on which he could at all events live at a pinch. The guilds were so organised that the journeyman of today became the master of tomorrow.

But all this changed, as soon as the means of production became socialised and concentrated in the hands of capitalists. The means of production, as well as the product, of the individual producer became more and more worthless; there was nothing left for him but to turn wage-worker under the capitalist. Wage-labour, aforetime the exception and accessory, now became the rule and basis of all production; aforetime complementary, it now became the sole remaining function of the worker. The wage-worker for a time became a wage-worker for life. The number of these permanent wageworkers was further enormously increased by the breaking-up of the feudal system that occurred at the same time, by the disbanding of the retainers of the feudal lords, the eviction of the peasants from their homesteads, etc. The separation was made complete between the means of production concentrated in the hands of the capitalists, on the one side, and the producers, possessing nothing but their labour-power, on the other. The contradiction between socialised production and capitalistic appropriation manifested itself as the antagonism of proletariat and bourgeoisie; With this recognition, at last, of the real nature of the productive forces of today, the social anarchy of production gives place to a social regulation of production upon a definite plan, according to the needs of the community and of each individual. Then the capitalist mode of appropriation, in which the product enslaves first the producer and then the appropriator, is replaced by the mode of appropriation of the products that is based upon the nature of the modern means of production: upon the one hand, direct social appropriation, as means to the maintenance and extension of production - on the other, direct individual appropriation, as means of subsistence and of enjoyment" - Friedrich Engels

"The proletariat seizes the public power, and by means of this transforms the socialised means of production, slipping from the hands of the bourgeoisie, into public property. By this set the proletariat frees the means of production from the character of capital they have thus far borne, and gives their socialised character complete freedom to work itself out. Socialised production upon a predetermined plan becomes henceforth possible" - Friedrich Engels

"With the seizing of the means of production by society production of commodities is done away with, and, simultaneously, the mastery of the product over the producer. Anarchy in social production is replaced by systematic, definite organisation. The struggle for individual existence disappears. Then for the first time man, in a certain sense, is finally marked off from the rest of the animal kingdom, and emerges from mere animal conditions of existence into really human ones. The whole sphere of the conditions of life which environ man, and which have hitherto ruled man, now comes under the dominion and control of man who for the first time becomes the real, conscious lord of nature because he has now become master of his own social organisation. The laws of his own social action, hitherto standing face to face with man as laws of nature foreign to, and dominating him, will then be used with full understanding, and so mastered by him. Man's own social organisation, hitherto confronting him as a necessity imposed by nature and history, now becomes the result of his own free action. The extraneous objective forces that have hitherto governed history pass under the control of man himself. Only from that time will man himself, with full consciousness, make his own history - only from that time will the social causes set in movement by him have, in the main and in a constantly growing measure, the results intended by him. It is the humanity's leap from the kingdom of necessity to the kingdom of freedom" - Friedrich Engels

"The crisis consists precisely in the fact that the old is dying and the new cannot be born" - Antonio Gramsci; (In this interregnum a great variety of morbid symptoms appear Žižek uses it a lot, although he modifies it a bit: >The old world is dying, and the new world struggles to be born: now is the time of monsters)

"Without surplus product you cannot build the new system. It is necessary that the workers understand that under capitalism they are interested in what it is that they are getting. But under socialism they take care of their own society and this is what educates the worker. Income remains but it acquires another character. The surplus product is there, but it does not go to the exploiter, but towards increasing the welfare of the people, strengthening defence etc. The surplus product gets transformed" - J.V. Stalin

"In our country distribution takes place according to labour. We have qualified and unqualified labour. How should we define an engineer's work? It is multiplied simple labour. With us incomes are distributed according to labour. It cannot be that this distribution happens independently of the law of value. We think that the entire economy is run according to the plan, but it does not always happen this way. There is a lot of spontaneity with us also. We knowingly, and not spontaneously, make calculations according to the law of value. In their system the law of value operates spontaneously, bringing in its wake destruction, and demands huge sacrifices. In our system the character of the law of value undergoes a change, it acquires a new content, a new form. We knowingly, and not spontaneously, set prices. Engels speaks of leaps. It is a risky formula, but it can be accepted, if we correctly understand the leap from the realm of necessity into the realm of freedom. We must understand freedom of will as necessity recognised, where the leap means a transition from spontaneous inevitability to the recognition of necessity. In their system the law of value operates spontaneously and it leads to large-scale destruction. But we should conduct things in such a way that there are fewer sacrifices. The necessity resulting from the operation of the law of value must be used by us consciously" - J.V. Stalin

[Surplus product in a socialist society - the term is embarrassing] "On the contrary, we have to educate the worker that the surplus product is needed by us, there is more responsibility. The worker must understand that he produces not only for himself and his family, but also for creating reserves and strengthening defence etc. [In the Critique of the Gotha Programme Marx did not write about surplus product] If you want to seek answers for everything in Marx you will get nowhere. You have in front of you a laboratory such as the U.S.S.R. which has existed now for more than 20 years but you think that Marx ought to be knowing more than you about socialism. Do you not understand that in the Critique of the Gotha Programme Marx was not in a position to foresee!" - J.V. Stalin

"If I were asked about my predilection towards socialism I would answer: with regard to this issue what I aspire to is not to increase the wealth of factories but that of life. My concern is not that people should be equal in distribution of food but that every individual should be allowed to exploit his talents and potential. The labourer crushed by his misery may not find in socialism anything except a promise that he may take what he is deprived of, but I view it as continuous and generous giving, as giving to life many times what it has offered us" - Michel Aflaq

"A socialist economy is a planned economy, managed by its masters, the popular masses. It is an instrinsic requirement of a socialist economy that it be developed rapidly in a planned and balanced way in the common interests of the masses by increasing the creative enthusiasm of the working people and that equitable distribution be made according to the quantity and quality of work done" - Kim Il-sung

Race:

"I am a man and what I have to recapture is the whole

past of the world, I am not responsible only for the slavery involved in Santo Domingo, every time man has contributed to the victory of the dignity of the spirit, every time a man has said no to an attempt to subjugate his fellows, I have felt solidarity with his act. In no way does my basic vocation have to be drawn from the past of peoples of colour. In no way do I have to dedicate myself to reviving some black civilisation unjustly ignored. I will not make myself the man of any past. My black skin is not a repository for specific values. Haven't I got better things to do on this earth than avenge the blacks of the 17th century? I as a man of colour do not have the right to hope that in the white man there will be a crystallisation of guilt towards the past of my race. I as a man of colour do not have the right of stamping down the pride of my former master. I have neither the right nor the duty to demand reparations for my subjugated ancestors. There is no black mission. There is no white burden. I do not want to be victim of the rules of a black world. Am I going to ask this white man to answer for the slave traders of the 17th century? Am I going to try by every means available to cause guilt to burgeon in their souls? I am not a slave to slavery that dehumanised my ancestors. It would be of enormous interest to discover a black literature or architecture from the 3rd century B.C, we would be overjoyed to learn of the existence of a correspondence between some black philosopher and Plato, but we can absolutely not see how this fact would change the lives of 8 year old kids working the cane fields of Martinique or Guadaloupe. I find myself in the world and I recognise I have one right alone: of demanding human behaviour from the other" - Frantz Fanon

"It is not only the Blacks, but also the Whites who dare to defend them, such as Mrs. Harriet Beecher Stowe - author of 'Uncle Tom's Cabin' - who are ill treated. Elijah Lovejoy was killed, John Brown hanged. Thomas Beach and Stephen Foster were presecuted, attacked, and imprisoned. Here is what

Foster wrote from prison, 'When I look at my damaged limbs, I think that, to hold me, prison will not be necessary for much longer... These last 15 months, their cells have been opened to me four times, 24 times my compatriots have dragged me out of their churches, twice they have thrown me from the second floor of their houses; they have damaged my kidneys once; another time they tried to put me in irons; twice they have made me pay fines; once 10,000 people tried to lynch me, and dealt me 20 blows on my head, arms and neck...' In 30 years, 708 Whites, including 11 women, have been lynched. Some for having organised strikes, others for having espoused the cause of the Blacks. Among the collection of the crimes of American 'civilisation,' lynching has a place of honour" - Hồ Chí Minh

"We got to face some facts. That the masses are poor, that the masses belong to what you call the lower class, and when I talk about the masses, I'm talking about the white masses, I'm talking about the black masses, and the brown masses, and the yellow masses too. We've got to face the fact that some people say you fight fire best with fire, but we say you put fire out best with water. We're going to fight racism not with racism, but we're going to fight with solidarity. We say we're not going to fight capitalism with black capitalism, but we're going to fight it with socialism. We're stood up and said we're not going to fight reactionary pigs and reactionary state's attorneys like this and reactionary state's attorneys like Hanrahan with any other reactions on our part. We're going to fight their reactions with all of us people getting together and having an international proletarian revolution. That's what it has to be. The people have to have the power: it belongs to the people" - Fred Hampton

"If you can convince the lowest white man he's better than the best coloured man, he won't notice you're picking his pocket. Hell give him somebody to look down on, and he'll empty his pockets for you" - (Lyndon B. Johnson, on how the elite use racism)

"There are no socially significant inherited characteristics among different ethnic groups or nations. Blacks are in no way inherently more lazy, less creative, more musical or cooperative, Jews or Chinese are in no way inherently more crafty, sly, or intelligent; whites are in no way inherently antagonistic to people of dark skin; and no members of any socially defined 'race' or ethnic group have any inherent predisposition to identify or feel solidarity with other members of the same group and hostility to, or lack of solidarity with, members of other groups. All manifest differences between different people's, ethnic groups, nations, etc., are a product of the logic of the mode of production that generates 'races'; The relationship between capital and especially exploited menial workers (such as Blacks and Hispanics) in the U.S. is the essence of racism. This antagonist relationship is a source of considerable profit for capital. Such exploitative relationships can only be dissolved through revolutionary activity which destroys such antagonistic relationships. Capitalism generates a racist ideology which is not only used to legitimate the special exploitation of ethnic minorities and nations in the eyes of the exploiters, but also to convince the members of the majority ethnic group workers that it has 'white skin privilege,' i.e., that it has more in common with 'white capitalists' than it does with Black or Hispanic workers. This ideology is implanted both by control of the education and mass media which perpetuates racist ideologies, and by the ability of the capitalist class to structure the labour force in such a way as majority group workers have slightly better jobs, slightly better pay than minority group workers, and further receive somewhat better treatment by the police, in the courts, by welfare agencies etc. The illusion that all whites benefit from racist structures is thus created in both the majority group workers. But in reality, the ability of the capitalists to turn the different segments of the working class against each other seriously hurts the condition of all the working class, both its majority and minority members (although of course it hurts the minority group workers relatively more). The only beneficiaries of racist structures are those that employ minorities and thus make extra profits from: the special exploitation of minorities and, the weak class consciousness, lack of strong unions, absence of a militant socialist movement, etc., which racial divisiveness brings to the majority group. It should be remembered that white workers in the U.S. are the best off in states such as Michigan where their relative advantage over Black workers is the least in the country (and which have a strong militant interracial union tradition) and worse off in Mississippi where whites are at the same time the best off vis-a-vis Blacks. Where racist Ideology is strongest, working class solidarity is the weakest and all workers, white and Black are in much worse shape than where racist ideology has been overcome enough to allow multi-ethnic/national forms of class organisation to emerge and improve the conditions of the working class as a whole; It is the obligation of leftists to educate white workers about how they are being 'suckered' by the 'white skin privilege' argument of the capitalist class and how their own interests coincide with their fellow minority group workers" - Albert Szymanski

"The giant industrial monopolies, the big banks and insurance companies, the financiers and landowners, all spawn racism and use it as one of their chief class weapons to maintain and defend their regime of exploitation and oppression, of enmity among peoples, of imperialist wars of aggression. It follows that all democratic and antimonopoly forces, with the working class and Black liberation movement in the van, can effectively defend the interests of the vast majority of people only when they actively further the struggle against racism. This is an essential precondition for the development of a fighting alliance which will unite all democratic and antimonopoly [anticapitalist] forces in the country. Marx wrote long ago that 'labour in a white skin can never be free so long as labour in the black skin is branded.'

This profound observation points up the fact that racism is the consciously employed weapon of the white imperialist oppressors, who use it to create division in the ranks of the working class. And Marx correctly suggests that white workers must take the lead in the struggle against racism. This is the path which can lead to unity of Black and white workers in struggle, which can achieve Black equality and a real improvement in the conditions of all workers" - Henry M. Winston

"The race question is subsidiary to the class question in politics, and to think of imperialism in terms of race is disastrous. But to neglect the racial factor as merely incidental [is] an error only less grave than to make it fundamental" - C.L.R. James

"If a white man wants to lynch me, that's his problem. If he's got the power to lynch me, that's my problem... Racism gets its power from capitalism. Thus, if you're anti-racist, whether you know it or not, you must be anti-capitalist. The power for racism, the power for sexism, comes from capitalism, not an attitude" - Kwame Ture

"Referring to SDS's agreement to support the petition in the 'colonies' (black and brown communities) but not in the 'oppressor country' (white America), Hilliard wrote in the Black Panther: 'How abstract and divorced from the reality of the world around them they must be to think that the Black Panther party would allow them to leave their communities and begin to organise the colony; to control the fascists in the oppressor country is a very definite step towards white people's power, because James Rector was not shotgunned to death in the black community. It seems they prefer to allow the already legitimate reactionary forces to take roost or sanctuary in the white communities.' Stating that the 'Black Panther party will not be dictated to by people who are obviously bourgeois procrastinators,' Hilliard went on to imply that SDS, among other groups, was 'at best national socialist' (i.e., fascist)" - Jack A. Smith

Liberalism:

"Liberalism is extremely harmful in a revolutionary collective. It is a corrosive which eats away unity, undermines cohesion, causes apathy and creates dissension. It robs the revolutionary ranks of compact organisation and strict discipline, prevents policies from being carried through and alienates the Party organisations from the masses which the Party leads. It is an extremely bad tendency. Liberalism stems from petty-bourgeois selfishness, it places personal interests first and the interests of the revolution second, and this gives rise to ideological, political and organisational liberalism. People who are liberals look upon the principles of Marxism as abstract dogma. They approve of Marxism, but are not prepared to practice it or to practice it in full; they are not prepared to replace their liberalism by Marxism. These people have their Marxism, but they have their liberalism as well - they talk Marxism but practice liberalism; they apply Marxism to others but liberalism to themselves. They keep both kinds of goods in stock and find a use for each. This is how the minds of certain people work. Liberalism is a manifestation of opportunism and conflicts fundamentally with Marxism. It is negative and objectively has the effect of helping the enemy; that is why the enemy welcomes its preservation in our midst. Such being its nature, there should be no place for it in the ranks of the revolution" - Mao Zedong

Theory/Philosophy:

"This conception of history depends on our ability to expound the real process of production, starting out from the material production of life itself, and to comprehend the form of intercourse connected with this and created by this mode of production (i.e. civil society in its various stages), as the basis of all history; and to show it in its action as State, to explain all the different theoretical products and forms of consciousness, religion, philosophy, ethics, etc. etc. and trace their origins and growth from that basis; by which means, of course, the whole thing can be depicted in its totality (and therefore, too, the reciprocal action of these various sides on one another). It has not, like the idealistic view of history, in every period to look for a category, but remains constantly on the real ground of history; it does not explain practice from the idea but explains the formation of ideas from material practice; and accordingly it comes to the conclusion that all forms and products of consciousness cannot be dissolved by mental criticism, by resolution into 'self-consciousness' or transformation into 'apparitions,' 'spectres,' 'fancies,' etc. but only by the practical overthrow of the actual social relations which gave rise to this idealistic humbug; that not criticism but revolution is the driving force of history, also of religion, of philosophy and all other types of theory. It shows that history does not end by being resolved into 'self-consciousness as spirit of the spirit,' but that in it at each stage there is found a material result: a sum of productive forces, an historically created relation of individuals to nature and to one another, which is handed down to each generation from its predecessor; a mass of productive forces, capital funds and conditions, which, on the one hand, is indeed modified by the new generation, but also on the other prescribes for it its conditions of life and gives it a definite development, a special character. It shows that circumstances make men just as much as men make circumstances" - Karl Marx

"The charges against Communism made from a religious, a philosophical and, generally, from an ideological standpoint, are not deserving of serious examination. Does it require deep intuition to comprehend that man's ideas, views, and conception, in one word, man's consciousness, changes with every change in the conditions of his material existence, in his social relations and in his social life? What else does the history of ideas prove, than that intellectual production changes its character in proportion as material production is changed? The ruling ideas of each age have ever been the ideas of its ruling class. When people speak of the ideas that revolutionise society, they do but express that fact that within the old society the elements of a new one have been created, and that the dissolution of the old ideas keeps even pace with the dissolution of the old conditions of existence. When the ancient world was in its last throes, the ancient religions were overcome by Christianity. When Christian ideas succumbed in the 18th century to rationalist ideas, feudal society fought its death battle with the then revolutionary bourgeoisie. The ideas of religious liberty and freedom of conscience merely gave expression to the sway of free competition within the domain of knowledge. 'Undoubtedly,' it will be said, 'religious, moral, philosophical, and juridical ideas have been modified in the course of historical development. But religion, morality, philosophy, political science, and law, constantly survived this change.' 'There are, besides, eternal truths, such as Freedom, Justice, etc., that are common to all states of society. But Communism abolishes eternal truths, it abolishes all religion, and all morality, instead of constituting them on a new basis; it therefore acts in contradiction to all past historical experience.' What does this accusation reduce itself to? The history of all past society has consisted in the development of class antagonisms, antagonisms that assumed different forms at different epochs" - Karl Marx

"Without revolutionary theory there can be no revolutionary movement. This idea cannot be insisted upon too strongly at a time when the fashionable preaching of opportunism goes hand in hand with an infatuation for the narrowest forms of practical activity" - V.I. Lenin

"Needless to say, of course, all boundaries in nature and in society are conventional and changeable, and it would be absurd to argue, for example, about the particular year or decade in which imperialism 'definitely' became established" -

V.I. Lenin

"Unless the economic roots of this phenomenon are understood and its political and social significance is appreciated, not a step can be taken toward the solution of the practical problem of the Communist movement and of the impending social revolution" - V.I. Lenin

"Contrary to metaphysics, dialectics does not regard nature as an accidental agglomeration of things, of phenomena, unconnected with, isolated from, and independent of, each other, but as a connected and integral whole, in which things, phenomena are organically connected with, dependent on, and determined by, each other. The dialectical method therefore holds that no phenomenon in nature can be understood if taken by itself, isolated from surrounding phenomena, inasmuch as any phenomenon in any realm of nature may become meaningless to us if it is not considered in connection with the surrounding conditions, but divorced from them; and that, vice versa, any phenomenon can be understood and explained if considered in its inseparable connection with surrounding phenomena, as one conditioned by surrounding phenomena" - J.V. Stalin

"Whether or not one's consciousness or ideas (including theories, policies, plans or measures) do correctly reflect the laws of the objective external world is not yet proved at this stage, in which it is not yet possible to ascertain whether they are correct or not; For it is this leap alone that can prove the correctness or incorrectness of the first leap in cognition, i.e., of the ideas, theories, policies, plans or measures formulated in the course of reflecting the objective external world; Such is the Marxist theory of knowledge, the dialectical materialist theory of knowledge. Among our comrades there are many who do not yet understand this theory of knowledge. When asked the sources of their ideas, opinions, policies, methods, plans and conclusions, eloquent speeches and long articles they consider the questions strange and cannot answer it.

Nor do they comprehend that matter, can be transformed into consciousness and consciousness into matter, although such leaps are phenomena of everyday life" - Mao Zedong

"Civilise the mind and make savage the body; This is an apt saying. In order to civilise the mind one must first make savage the body. If the body is made savage, then the civilised mind will follow. Knowledge consists in knowing the things in the world, and in discerning their laws" - Mao Zedong

"If there is to be revolution, there must be a revolutionary party. Without a revolutionary party, without a party built on the Marxist-Leninist revolutionary theory and in the Marxist-Leninist revolutionary style, it is impossible to lead the working class and the broad masses of the people to defeat imperialism and its running dogs" - Mao Zedong

"The old logic, coming up against the logical contradiction that it itself brought to light just because it rigorously followed its own principles, always baulked at it, retreated to analysis of the preceding movement of thought, and always strove to find an error or mistake in it leading to the contradiction. For formal logical thinking contradictions thus became an insurmountable barrier to the forward movement of thought, an obstacle in the way of concrete analysis of the essence of the matter. It therefore also came about that 'thought, despairing of managing by itself to resolve the contradiction into which it had got itself, turns back to the solutions and reliefs that were the spirit's lot in its other modes and forms'. It could not be otherwise, since the contradiction did not develop through a mistake. No mistake, it ultimately proved, had been made in the preceding thinking. It was necessary to go even further back, to uncomprehended contemplation, sense perception, aesthetic intuition, i.e. to the realm of lower forms of consciousness (lower, that is, in relation to conceptual thinking), where there was really no contradiction for the simple reason that it had still not been disclosed and clearly expressed. (It never hurts, of course, to go back and analyse the preceding course of argument and check whether there has not been a formal mistake, for that also happens not infrequently; and here the recommendations of formal logic have a quite rational sense and value. It may turn out, as a result of checking, that a given logical contradiction is really nothing but the result of committing an error or mistake somewhere. Hegel, of course, never dreamed of denying such a case. He, like Kant, had in mind only those antinomies that developed in thought as a result of the most formally 'correct' and faultless argumentation)" - E.V. Ilyenkov

"Lenin had been writing his book not only during these months, but throughout his entire preceding life. Prior to the day when he actually set pen to paper, he had already endured and suffered over this book. Throughout long winter months in Shushenskoe, where, according to the memoirs of N.K. Krupskaya, he studied the classics of world philosophy, including Hegel and his Phenomenology of Spirit; over long conversations with Plekhanov; throughout the correspondence with Lengnik and Bogdanov, in the course of which Lenin's letters (which, alas, have been lost) grew into 'whole long treatises on philosophy' measuring 'three notebooks'... And, finally, the last meeting with Bogdanov and his friends on Capri in April 1908, which once again convinced him of the urgent and inescapable necessity of giving open, final and decisive battle to Machism" - E.V. Ilyenkov

"All levels of society contribute to the impetus for social revolution. Within the base, advancments in the means of production precipitate conflicts with the relations of production. The inherent revolutionary nature of capitalism at work within the means of production runs counter to the institutional path dependencies found in the relations of production. This conflict ultimately provides the magnitude of revolutionary impetus but no direction. Direction emerges as the resultant sum of all applied ideological vectors emanating from the superstructure. Chief among these vectors is the reactionary. This is the tendency which must be overcome" - Louis Althusser

"'Materialism' as a term and as a concept is booby-trapped by its functional association with the eighteenth-century bourgeois Enlightenment and with nineteenth-century positivism. Whatever precautions are taken, it always fatally ends up projecting a determinism by matter (that is to say, the individual body or organism in isolation) rather than - as in historical materialism - a determination by the mode of production. It would be better to grasp Marxism and the dialectic as an attempt to overcome not idealism by itself, but that every ideological opposition between idealism and materialism in the first place. The work of both Sartre and Gramsci is there to argue for some position 'beyond idealism and materialism,' and if one does not like the projected new solution - called 'praxis' - then at least it would be desirable to search for something more adequate" - F. Jameson

Manufactured by Amazon.ca
Bolton, ON